I thought Star ██████████ *ul journey. It* ended up taking ▪▪▪ ▪▪ gripping and very, very clever. It interweaves philosophy, mysticism and some home truths in an ▪▪▪▪▪▪▪ ▪▪▪▪ The Da Vinci Code ▪▪▪ ▪ ▪▪▪▪▪ tale and thought prov▪▪▪ ▪ ▪▪ is not just another good read, it deserves its place on the bestseller list. Sheer genius. **Paul Salmon**, Eternal Spirit magazine

I was completely unprepared for the effect Star Pilgrim would have on me. From the word go, my imagination was captured. I went back to a time in my childhood where a story was so powerful that I could do nothing but keep reading until the end. Much more important than the brilliantly crafted story, however, is the simple message hidden in the book. Star Pilgrim is important, it is timely and needs to be read. **Mary Anderson, Scientist, St Patrick's Hospital, Dublin**

Star Pilgrim is a wonderful work of fiction that reminds us of some deep truths - which we already know if we look deeply enough within. **Timothy Freke,** author of The Jesus Mysteries

From the first page Star Pilgrim grabs you by the arm and takes you into a mystical sci-fi labyrinth, not letting go until the very end. With a baptised imagination the author manages to achieve the near impossible - entertainment and enlightenment simultaneously. Star Pilgrim is a journey of the soul, a combination of Arthur C. Clarke and Paulo Coelho. At once an epic "close encounter" adventure and a quest for the very meaning of life. **Mark Townsend**, author of The Path of The Blue Raven (O-Books)

A colossal achievement! Star Pilgrim somehow manages to combine a brilliantly written "page turner" with a spiritual handbook a la Eckhart Tolle. Elegantly embedded in the arc of the story, Star Pilgrim offers new responses for us all as we negotiate the opportunities of the coming years. **Steve Coe**, Song Writer, Music Producer and Film Maker

Star Pilgrim

A Story of the Deepest Mysteries
of Existence

Star Pilgrim

A Story of the Deepest Mysteries
of Existence

Simon Small

BOOKS

Winchester, UK
Washington, USA

First published by O-Books, 2011
O-Books is an imprint of John Hunt Publishing Ltd., The Bothy, Deershot Lodge, Park Lane, Ropley,
Hants, SO24 0BE, UK
office1@o-books.net
www.o-books.com

For distributor details and how to order please visit the 'Ordering' section on our website.

Design: Stuart Davies

Printed in the UK by CPI Antony Rowe

We operate a distinctive and ethical publishing philosophy in all
areas of our business, from our global network of authors to
production and worldwide distribution.

www.starpilgrim.com
www.simonsmall.info

Also by Simon Small in O-Books (non-fiction)

From the Bottom of the Pond: *The forgotten art of experiencing God in the depths of the present moment*

Waiting.

Feeling the currents of time brush past.

A still rock in a flowing river.

Ancient thoughts and memories about to give birth to a new future.

All around, beautifully lit, subtle-hued grey dust undulating gently toward a not-too distant, fiercely delineated horizon.

To one side, the dust is disturbed and trodden. Alien-looking metallic shapes loom, shrines to the god of light and lyre, emanating stark coal-dark shadows. Beyond the disturbance, all is tranquil. A place chosen for its multilayered meaning.

Above is star-studded blackness, broken by a crescent of blue-white light, the only visible sliver of an invisible sphere. But he can sense the sphere in other, deeper ways. The swirling kaleidoscope of swarming consciousness that coats its surface impinges on his mind, as a gentle breeze on bare skin. One particular mind-spark draws his attention. Their thoughts have touched frequently in recent times and in a few moments they will entwine again.

Then everything must change.

For soon they must meet at another level, as once they did long before, as an ancient cycle is completed. It is this meeting for which he comes, so they may together serve that which is infinitely greater.

Beyond the hidden sphere, still visible, though not for much longer, a disk of fiery incandescent light hangs motionless, the fulcrum of all it knows. For a brief second he becomes aware of the strange companion who waits with him. Instantly the light is transformed and becomes a pulsating cauldron of aliveness. Then it fades as, with great effort, he refocuses on the darkened world that hangs before him.

It is time

He reaches out with his thoughts and touches the mind-spark, which feels both alien and familiar.

The waiting ends.

Chapter 1

With dawn only a little way off, Joseph dreamed.

It was very strange, for he knew it was a dream. He had awakened within it. He knew that he was still asleep, yet was profoundly awake.

He was flying, or rather floating. He sensed that he was being shown something that was very important, but did not know who the invisible teacher was, except that it was someone closer to him than a heartbeat. Joseph knew that they had met many times and there was a familiarity and intensity to the relationship that soothed an ancient grief, which had ached for longer than he could remember. He also had an intuition that the relationship was just as essential to the Teacher as it was to him, in that through their shared experiences, from very different perspectives, both evolved and grew. And in their journeying together, they came into even closer relationship.

Joseph floated above the canopy of an oak forest that stretched away as far as the eye could see, the green quilt made uneven only by the rise and fall of the ground. It was one of the gifts of the dream that somehow he was able to see in all directions at once. The sweeping panorama of verdant green set against a blue sky filled him with its beauty. He was aware, without knowing how, that it was England in its glorious summer robes. Yet also, inexplicably, he knew that it was not yet England, as it had still to fully express that essence. He sensed that the consciousness of this place was in transition from one age to another.

He found himself giving close attention to the area of the forest below where he drifted. The first thing he noticed was that he was directly above a hill, roughly oval in shape. He had not seen it at first, as its steep sides were camouflaged by the thick covering of trees. He now saw that below to the south was a deep, wide valley, within which flowed a narrow river, almost entirely hidden by the trees. As he took in more of the landscape, he saw that the hill was actually only steep on three sides and that its northern slope tapered off gently into the distance. The hill reminded him of a promontory projecting out into a gentle sea. He also sensed it as a wild and mysterious place, looming above the more sedate valley.

Joseph looked closer and saw that on the hill below him the perfect flow of the forest was broken by an open space, so small that the boughs of the surrounding trees almost enclosed it as in an arched roof. The trees seemed to have been cleared to form what was, to the eye, a nearly perfect circle. It had the feel of a sanctuary; a sacred place; somewhere set aside. Joseph realized that the clearing was located close to the front edge of the escarpment, just before the ground fell away sharply towards the valley. At this time of year, there would be no view over the valley from ground level because of the thick foliage. But Joseph saw that in winter, when the trees were bare, the view would be wonderful.

He then knew that he had to find whoever had created the clearing. It mattered enormously to locate them, but he did not know why. He found himself drifting northwards over the forest for a few hundred yards and then glimpsed through the trees what he was looking for. There, scattered between the trees, across a wide area, was a group of twelve simple rectangular wooden huts with sloping roofs made from thatched dried grass and mud. They were very small and Joseph could not imagine more than one person being able to live in each. The dwellings looked deserted and Joseph could detect no sign of life. But there was life. He could sense it.

The slow, faint tolling of a bell gave him the clue he needed. It took a few moments, but then he saw the stone building resting quietly at the approximate center of the collection of huts. It was almost invisible, covered as it was by thick lichen and moss. Joseph immediately sensed how old it was. It had been there a long time, unchanging while the world evolved around it, serving in many different ways the same purpose. Again, without knowing how, he knew that it was now a church, but in ages gone by had served as a gateway into the mystery of existence for other, long forgotten creeds. Church was probably too grand a word for what he beheld. Although significantly larger than the huts that surrounded it, Joseph judged that it would struggle to hold more than a handful of people. The tolling bell drew his attention once more. Looking closely, he saw that the bell was concealed within a small turret, which rose out of the west end of the building. It was being rung with a very slow rhythm. Whoever lived in the huts must be in the church.

At that moment, as though responding to his thought, the door to the church opened and eleven figures processed out. They were led by a solitary, tall, stately figure, who walked slowly setting the pace for the others. His hands, clasped together over his solar plexus, were almost lost in the voluminous sleeves of the garment that he wore. Behind him, the others followed in pairs. Each monk, for this was clearly what they were, was dressed in a long brown, rough looking robe, with a raised hood obscuring the face. Joseph could catch only occasional glimpses of features in the enfolding shadows. The robe of each was gathered around the waist with a rope girdle. He did not recognize the religious order to which they belonged and felt the Teacher telling him that they were maverick, outside the authority of the wider church, living out their lives in this lonely place. He sensed something esoteric, hidden, which sought safety from a hostile world in self-imposed seclusion.

Behind the leader, the front pair each carried an object held out before them in ceremonial fashion. One carried a gleaming silver chalice and Joseph glimpsed what he knew to be red wine gently moving about inside. The silver and red made a startling, evocative contrast. The other held a small silver plate, or paten, on which rested a circular piece of bread. Joseph was now sure that these were Christian monks, for he was seeing the bread and wine of the Mass, the deeply mysterious primal rite at the heart of the Christian faith.

Yet it was what the remaining monks conveyed between them that stirred his heart. As soon as he saw it, Joseph felt powerful, confused emotions erupt from deep within. He knew that the Teacher sensed this and had moved closer to steady him. For on a litter was a dead body. It was a monk, dressed as the rest were, with the hood pulled up obscuring the face and hands clasped over the breast. The brothers had lost one of their own. There had been twelve, now there were eleven. He could suddenly sense their sadness. One of the huts he had seen earlier would now be empty and would never be occupied again. This was the beginning of the end of an era. All was passing. All was impermanent. The community had served its purpose and would gradually fade away. This death was the first dimming. He then understood that their sadness was not just personal for the friend they had lost, but for what the death presaged. Joseph did not know how he was aware of all of this, but did not doubt its veracity. But he also knew something else. That in this ending something new and powerful would be born, that transcended time and would serve a great purpose. This was a deep knowledge within him, which was simply present without preamble.

Joseph followed as the procession wound its way between the trees. He guessed that the monks must be following some kind of path, invisible from where he floated above. They clearly knew where they were going. At first he wondered if they intended to return the dead monk to his hut, so that it might serve as his last resting place, thus symbolizing the meaning of his life. But as they progressed beyond the outermost of the dwellings, he knew that they must be heading somewhere else. As he traced the direction of their journey, he saw that they were travelling south towards the sun that blazed high in the sky. Suddenly he could hear the birds singing and the beauty of their song filled him with a feeling of poignancy as he watched the sad procession below. Then he knew where they were going and, as he thought of the place, he was there in an instant, floating once more above the almost hidden clearing on the edge of the hill, arched over like a green cathedral by the surrounding trees. This time, however, the foliage did not seem to inhibit his sight and he was able to see clearly into the heart of the sacred space. And he saw something that once more stirred powerful feelings inside. There, at the center of the clearing, a grave had been dug with the earth piled up to one side, dark brown against bright green. Joseph found it difficult to breathe for a few moments, as the sight impacted on him. At one level he thought he knew why this was, but he could also sense his teacher trying to get him to push beyond the obvious, for there were deeper currents at work. He felt himself being pushed closer and was suddenly at ground level looking into the grave, which had been dug very deep. It would be a long time before any body placed within would be disturbed. He became aware of the Teacher telling him that it was important to contemplate the grave, to give it profound attention. He was reluctant but tried his best to comply. All at once he felt himself falling into swirling eddies of confused consciousness. Images flashed across his mind of faces, experiences and incidents, but in no coherent order. He felt himself starting to be pulled down into the surging mind waves, as though drowning. Then he was back at the graveside, disorientated and unsteady, with a deep sense of the Teacher, intangible but unseen, holding him firmly. He was being told that what had just happened was important and that it had unlocked doors in the inner recesses of his mind that had long been sealed; that the understanding that lay behind those doors would seep into his consciousness in the days to come and would guide him in something that was about to happen. Then there was silence for a moment, until once more he could hear the birds singing and could almost feel the warm sun on his skin. He was aware that the Teacher had pulled back and stood a little way off. Joseph remained at the edge of the grave for a little while allowing equilibrium to return, until approaching footsteps told him the monks were not far off. He found himself stepping back to the edge of the clearing until he stood just inside the ring of trees. For reasons he did not understand, he wanted to witness what was about to happen from ground level rather than from above. He wanted to be a part of events, not just a dispassionate observer.

A few moments later the tall, stately monk led the others into the clearing. The litter was laid reverently on the grass with the head of the deceased monk facing the sun. The senior monk, for this is what he seemed to be, stood behind the head, between the chalice and paten bearers. The remaining monks lined up on either side. No words were said as, for one of those immeasurable periods of time that are common in dreams, there was only silence and stillness. Then the leader turned to his left and took the bread from the paten. Holding it in both hands, he raised it heavenward for a few moments and then replaced it on the paten. Very carefully and gently he broke it into pieces. He took one of the pieces and, turning to his left, dipped it lightly in the chalice, allowing a tincture of wine to stain the bread a light red. Bending over, he pulled back the hood of the dead man, exposing the face for the first time, and placed the fragment of bread into the mouth, softly closing the jaw when he had done so. He then returned to his place, took another piece of the broken bread, dipped it in the wine, but this time consumed it himself. Then, in quiet succession, each of the other monks did the same before returning to their place. Once more there was stillness. Joseph watched on transfixed, utterly caught up in what was happening. He very much wanted to see the face of the departed monk, but the others obscured his view. Then, without any apparent signal, the circle of monks broke-up. The ones who had carried the body walked to the pile of earth that stood to one side and, reaching down behind, produced long ropes which had been placed there in preparation for this moment. At first Joseph's eyes followed them, distracted by what they were doing, but then he looked once more at the body. And this time he could see the face.

The shock ran through him like a bolt of lightening. He felt the Teacher move closer in support. He knew the white, wax-like face that lay framed against the brown of the robe.

It was his own.

There was no exact resemblance. The features of the face echoed his own, as a child's can hint at those of a parent or grand parent. But it was not this that left Joseph in no doubt as to the identity of the corpse. It was recognition. It was deep memory. He knew what he was looking at because he knew. Even though part of him accepted that he was dreaming, it was a shocking moment. He almost could not take it in, for the mind cannot grasp its own apparent non-existence. It is a denial of its deepest conviction about itself. Suddenly, as at the graveside a little earlier, Joseph found himself plunging into fragmented memories and surging, confused emotions, being thrown around like a leaf in a storm. Then he felt, almost physically, a hand grab him and heave backwards. In a moment he was once more on the edge of the clearing, aware that the Teacher, his unseen companion, stood close by his side. His mind was full of questions, but all he could sense from the Teacher was to be still and watch. He gathered himself and tried to focus again on what was happening.

The leader still stood at the head of the deceased with the paten and chalice bearers on either side. Joseph watched silently as the others moved to position themselves around the body. The ropes were passed under the litter, there was a slight pause and then in one unified movement it was lifted off the ground and carried to hang over the open grave. The leader and his two companions followed until they stood once more at the head of their dead brother, with the sun blazing on their faces. Joseph saw the tall figure nod his head imperceptibly and the litter was slowly lowered out of sight. A chill ran through him as the body disappeared. It was so final, so real.

Suddenly Joseph could not bear to watch any more. He did not want this dream and tried to wake up. But he felt the Teacher gently urging him to stay a little longer. Again he sensed the importance of what he was seeing. With a mighty effort he refocused his awareness on the clearing and was stunned by what he encountered. They were looking directly at him. They knew that he was present. The monks, with their leader and two companions at the center, had formed an arc between him and the still-open grave. From within their concealing hoods he was been regarded with deep compassion. Joseph felt his heart swell with a response that came from a distant but powerful place within. Without thought, he stepped into the clearing and walked over to stand before the tall figure at the center of the arc. He found himself smiling for no obvious reason, except for an overwhelming feeling of loving reunion after a long absence. Without a word, the senior monk took a final piece of bread that lay on the paten, dipped it in the wine and placed it in Joseph's mouth.

In that moment his mind seemed to shatter and he plunged into a warm, formless sea.

Chapter 2

On the other side of the world from where Joseph slept, the night was still young.

Noelani felt guilty as she removed the telescope from the trunk of her battered Toyota. She looked furtively around the small car park and then got annoyed with herself. She was doing nothing wrong. The others at the University of Hawaii Educational Telescope on Mauna Kea would not miss her. There was too much excitement and talking for that. She had managed to slip out unnoticed and would go back a little later. She could always say that she had needed the ladies' room and endure the inevitable student-type jokes that would come her way. But she needed to see what was about to happen for herself, in peace and quiet. It felt important.

Noelani had been given the telescope as a surprise birthday present when she was twelve and it had quickly become the center of her life. She had always been enchanted by the night sky. Since she was a small child it had evoked something nameless deep within her. The telescope had been a gift from her grandmother, the matriarch of the family. When asked why she had bought it, all Grandmother would say was that she had seen it in a dream. This was her way, rooted in ancient Hawaiian spirituality. It was also how Noelani had acquired her name, seen in a dream by Grandmother. The telescope had taken Noelani's interest in the night sky to a new level. It had become for a while all she could talk about at the dinner table, until she began to suspect that she was straining the patience of even her most loving of families. From that time she had never had any doubt that one day she would be a professional astronomer. Now here she was, eight years later, an astronomy major at the University of Hawaii, standing on the summit of the extinct volcano that hosted the world's largest observatory. Over a dozen working telescopes being operated by scientists from eleven countries. It was Noelani's favorite place in the whole world. It was where the sea of space lapped gently on the shore of Earth.

She lifted the telescope onto her shoulder and closed the trunk as quietly as possible. Then she began to walk across the car park towards the secluded area of flat rock just below the summit that she had discovered a few days before. She was immediately grateful that she had dressed warmly in thick jeans and a padded jacket. She had pulled the hood up as soon as she had left the observatory and all that could be seen of her long dark hair was a few wisps that whipped in the wind around her Polynesian face. As she walked she looked up at the night sky, beautifully clear at this altitude, the stars dominated by the full moon that shone brightly with reflected sunlight. Looking down she could see patches of white billowing cloud lying below the mountain's peak. She felt as if she was on an island in the stars. She turned her head and could see on the summit the upper parts of some of the buildings that housed the many telescopes. They glowed in the silvery light of the moon.

Noelani reached the end of the car park and began scrambling across bare rock. Over the years she had carried her telescope to all kinds of remote places to obtain the perfect view of her latest cosmic obsession, so a short climb over rocky ground was not a problem. After about fifty yards she turned a slight corner and found herself between two shallow spurs that projected from the side of the mountain. She quickly located the large area of flat rock and began to set up the telescope under the light of the moon that hung clearly above. The task only took a few moments. She checked her watch; just a couple of minutes to go.

Noelani had seen lunar eclipses before on numerous occasions. But this was her first opportunity to see one from such a fantastic viewing point, through crystal clear air at high altitude. Moreover, tonight would be a total eclipse when the moon would pass fully into the Earth's shadow and be illuminated only by indirect light refracted through its larger neighbor's atmosphere, painting the moon strange and wonderful colors. It thrilled Noelani to know that within a short time the mighty dance of the Earth, sun and moon would align them almost exactly, with the planet on which she stood in the middle. Whilst both the scientist and the human being in her were fascinated to see what was about to happen, it was the latter that had persuaded her to sneak her own telescope up the mountain and slip out of the observatory where her fellow students would be viewing the event. They would not be alone as, all over the night side of the planet, stargazers of all types would also have their instruments focused on the Earth's largest satellite. Despite the party that was developing in the absence of any tutors, her colleagues would be taking the opportunity to make measurements of the refraction that would occur. Each eclipse produced different colored effects on the moon's surface, which as yet could not be predicted with any accuracy. Normally she would find making such measurements an absorbing experience, but tonight something else was at work in her that had been building for days. It gently demanded that she connect with the eclipse directly, alone and in silence with her feet firmly rooted on the ancient rock of Earth. It was the side of her that arose from the deep mysticism of her Polynesian ancestors, which still ran strongly in the veins of her family. It did not deny the power of science, which she adored, but was simply another way of knowing. Both were powerfully present within her, ebbing and flowing in turn, in deep relationship, but tonight it was the inner silent voice that guided her.

Noelani's thoughts were interrupted by an almost imperceptible change in the quality of the moonlight. She quickly looked through her telescope and immediately saw a slowly expanding blackness starting to move across the upper left quadrant of the still bright full moon. The eclipse had started. Losing all track of time, she watched spellbound as the blackness rolled its ink-like way diagonally across the lunar surface. As it did so, the wonderfully bright light that had illumined everything around her dimmed and became deep shadow. As the moon slowly disappeared, Noelani wondered whether there would be any colors. This eclipse seemed too total. But then, as the blackness seemed about to cover the whole surface, the remaining slice that was still in sunlight brightened and suddenly the darkened surface had a green tint, which almost immediately began to shift into a pale red. Noelani looked on enraptured as slowly the lunar surface became visible once more, but now tinged a breath-takingly beautiful red, which gradually fluxed through the most delicate shades. She thought it was the most wonderful thing she had ever seen. She lifted her head from the telescope for a few moments to find that her rocky island above the clouds was no longer moonlit silver, but an eerie alien color that she found difficult to name. It was almost a mixture of pink and maroon, if such a thing were possible. She returned to the eyepiece of her telescope and sank once more into the extraordinary vision that it offered. All thoughts of sneaking back into the observatory before she was missed were forgotten in the quiet ecstasy of the moment.

Her mind did not at first register the brilliant point of white light when, without warning, it flashed into existence. Perhaps it was too out of place, too unexpected. But it took no more than a few seconds for her to realize that something was wrong, or rather was not as it should be. She lifted her head for a moment and then bent over the eyepiece again. It was still there, in the Sea of Tranquility, just above the moon's equator, slightly to the east. A dot of the most intense light she had ever seen, which to her keen vision seemed to be pulsing slowly and rhythmically. Her ecstasy was replaced by puzzlement. The scientist in her immediately began to offer mundane explanations for what she was seeing and methodically she checked the lenses of the telescope for anything that could be producing a false image. She also examined the sky closely for any passing aircraft that could account for the light, but could see and hear nothing. She returned to the image in the telescope and caught her breath. Even though she had only been away for a few moments, a change was clearly discernable. The point of light had grown significantly and was now gently pulsing even more brilliantly against the pinky red background of the moon's surface. Noelani quickly tried to estimate how big the light must be if were really coming from the lunar surface, based on her knowledge of the size of nearby craters, but her mind was reluctant to process the calculations. There was something deep within that was telling her to absorb what was happening, to join with it and not be a dispassionate observer. For a moment, Noelani seemed to almost feel the presence of her grandmother, but then it was gone.

The light began to move, slowly and gracefully and, as Noelani watched, hypnotized, it started to inscribe a simple pattern. From its point of stillness it moved in a straight line, which then became the radius of a circle. As the circle was completed, the light returned to its original location and became still for a few moments. Then the process repeated itself, but with a new radius. The import of what she was witnessing suddenly hit Noelani and she leapt backwards from the telescope in shock. With a struggle she calmed her whirling thoughts and tried to analyze rationally what she was seeing. It was clearly intelligent behavior. There was nothing random in the light's movement or in the timing of its appearance when eyes all over the world would be trained on the moon. Then her inner skeptic asserted itself. It had to be a hoax, perhaps even by a group of students such as the one to which she belonged. But how? Try as she might, no obvious way of producing such effects would come to mind. A laser perhaps, fired at the moon from Earth, bouncing back off reflective material. But would not the reflective material need to have been pre-positioned with great accuracy – and on the moon? And would not the return beam be only visible at a very precise location on Earth? And would not an inconceivable amount of power be needed to produce such a sustained and brilliant effect? Noelani shook her head in bewilderment, not yet ready to grapple with the obvious, yet world-shattering explanation that patiently awaited her attention. She took a deep breath and calmed herself once more. She reminded herself that countless other pairs of eyes were watching the moon that night, many far more knowledgeable than hers. She would just watch what was happening and no doubt it would all be explained in the next few days. But deep within, she knew that it would not be that simple.

Noelani bent over again to look through the telescope and after a few moments a shiver went down her spine. The eclipse was now gradually coming to an end, but that was not what had sent a jolt of electricity through her. The point of light was now getting steadily bigger, gradually obscuring the Sea of Tranquility. It was moving towards her, towards Earth. She suddenly became very still inside, and in the stillness something ancient moved and remembered. A distant song that could not yet be heard, merely sensed. But it was a joyous song. Somewhere in the stillness, for no apparent reason, the fact that her name meant "beautiful girl from heaven" suddenly seemed very important to Noelani.

Her absorption was so total that she did not hear the distant shouts that erupted from different parts of the observatory complex. Neither did she hear the occasional slamming of car doors.

Three thousand miles to the east, Professor Jim Carrick of the Apache Point Lunar Laser-ranging Operation in New Mexico was staring at the screen of his computer incredulously, ignoring the telephone that was ringing on his desk. It had been ringing for a while, but he was lost in what he was looking at. Professor Carrick was a very ordered scientist and, for an astronomer, remarkably unimaginative. A predictable clockwork universe appealed to him very much. It was how things should be. It felt right. But tonight everything felt very wrong.

He had taken the opportunity of the eclipse to test the latest equipment and software that had just been installed at the observatory. For decades, Apache Point and other specialist observatories around the world had been measuring the distance from the Earth to the moon using laser pulses. Starting with Apollo 11 in 1969, numerous missions had left reflectors on the moon that, if hit accurately at the right time, would return the pulse to Earth. Using the speed of light, it was then possible to calculate how far the pulse had travelled through measuring the time taken for the journey. That night he had aimed the new equipment at the original reflector left by Apollo 11 at its base on the Sea of Tranquility, but right from the start he had experienced problems. It was as though something was in the way, interfering with the pulse. He had run all the diagnostic programs that he had, but they just kept saying that the equipment was working fine.

Then, suddenly, the problem seemed to correct itself and he was now getting clear readings on his monitor. But what he was seeing had only increased his puzzlement. If the figures were correct, the moon was moving towards the Earth. Obviously, this could not be right. Unfortunately, the only other explanation he could think of was that something between the Earth and the lunar surface was reflecting back the laser pulses and this was what was approaching. But what ever it was, judging from the first distance readings, it must have started its journey on or near the surface of the moon. Also, the laser pulse was very narrow when compared with the lunar surface and the distance that it was travelling. The object, if it existed, must be moving very precisely along the beam. The odds against something like this happening by chance were enormous. None of this made any sense to Jim's very methodical mind.

And there was something else that puzzled him even more.

The returning laser pulse was subtly different to what was being sent out. It had been changed in a way he could not identify. It was as though it now had hidden layers.

He leaned back in the chair, removed his glasses and rubbed tired eyes. If only the telephone would stop ringing he might be able to think.

A little while later, about two hundred miles to the south of Apache Point, Sergeant Marianne Webber of the United States Air Force could also hear telephones ringing with an air of urgency. The duty officers seemed to be rushing about with worried-looking faces. This was most unusual, if not unknown, where she worked. Despite the fact that many people found its name humorous, the Air Force Space Surveillance receiving station at Elephant Butte was a serious place, with an air of disciplined concentration. It was part of a network of radar transmitters and receivers, known colloquially as Space Fence, spread out across the United States of America, which tracked objects in near Earth orbit.

Sergeant Webber, however, was determined to ignore the disturbance and concentrate on the radar screen in front of her. She had only started her new posting three days earlier and had worked long and hard to achieve such a prestigious job. She was determined that in the future she would be one of those officers and burning ambition demanded that she perform her job without blemish. The duty officers that night were quite junior and she had no doubt that the disturbance was just some minor administrative panic over nothing at all. She was not going to let herself be distracted. Just for a moment the focus of her eyes relaxed a little and she caught a glimpse of her face reflected in the screen in front of her. She had been told more than once that she looked like a young Diana Ross and she had to admit that there was a definite resemblance. But whereas most women would have been delighted by such a comparison, the recollection made Marianne scowl. She wanted to be taken seriously, very seriously, and she had already learned that being pretty did not always help in the Air Force. In the few moments that she stared at her image in the screen, all she wanted to see was an officer's uniform, complete with braid. She sighed a little and then refocused determinedly on the radar screen.

The problem was that the screen was not cooperating with her ambition. Something odd was happening and that was the last thing she wanted just three days into the job. She would feel humiliated if she had to call one of the officers over to sort out the problem. They were no older than her and one had already been getting a bit too familiar. Anyway, if they had been doing their job properly they would have noticed already that something was wrong. She looked hard at the images before her and tried to work out what was happening. Normally all she would be looking at would be tracks of satellites and the vast amount of debris with which human beings had already managed to litter space. Even in just three days, Marianne had become highly sensitized to the flow of traces that crossed her screen on a regular basis. It had taken only a moment to realize that out in space, at the limit of the system's range, something new had appeared. And it was something that was behaving oddly.

As surreptitiously as she could, Marianne had run every database cross-reference, diagnostic check and calibration of which she could think, but just like Jim Carrick she had found that it made no difference. The system appeared to be working perfectly. The object was new and refused to go away. But it was more than the mere presence of the object that was causing her concern. It could easily have been just a repositioned Chinese satellite or an uncatalogued item of space junk, perhaps knocked into a new orbit following a collision with another piece of debris. Both things had happened before. The problem was that neither space junk nor satellites behaved like this trace.

First, it was not in orbit. Astonishingly, it seemed to be

holding position around a particular coordinate. Marianne was not an astrophysicist, but she knew that if at that altitude it was not in orbit it should be falling to Earth, pulled down by the planet's gravitational field. Yet it was another oddity about the trace that concerned Marianne the most. It was actually bizarre and was what had made her so reluctant to report the problem. The object was slowly weaving a pattern in space around its central coordinate. From its point of stillness it moved in a straight line, which then became the radius of a circle. As the circle was completed it returned to its original location, became still for a few moments and then repeated the process with a new radius. When she had first seen this, Marianne's initial thought had been that someone was playing a prank on the rookie; had perhaps downloaded illicit code into the software of her equipment; but she had quickly dismissed the idea. No one would do such a thing. The work was too important and the consequences for the individual, if caught, would be horrendous.

Marianne cleared her mind and tried to allow what she was seeing to make a fresh imprint. She thought that this might help her to finally understand exactly what it was. It was then that a tingle of shock went through her and a sheen of perspiration appeared on her furrowed brow. Cleared of all its technical questions, the most obvious explanation suddenly occurred to her. She was watching a powered craft on the edge of deep space, maneuvering with the clear intention of getting itself noticed. Marianne did not want to acknowledge the implications of this realization. She found herself hyperventilating slightly, until what happened next froze her in her chair. The trace suddenly started to move in a new way. It began to lose altitude. It was moving slowly and deliberately towards the surface of Earth. For one irrational moment, Marianne was convinced that it had waited until she had finally been willing to acknowledge the truth of what she was seeing. Her mind was numbed. She did not know what to do.

Marianne was saved by one of the young duty officers entering the room and asking in a strained voice if anyone was seeing something odd on their screen.

Marianne managed to raise a shaky hand.

Chapter 3

Joseph awoke alone.

For a few moments he was confused and disorientated by the power of the dream and his sudden awakening. But even in the midst of his swirling thoughts, he knew one thing with absolute clarity. He was alone. It was the first thing he knew every morning.

He rolled over in the large double bed and, with a struggle, opened his eyes. It was still dark and he could hear the quiet gurgling of the central heating as it fought against the mid-winter freeze. In his still drowsy state Joseph knew this meant dawn could not be far away. The occasional rumbling sound of distant traffic suggested that for some the new day was underway already. He sighed, knowing that soon he must get up. He had commitments, things that must be done, which was good. Otherwise he might spend too much time with his thoughts, with his sense of loss and, worst of all, with the anger. The anger was the most difficult to deal with because it was a road to nowhere.

He sat up in bed, opened his eyes fully and switched on the bedside light. As his vision adjusted, he took in the familiar room. His eyes paused at the two wardrobes against the far wall, one now emptied. They paused again at the small chair that once would have had clothing draped over, but now was bare. This was his morning ritual, but one from which he would happily escape. But its hold over him was too strong. For many years ritual had been at the heart of his life, feeding and nurturing him. It was a new discovery to find that it could also slowly crucify.

Then, just for a moment, he thought he smelt coffee. This happened sometimes and, even though he knew that it was just his mind playing tricks, it gave the ritual its own particular incense. Every morning Clare had brought him a cup of coffee while he lay in bed adjusting to the new day. The aroma had become one of those seemingly insignificant details of married life that in loss revealed an unsuspected power. He closed his eyes again for a few moments and recalled how the clunk of the coffee cup on the bedside table would often be what woke him up. As he carefully, and with difficulty, eased his eyes open there would be the steaming mug in front of his face. He would listen as Clare moved to her side of the double bed, put down her own drink and removed her dressing gown. The mattress would sag as she climbed into bed. Then they would sit together with their coffee, usually in silence, gently adjusting to the new day. Sometimes he would find himself looking at her. Her brown mousy hair would already have been brushed and be resting on slim shoulders. He would often notice that she had already managed to spill a few drops of coffee onto her long sleeved cotton nightdress. Such accidents were an everyday part of Clare's life, yet she always seemed surprised by their occurrence.

A sob rose into his throat and with it came the anger once more. Anger at the man who had taken her away from him and anger at all such men, of whom there seemed to be so many. When days started like this they usually went relentlessly downhill. For the past couple of months he had been coping much better and had dared to hope that the worst might be over. But the pain was back this morning, as bad as before. And he knew why. It was the dream and what the dream was a part of. Only Clare had known what was happening to him. Only she had been able to soothe the deep disturbance that the experience brought with it.

Joseph sat in bed as a faint ghostly light began to penetrate the drawn curtains. He found his thoughts going back to the evening three years before when he had first felt the presence of the Teacher in his mind. He and Clare had been sitting in bed reading, as they often did. It was spring time and still light outside. They liked to go to bed early and then to read and talk for a long time. In their different ways they only ever read around one subject. They were both entranced by the mystery of being, by the extraordinary fact of existence. Something within them was set ablaze by the exploration of the greatest mystery and it was a fire that neither of them could have quenched, even if they had so wished. Neither could say why the hunger was so strong. It surged up from their very roots. It was what had drawn Joseph into religion and Clare into what she would rather call spirituality. For both of them, these were ways of exploring, of getting better questions rather than easy answers. Their interest was drawn to whatever gave new insight into their quest.

But that night the Teacher was suddenly there in his mind.

Not in an overpowering way, making no attempt to take him over; just there, waiting politely to be heard. He had not even been aware of the moment of arrival. Up to that instant of Joseph's life there had been nothing like it. Then, in less time than a thought could surface, the presence was palpable and indisputable. They had been talking about something she had just read when, without any apparent break in the conversation, Joseph was aware of answers and even more questions erupting into his mind. He had found himself speaking with an authority that could almost be felt physically in the room. He had been both one and two in the same moment. Present fully as Joseph, yet also Joseph and the Teacher. Eventually he had to stop himself speaking by an act of will. He was afraid to do this in case the Teacher left, but he seemed to accept Joseph's wish with respect and good humor.

Clare had stared at him for a full minute and then simply said, "Wow!"

Joseph did not know what had happened or how to describe what he had felt. Clare had questioned him unrelentingly, her eyes shining with excitement, but there was little that he had been able to say. All he knew in that moment was that it had been the most extraordinary experience of his life and that the Teacher was utterly benevolent, profoundly wise and came with a powerful sense of unknown purpose. Beyond this, Joseph had no idea who or what the Teacher was.

From then on the Teacher had appeared frequently in Joseph's mind. Sometimes it was in full consciousness, as with their first encounter. On other occasions in vivid dreams, as with the one he had just awakened from. In the dreams he had strange encounters and conversations, made remarkable journeys and visited particular, but unknown places. One location seemed to be especially important and he frequently found himself in a great city in ancient times, situated between two great rivers. There he would meet someone. When he woke up, he could never remember what the person looked like or what had been said, but he always felt transformed, as though some fundamental break-through in understanding had occurred. There had also been other moments of connection, at the edge of consciousness, so subtle that it had taken Joseph a while to realize that it was the Teacher's influence. He would find himself being drawn to books, people and places without knowing why.

There was something else which the Teacher's arrival seemed to trigger in Joseph. He sometimes found himself experiencing feelings of profound connection with existence. It was as though the rock-solid boundaries that had always walled him off from everything and everybody else would blur and he would taste the unity, the oneness from which all sprang. It was as if his mind became illumined, expanded, transformed into a new and deeper consciousness. It would not last long before fading, but each experience left an indelible mark on his memory – together with a poignant sense of loss.

And there had been moments, extraordinary and strange, when he had no longer been sure whether it was the Teacher who inspired and guided or a deeper part of himself. He had, very occasionally, seemed to reach a depth where identities blurred and something else emerged.

The journey with the Teacher had in time become an almost bipolar helter-skelter ride, with moments of incredible inspiration and insight too often followed by feelings of melancholy and lack of purpose. Joseph naturally found the everyday world a difficult place to be. He struggled with the mundane demands of life and had come to despair of people, collectively and often individually. From the terrible things he witnessed on the television news, to the thoughtless and sometimes cruel behavior he saw in his local community, to the aggression and politicking he witnessed continually among the people in whose midst he worked, he struggled to find any hope that humanity could evolve into something better. In his worst moments he wondered whether the universe might not be a better place without Homo sapiens. It was only his relationship with certain individuals, particularly Clare, which shone a light in the dark for him.

Then the Teacher had appeared, evoking a sense of somewhere else where beauty and hope reigned, but in so doing had made it even more difficult for Joseph to live in the world.

Sometimes he had resisted the whole experience, but had inevitably given way in the end. He became increasingly agitated until he allowed the Teacher back into his mind. Something deep within knew that the relationship was of immeasurable importance.

As time passed the experience became difficult in another way. He could not help but sometimes question its reality. He had always been highly imaginative and this knowledge brought doubts and self-questioning. His moods swung wildly at times from complete belief to discounting the experience entirely. Clare never had this problem. For her its reality was never in doubt. She had a deep faith that eventually always communicated itself to Joseph. She had always been able to reassure him that something extraordinary was happening and that he had not lost his sanity.

Although it did not make matters any easier, over time Joseph began to suspect an underlying purpose in the process. It was not to fill his mind, but to empty it. He began to see that each encounter, each experience of illumination, left him with more questions than answers. Everything he thought he knew, whether consciously or unconsciously, was being undermined. At times it left his mind reeling, with a growing sense of vulnerability. It was as though his mind was being methodically opened, cleared and made ready for … something.

In the end, the journey with the Teacher had become the most real thing in his life, yet also the most unreal. Beside him all the way had been Clare, the only other person who had known what was happening to him. There was no one else he could have talked to, especially because of his role in life. Then she had gone and he had been forced to cope with the experience as best he could. The Teacher had simply continued as before, seemingly oblivious to the shattering of Joseph's life. He could not help but feel resentment about this.

Joseph thought about the dream of the forest monks. Its power and clarity had been greater, more focused than anything that had come before. He realized that it was this that had left him so disturbed. Something had changed. Then, suddenly, as though he had been waiting for this thought to arise in Joseph's mind, the Teacher invisibly erupted into his awareness. Never had he felt so close, so tangible. Joseph gasped, feeling almost overwhelmed. Without being conscious of it, he clutched his head in his hands. Then the Teacher withdrew slightly, allowing Joseph to regain some equilibrium. With great effort, Joseph tried to focus his mind. He sensed that the Teacher was trying to tell him something, yet did not wish to speak. Joseph closed his eyes and tried to communicate with the inner presence, but all that came back was deep intuition of warning, or rather of being alerted. The conviction that this day really mattered came across with irresistible force.

Then the unthinkable happened.

Without warning, with an extraordinary sense of finality, the Teacher was gone. Joseph knew that he would not return. He knew this with utter conviction, without knowing how. It was utterly shocking and felt like a foundation stone had been removed, another link with Clare broken, another anchor in this difficult world wrenched away. Joseph's mind was thrown into confusion and despair. He found himself reliving the moment, trying in vain to reconnect.

He felt his frustration turn into anger.

But he did not want that.

He was weary of anger. It was eating away at his soul. Yet he wanted the alternative even less. As the anger moved into the background, the sadness came.

He had never felt so alone.

He knew that he had to go and find Clare.

Only she would understand.

He knew that this would bring as much pain as balm, but on this morning he needed her.

Chapter 4

Thousands of miles away, the night was no longer young.

On the other side of the world, at Cheyenne Mountain in Colorado, there were no ringing telephones or harassed-looking officers in the NORAD control room. There was, instead, an intense mood of concentration and seriousness. In his nearly thirty-year association with the North American Aerospace Defense Command, Lieutenant General David de Lafitte of the Canadian Air Force had never experienced an atmosphere such as this. Even in 1980 when a computer failure had indicated that a nuclear attack was in progress, the suddenness of the warning and the almost immediate realization that it was false had not allowed any great sense of emergency to develop. But this was different. This time they knew something was coming and the waiting was allowing the tension to build. It was also different because in 1980 he had been a young, very junior officer on his first posting, carrying little responsibility. Now he was the Deputy Commander, fully in charge in the absence of his chief. It had been agreed in 1958, when NORAD had been established by the governments of the United States and Canada, that the commanding officer would always be American and the deputy Canadian. General de Lafitte had always quietly resented this junior status for his country, but now a bit of him wished mightily that his US Commander was not away on leave.

The unthinkable for which they had prepared seemed to be happening. Not a nuclear attack by an enemy state, but something else that had been long planned for, without anyone being quite able to believe that it would ever come to pass. The general had been on secret seminars over the years to develop protocols for a moment such as this, but had struggled to take them seriously. This was not only because he believed the eventuality was extremely unlikely, but also because he doubted that it was possible to prepare for something of such extreme strangeness. Yet now, as the unthinkable seemed to be happening, he was grateful for those protocols. Perhaps, despite all of the evidence to the contrary, the object would prove to be a false unknown. But the protocols gave him something to hold on to in a place without reliable points of reference.

So far, since the incoming target had first been detected and its likely nature shockingly confirmed, he had followed the protocols to the letter. Ground defenses were on high alert and aircraft were deployed in the estimated area of atmospheric entry. But these actions were precautionary only. Offensive action could only be taken on the direct order of the President and Prime Minister, both of whom were being rushed to secure locations. In reality, de Lafitte had no doubt that his orders would come from the President. Only if the actions of the incomer were clearly and instantly hostile could the general order retaliation on his own authority. The protocols had been written on the unequivocal understanding that should a day such as this ever come, they would be dealing with an unknown of awesome technological achievement and probable overwhelming power. It was also considered possible that an intelligence formed and shaped in unimaginable conditions might easily misinterpret well-intentioned actions, so treading softly was the theme that ran through the guidance. His aircraft were firmly ordered, therefore, to keep well clear and simply observe from a distance. All that was left now was to watch and wait. The object would enter the atmosphere somewhere over the northern Rocky Mountains and should be detected almost immediately by both ground and airborne radar. Its arrival was imminent.

General de Lafitte stood solidly on the raised command platform looking out over the control room where his staff focused on the screens in front of them, an imposing figure in his immaculate uniform and close-cropped hair. He was determined to exude an air of calmness, despite the fluttering of his stomach and the perspiration trickling down his back. He knew from experience that his people would sense his calm, even if they could not directly see him. On the opposite side of the control room from where he stood, the entire wall was covered with a real-time display of all aerial activity over North America and its surrounding airspace. His eyes were fixed on the display at the point where it was expected that the first trace of the object should appear.

And then, in a moment, without preliminaries, there it was, a white dot moving across the display. Something akin to a jolt of electricity went around the room. Numbers began to flash onto the screen. After his many years of experience the general understood what they meant, but he took the opportunity to break the silence by asking for an explanation. He wanted to create a feeling of normality as soon as he could.

"The object is slowing rapidly, Sir. It's already down below one thousand miles per hour." There was a brief pause. "That should not be possible, Sir ... it should be burning-up."

The general could tell that the junior officer was trying to keep his voice calm. "Not possible" was something of an understatement. The object, like the other strange traces they had tracked over the years, was doing the impossible. But on this occasion it was different. Now there seemed to be real intent, rather than just some kind of random display. The demonstration on the moon, and its deliberate drawing of attention to itself, left little doubt that this time it meant business.

"What reports do we have from shadowing aircraft?" the general asked in a measured tone. Whilst it was still the middle of the night, he knew that the planes were equipped with powerful radars of their own, together with enhanced night vision equipment. Another officer answered.

"They've picked it up on their radar, Sir, and have visual contact. They report an intense white light, but not the same as that given off by a super-heated re-entry."

"Thank you. Okay people, let's just watch and be prepared for anything." A murmur of assent went around the room.

He watched as the dot on the wall display continued to move across the map of North America. He could tell from the numbers flashing underneath that it was both descending and slowing at a rapid rate. Before long, it appeared to be merely crawling across the screen, before disappearing completely. He knew what had happened. It had dropped below the level at which ground radar could track it. It was at this point that the surveillance aircraft became very important. He was about to ask what they could see, but was cut off by one of his staff.

"Sir, aircraft report that the object has come to a halt and is hovering at very low altitude. Estimated height, three hundred feet."

"And where is this please?"

There was a short pause as the officer waited for more information from the aircraft. Then the reply came. There were a few sharp intakes of breath around the room. General de Lafitte thought for a few moments and then was forced to smile at what the object seemed to be doing.

"Well people," he said with a sigh, "there'll be no hiding this one."

Chapter 5

Joseph never used the front door of the old house if he did not have to. He much preferred to enter and leave via the venerable and aged French windows that opened onto the wonderful garden at the rear of the property. Garden was perhaps too grand a word for what was basically a large sweeping lawn, surrounded by ancient trees that reached all the way from the house to where the land fell sharply away towards the town spread out in the valley below. The drop at the end of the garden was precipitous and long, a mixture of dangerously loose gravel combined with large limestone outcroppings.

The garden was a sacred place for Joseph. It was where he reconnected with his oldest and deepest yearning, a great theme of his life which had been an essential and mysterious part of his being for as long as he could remember. From the first moment when, as a child, he had looked up and seen the stars silently twinkling against their dark velvety backdrop, he had wanted to leave the confines of Earth and plunge into that fathomless ocean. Something had drawn him. It had filled his dreams and imaginings. As he grew older and read about people marooned on desert islands, he thought he knew how they must have felt. He experienced the world on which he stood in the same way.

As an adult he had tried to interpret this yearning in more psychological terms, as a response to mundane human life that could never fulfill him in the same way that it seemed able to for others. Yet he knew, deep down, that this alternative explanation could at best be only partial. There was something else at work, real and powerful, that made him feel as if he was trapped in a rock pool while the mighty ocean pounded just a short distance away, but out of reach. He had done his best as an adult to suppress this great yearning, for it could only end in frustration, but it would not be held down for long. The garden on a clear night was the place where it always burst forth once more and he allowed himself to delight in the experience. Clare and he had shared many such nights.

The garden was also the place, however, which brought the second great theme of his life into focus. He had long ago concluded that most of the inhabitants of the rock pool, with some notable exceptions, seemed to share a collective insanity. At worst he had a constant, nagging background fear of them, reinforced by everything from personal experience through to the nightly television news. And the loss of Clare had only confirmed what he already believed about humanity. He did not want to think in this way, but daily living only reinforced the deep primal feeling.

Yet he had chosen a profession that sought to serve others, which meant that he was always in the midst of the world. At an individual level he often met people he liked and admired, who exuded goodness and kindness, but still the deeper distrust remained. He often thought that he was a confused mess.

At best, he could not understand how people could be so absorbed in their tiny firefly lives, when all around, hidden in plain sight, was the breathtaking enigma of existence. Joseph would sometimes stand at the end of the lawn and look out over the town, imagining the stories that were out-flowing unseen below, so important to the people concerned, yet over in a flash and forgotten just as quickly. Very occasionally he met others who had the same relationship with the world as him and it was an unspeakable relief not to feel different, cut off and alone. Clare had been such a one.

Yet, sometimes, on a clear night he would look upwards at the blazing stars, become conscious of the majesty at which he gazed and his mind would still. As he did so, paradoxically, a sense of the wonder of human life and an intuition of its limitless potential would arise within him. This would leave him even more confused as he then looked down into the valley.

He closed the glazed door behind him with difficulty. The wood, though well-seasoned, had warped over many years and no longer fitted snugly into the frame. He leaned his body against the door to force it in a little more and was able to turn the key in the lock. He turned around and gazed out once again over the lawn. He loved the garden with its sense of spaciousness and the ancient, almost timeless trees that formed a kind of amphitheatre that presented to the eye the majestic view that erupted where the lawn finished. There was no clutter. Nothing was wasted. Everything was focused to nurture a deeper consciousness. For Joseph it was a kind of Celtic Zen garden in the heart of England. He had no idea if it had been planned with this in mind, for it had been that way when they moved to the house, yet this was the effect. But Joseph had to admit, with some slight pangs of guilt, that the garden was marred. The magnificent lawn was not as perfect as it should be. The grass was long and straggly, as it was a while since it had been cut. It had been Clare's pride and joy, and it was she that had looked after it. When he had lost her in the middle of the previous summer, he had been unable to bring his mind to such things and the lawn had run wild. He regretted this now as he knew that, somehow, it really mattered to his state of mind that the garden and lawn continued to be loved and cared for. That it had not been for the last few months disturbed him. Part of this feeling was connected with Clare and the memories of her that the garden brought back, but there was also something else, much older and more powerful that urged him to care for this place. Joseph resolved there and then that, come the spring, the garden would be restored to its best. He had complete clarity on this resolution and knew that he would act on it. He had rarely experienced clarity over the last few months and his mind felt for a few moments refreshed and clear, before the numbing sadness returned.

Joseph took a deep breath and walked across the small, irregularly paved patio and down a few steps onto the frozen grass with its milky-white frosty sheen. He paused for a few moments and considered walking to the end of the garden to gaze out over the valley for a while. It was now fully light as he had taken his time over showering and getting dressed that morning, despite his urgent need to get out. He had even managed a bit of breakfast. He had made himself do this. The basics of everyday living could easily seem overwhelming in a state of mind such as his and be neglected. He knew this was not a good habit, which once established could be difficult to break. In the early days after Clare had gone he had started to slide, but had been fortunate in having someone who had cared enough to talk bluntly to him. It was strange, because he had never really warmed to the bishop with her forthright way of speaking and horribly rational mind. Now he was grateful for her honesty and courage. Joseph stood, his cold breath billowing before him, and felt tempted to walk forward and contemplate the familiar view. He resisted, for he knew that the urge did not arise from the mysterious contemplative impulse that was so often at work within him, but from prevarication. His mind knew it was about to do something difficult and was using evasion tactics.

He sighed, turned to his right and began to walk slowly around the rear of the house, his shoes crunching on the grass. As he walked he looked up at the house and, even now, could not help but be quietly entranced by its evocative appearance. Large, with a slightly gothic impression, it was a strange mixture of different periods. Its origins were unclear. The earliest parts were almost certainly Tudor, but it was the large Georgian windows that dominated its external appearance, while the interior was typically Victorian. Its uncertain history had resulted in a collection of myths and legends being associated with it, which Clare had researched as well as she could. She had always been fascinated by such tales. And it was, of course, here that the Teacher had first made himself known. Clare and he often wondered whether the house, or rather the grounds on which it stood, had some kind of power. There had been times when both of them had sensed that the veil was a little thinner in this place.

He reached the corner of the house and turned along the narrow gravel path that ran along its side. His feet now crunched on gravel, rather than frozen grass. Just before he reached the front corner of the building, he turned left through the wooden gate that gave the house its own special access to the churchyard. He crossed the narrow potholed lane that came to a dead end a dozen or so yards to his left, just out of sight beyond a bend. Sometimes people attending the church insisted on using the turning circle where the lane finished as somewhere to leave their car, rather than use the large designated car park on the other side of the churchyard and so having to walk a little further. The resulting chaos as cars, unable to turn, reversed back along the narrow lane and met vehicles coming the other way was amusing to watch, but not to be involved in. On the other side of the lane, Joseph opened another rickety wooden gate and found himself on the long curving path that led through the maze of ancient and modern graves to the church. He did not follow the path, but turned to the left and, once more crunching over frozen grass, followed the boundary hedge to where he knew he would find Clare. As he walked, he was aware of each of the graves that he passed. Each life that was represented had its own story, seemingly so powerful and important at the time, yet now gone. He had tasted for himself what this meant.

It did not take him long to reach Clare. She lay at the far edge of the churchyard, looking out over the valley, forever at one with the view that had meant so much to them. At this point the hawthorn hedge dropped away down the slope, until it petered out a short distance further on. It was an area of the churchyard that had been reserved for future burials, but Joseph had used his authority to insist that she be laid to rest in this place. No one had wanted to argue. It would be many years before anyone else would be buried in the vicinity. This was fine by Joseph as it meant that he could always feel that he was alone with her when he came to talk. This was how it had been when she was alive. They had been soul mates, utterly fulfilled by their relationship, having no great need to be part of a wider social network. They were genuinely friendly with many people, but without needing to go beyond this. Both were quietly, but deeply, unconventional and only managed to function in normal society with difficulty. But they had each other, so it was fine – until the day when in the town below the hill a group of drunken young men, mostly teenagers, had stolen a car for a bit of fun and gone speeding through the streets pursued by the police. Losing control, they had mounted the pavement just as Clare was leaving a shop. Joseph had known the police officer who knocked on the door. It had made things no easier. In one moment his whole life had fallen apart.

He had not said goodbye to Clare that day.

He had been working in his study.

In court the driver had shown no remorse and had projected an air of boredom throughout the proceedings. The rational part of Joseph had known that this was merely an act, the way that an immature youth was coping with fear and terrible guilt. But reason had not helped him to feel any less angry. It had fed a thousand-fold his sense of a humanity fundamentally flawed. The many individual acts of kindness that had showered upon him since that day, for which he was profoundly grateful, had been unable to heal this conviction. He did not want to believe that this was true and still tried sometimes to see the best, but deep down he knew that he was pretending. Not that anyone would have guessed, for he covered his feelings well. He had spoken to the bishop several times about how he felt and had been listened to with great kindness and wisdom. The advice had been to let life unfold and, perhaps, it would of itself bring the answer to Joseph's struggle. He had worried too about his vocation. Not his relationship with the mystery of God, which he sensed in every moment, but whether such disillusionment and anger still allowed him to be alongside people who were in need. Once more the bishop's advice had been to be patient and allow life to evolve as it would. Again, Joseph had deeply appreciated her patient insight and had come away reassured to some extent. But there were other matters that he could never discuss with a bishop and they were why he was here on this cold morning.

Joseph sat down on the bench that he had placed by Clare's grave, beneath a couple of ancient, gnarled, sinewy yew trees, which had been in this place since before even the locals could remember. Directly in front of him was the simple marble stone that marked where she lay, which gave only her name and dates. She had been a few years younger than him and had taken mischievous delight when he had turned forty. He had been grateful that she was an only child, whose parents had died years before with no close relatives. He had not been required to discuss and compromise about the stone or anything else around her death, but had been able to do exactly as he pleased. This had made matters a little easier. He had been an orphan, raised by a series of foster parents with whom he had never bonded, despite their undoubted kindness. He had been terribly shy and uncertain as a child, and school had not been an easy experience.

He contemplated the stone for a few moments and then lifted his eyes to look out across the valley towards the far horizon. Then very quietly, barely in more than a whisper, told her about the dream and that the Teacher had gone. As he told her, the weight on his shoulders gradually lessened and thinking became a little easier. After a while Joseph found that there were no more words and he sank into silence. There was a kind of peace. He closed his eyes and in his mind he could suddenly see her face, the hazel eyes with a scattering of freckles around the nose, assuming the wonderful intensity it had when she was listening to something important. It was too much and he quickly opened his eyes and focused on the horizon.

The hill on which the house and the church stood was curved and from this part of the burial ground the town in the valley could not be seen. Instead there was just a panoramic view across farmland to where the ground and sky seemed to meet in the far distance. He had often thought what a remarkable symbol the horizon was. A false boundary that could never be reached.

His thoughts were interrupted by a sound from behind. He turned and in the distance, at the other end of the burial ground by the church, he caught a glimpse of Leola Lambert approaching the vestry door. Since anyone could remember she had prepared the church every Wednesday morning for the mid-week Mass. She appeared not to have seen him, but Joseph knew that her eyes missed nothing. She would have spotted him sitting by Clare's grave but, with her innate sensitivity, would never intrude. He also knew that, unlike most of the other old ladies who attended the church, the fact that the rector had once more been discovered sitting by his dead wife's grave would not become the latest item of gossip.

It had taken him a while to appreciate Leola after he had moved to the parish. At first he had just seen her as one of the group of widowed elderly ladies who, as with so much of the Church of England, made up a substantial caucus of the congregation. Gradually, however, he had discovered what a remarkable and mysterious person she was. She had lost her husband years before after a long marriage and, although he could not be certain, Joseph guessed that she must be in her eighties. He also sensed that it must have been a happy marriage for, although she never mentioned him by name, there was something in her voice on the odd occasions when, in her broad rural accent, she referred to "the old man" that conveyed more than words ever could. There was also the moment at Clare's funeral when she had taken both of his hands and looked deeply into his eyes. In that moment there was no doubt that she knew his pain and was telling him so. But there had also been a glimpse of something else, a power that resided in her that was more than the Leola he had come to know in daily life.

Although she did not talk about herself very much, he knew that she had been born locally to farm laborer parents in an age when such people lived and died without ever leaving the area where they had come into the world. And slowly he learned other things about Leola, things that had come to him in whispered fragments that, over time, he had eventually pieced together. She was what country people called a "wise woman", someone profoundly at one with the land, nature and the essence of life. Someone they went to for counsel and healing. Someone who knew and practiced the "old ways" alongside a deep and genuine relationship with the figure of Jesus – and saw no contradiction in doing so. When he had realized this about her, much had fallen into place. He had noticed previously how members of the congregation whose families had lived in the area for generations treated her with a quiet respect, how they fell silent when she spoke and how pleased they looked if she chose to sit beside them. Joseph, and especially Clare, had been delighted by this discovery. For them it was an opportunity to explore the mystery of existence from a different direction, to hear a fresh voice.

It had had not been easy, for Leola and her forebears had learned the hard way to be discreet about their activities. Around Joseph she had been tongue-tied, but she had been willing to talk to Clare. At first, Clare had shared with him what Leola told her, but soon she too had become coy. This was a new experience for Joseph. They had always shared everything, but something deep within had told him to accept the situation and he had found peace with the exclusion. One thing, however, had gradually struck Joseph about Leola - how differently she experienced the world. It had been brought home to him when he and Clare had gone for a walk with her across some fields to pick blackberries. It had become apparent that, for Leola, every blade of grass, every stone, every pool of mud was alive in its own way. Indeed, for Leola they shone with the same life force that burned in her. The walk with Leola had reminded Joseph of his times of illumination since the arrival of the Teacher. But these had been just fleeting experiences, whereas for Leola such deeply connected consciousness seemed to be a sustained condition wherein the world was part of her and she was a part of it. They emanated each other. Leola could never have explained it in this way, even if she had possessed the language and education, for it was not something of which she was consciously aware. It was her natural state of being.

At one point on their ramble a beautiful roe deer had burst from some trees and Leola had frozen, eyes shining with delight. The deer and Leola had regarded each other for a timeless moment, clearly in profound relationship, before the animal had casually turned and walked back into the trees. Months later, by chance, Clare had discovered that "Leola" was an Anglo Saxon name meaning "deer". To Joseph, it somehow felt right that Leola should be so profoundly connected to an animal that had walked the land of Britain for thousands of years, since before the Mesolithic age.

This walk had been important for Clare. It had awakened a realization that she experienced the world in the same way as Leola. But whereas Leola had been raised and nurtured in a culture where this was accepted and venerated, Clare had been isolated among minds that could never understand. That day had been the start of a close relationship between the two women, one old and one young, one a link to a simple and unsophisticated past and the other the product of the modern educated world. Joseph had often wondered to what extent he figured in the long, intense conversations they shared and what happened on those days when they disappeared off into the country together. But it was the one area of her life that Clare would not share with him, explaining once with mischievous eyes that it was too sacred. Joseph could see that her discovery of

Leola had clearly made Clare happy and this had helped him to accept the situation. Yet he was often curious. Somehow, mysteriously, Clare's death had left behind a strong unspoken bond between Joseph and Leola and there were occasions when he suspected that she knew far more about him, than he knew about her.

Leola's arrival meant that he could sit with Clare no longer. He rose and walked towards the church, watching as Leola struggled with the large old-fashioned key to the outer Vestry door. Her arthritic hands made it difficult to grip anything too tightly and the lock was stiff with age, despite the liberal amounts of easing oil that were frequently applied. He walked slowly, winding his way through the tombstones. It was a large churchyard that had developed in an unplanned manner down the centuries. There were no straight lines or neatly drawn plots. The gravestones were of every size and shape imaginable, with many bearing inscriptions that had worn away to just faint impressions. It gave the place a sense of the ancient and mysterious, which Joseph liked. He trod carefully across the still frozen grass, his long black cloak and cassock brushing the surface and becoming progressively wetter in the process. His white clerical collar could just be glimpsed. Clare had been amused that so unconventional a priest had dressed in such a traditional manner, but he felt that the symbolism was important and changed the nature of his relationship with people. Sometimes it could be an obstacle, but he had lost count of the deep conversations that had unexpectedly occurred, often with complete strangers and in the most unlikely of circumstances, because of the clerical garb. Also for Joseph, which was very important, it represented a living tradition going back millennia and had its origins in ancient monastic attire. It was something not of the modern world with its passing fashions, but pointed to something eternal. This gave it an unspoken authority.

As Joseph walked towards Leola, he glanced up at the church.

St Petroc's was, as the name suggested, originally a Saxon place of worship, but which had been extensively altered and enlarged by the Normans. The dedication to this particular saint was interesting for, as was common with the legends of Saxon saints, Petroc had been required to deal with a threatening dragon. But whereas most of his brother saints had destroyed the terrifying creature, he had simply whispered a prayer in its ear after which it had swum out to sea in search of new lands. As the dragon often symbolized for Christians the indigenous pagan culture of Britain, the legend suggested that Petroc had a more gentle and subtle way of handling the encounter than was commonly the case in his age. Some years before Joseph arrived as its priest, drainage repairs had revealed archaeology suggesting that the hilltop on which the church and his home, the rectory, stood had been used for religious ritual for several thousand years. To Joseph's mind, this should have come as no surprise, as the prominent, unusual hill had an air of the numinous to it – something indefinable that few locations possessed. It was natural that it should have spoken to generations of souls. The choice of Petroc to be patron to the site when it became Christian hinted that the new religion in this area had found an accommodation with the old. Joseph glanced up as he slowly walked towards Leola, and wondered if he was seeing in her a living symbol of this act of maturity and humility.

The hill stood over the town below and the church tower was visible from almost every street. For centuries it had quietly dominated the minds of those below, pointing upwards to strange mysteries. The church and the rectory were the only buildings on the hill, with access being along a steep road which wound its way upwards around the back of the hill from the valley. In years gone by there had been a more direct footpath up the slope from the town, but it was steep and tiring and with the coming of the motor car it had fallen into disuse. At some point what remained of it was washed away in a winter storm. Leola had a car almost as ancient as she was and, blissfully unaware, caused mayhem wherever she drove.

The church's southern face stood before him, massive and solid, with the large square tower at its western end. The entrance was through imposing, iron-girded double doors at its base. The main building ran off to the right of the tower as Joseph looked at it, basically rectangular, but with various additions tacked on at some point in the past, such as the vestry that Leola was trying unsuccessfully to enter. The roof was flat with a crenulated border, above stone walls darkened with age. Large windows, tapering to typical Norman arches, rounded off the building's majestic appearance. Like the clerical dress that he wore, it had seen the ages pass and remained unmoved by humanity's trifling dramas. As Joseph approached up the slight rise of the graveyard, the church appeared to him set against the brilliant blue winter sky which lay behind it. It was a powerful and inspiring sight.

Joseph reached Leola, deliberately pushing down thoughts of Clare and the Teacher as he did so.

"Good morning Leola. Having trouble with the lock?"

"Morning to you, also, Father Joseph," Leola replied in her wonderful rustic accent. Despite his many requests, she would never just call him "Joseph". She had been shaped in an age of deference, when the clergy were always addressed formally. It was not a deference that came from weakness, however, but from an inner strength. "I'm thinking that this old lock, he'll have to be replaced before long."

With these words, she looked up for the first time and was clearly startled by what she saw. She turned towards him completely and Joseph found himself being closely examined by the bright blue eyes that shone with life from Leola's weathered leathery face. She looked at him intently for what seemed an age without saying a word. Then she leaned back with a look of awe on her face. She took his hand firmly in one of hers.

"I don't know what's going to happen lad, but always remember that you're never alone," she said without preamble, her eyes once more fixing on his. Then, as though nothing had happened, she turned back to the door and, without any apparent difficulty, turned the key in the lock and walked into the vestry, leaving a stunned Joseph standing outside. Stunned that she had called him "lad" and more stunned by the intensity of her enigmatic message.

He pulled himself together and followed her.

Waiting once more.

Yet in a familiar place this time, not so alien or desolate and, above all, not so dry.

He felt the surging water below and it delighted his soul. It evoked far-away home and those whom he loved. He imagined what it would be like to be carried along by those currents, twisting and turning, diving and soaring without any purpose other than sheer joy. For a while he lost himself in reverie.

It was the pressing of so many minds that brought him back. The sea of consciousness that surrounded him pressed in with ever increasing force, as his presence became the focus of intense awareness. This was good, for it was what had been intended. It was important that all minds on this world should be opened. Yet it was still not easy to be at the center of such confused, fragmented thinking. It was one of the reasons he had chosen to wait here, where the feel of the water would help anchor him. But there were other reasons too. Above all, it was a place where his presence could not be hidden. No one would be able to control knowledge of him. Also, it was a place of symbolic meaning, where minds met and learned how to work together.

He reached inwardly and sensed the presence that was his travelling companion. Familiar and yet also so strange. No communication was needed, for it would be a while before they needed to move again.

He felt himself drawn once more to the energy of the water rushing below and saw in his mind the vast melting ice sheets that had carved out this place, unleashing torrents of water as their existence faded away.

Soon he was back in reverie.

Chapter 6

This moment was why Joseph was a priest.

In front of him on the altar were the bread and wine that he was about to consecrate as the culmination of the Mass. The silver paten and chalice that held them glinted in the flickering candlelight. Around him in the streaming sunlight the stained glass windows of the church threw colored motifs on the flagstones; blues, greens and reds painting ghostly shapes.

Years before, one Christmas Day, on a sudden impulse, he had gone into a church vaguely seeking some meaning in the midst of the spending, eating and drinking. He had sat down at the back in the fervent hope that he would not be noticed. To start with, as he looked around at the sea of respectability, he had regretted his spontaneity. He had felt completely out of place. But when he had watched the priest consecrate the bread and wine, and had then gone forward to receive, something within had awakened. As he had walked away from the altar rail he had known his future.

Joseph knew that he would never understand what had happened on that day, for it was beyond any understanding. The Mystery that lay at the heart of existence, which many people liked to call God, had reached out and touched him. The Mystery was no stranger to Joseph. All of his life the breath-taking wonder of existence had filled him. He had never been able to understand why most other people did not seem to see it. They appeared so lost in their life story that they could not see the miracle that was in front of their face. Now the Mystery had demonstrated that in its depths there was a living meaning and purpose.

And meaning and purpose were what Joseph had sought since he was a child.

It was the third great theme of his life, confusingly interwoven with his despair of humanity and his yearning for the stars.

Deep within, since he could first remember, there had always been a pressure, a sense that there was something he must do, but which he had never been able to identify. Occasionally, though, he discovered something that, whilst not the thing itself, seemed to take him closer to his ultimate purpose. Becoming a priest had felt like a huge step in the right direction, for reasons he could never explain. He had walked forward into his new life in faith rather than certainty.

On that Christmas Day, the Mystery had for Joseph acquired a face and a name. From that day he had known that he was a follower of the extraordinary figure known as Jesus. He had no idea who Jesus was, except that he was the Mystery embodied. All Joseph knew was that when he contemplated the stories of the Christ's life and communed with him in prayer, his heart caught fire. He accepted that this was not the case for everyone and had never doubted that the Mystery reached out in innumerable ways to other people, wearing many masks and known by many names. His was just one thread in a multicolored tapestry.

This conviction had been confirmed the first time he encountered Clare. She had been sitting underneath a yew tree outside a church where he was a priest. He had said a perfunctory "Good Morning" as he had walked past, his mind absorbed with what he had to do that day. But when she had raised her head to return the greeting, his thoughts had been swept away in an instant as he saw the Mystery shining from her eyes. He had been completely thrown and had mumbled something about having to go inside. He had stumbled through the door into the church and had tried to go about his business. Yet he had been unable to get those eyes out of his mind and, very nervously, after pacing up and down with indecision, he had gone outside again, desperately relieved to find that she was still there. She had smiled, a smile that told Joseph that she had been waiting for him. Clare had been a spiritual seeker, exploring any teaching or practice to which she felt drawn. Joseph had joined with her in the great quest and had seen the Mystery shining in many different places. Together they had learned to be grateful for any insight into its nature, whether from the power of science, the questioning of philosophy, the depths of spirituality or the inspiration of art.

The journey with Clare had not changed Joseph's acceptance of what he was, but had reinforced his profound sense of the unknownness of existence. This could only nurture a deep humility. Through being utterly conscious of how much he did not know, a generosity and openness to other insights into the wonder of existence arose naturally. The lust for certainty that seemed to dominate so much of what was called Christianity saddened and bemused him. It could only come from a disconnection with the very nature of what the word "God" pointed to. Clare had eventually found herself settling into Buddhism, although more lately she had been increasingly drawn towards nature-based spirituality through her friendship with Leola.

And now Joseph stood, as he had done many times before, about to invoke the great prayer of consecration that lay at the heart of the Mass. The rite was the re-enactment of the Last Supper, Jesus' final meal with his friends in the upper room of a house in Jerusalem, just before his arrest and death. The prayer now told the story with awesome simplicity. He reached down to the altar and raised the paten with the piece of bread on it. As he did so, the beautiful gold cross that was embroidered on the front of his ceremonial robe flashed as the tiny jewels sewn into it caught the candlelight. As he proclaimed what had happened, his voice seemed to take on a deeper resonance.

"On the night before his death,
Jesus shared supper with his friends.
Taking some bread, he gave thanks to God.
He broke the bread and gave it to them saying:

49

Eat this; it is my body which I will give for you.
Do this in the future and remember me."

Joseph closed his eyes and paused to allow the words to sink in. As he did so, in his imagination, he was there in the room with Jesus and his disciples. This often happened when he presided at Mass. It took no effort on his part. It just seemed to be his natural response to the story. Yet the clarity this time took his breath away. He could almost believe that he was there, as the sights, sounds and aromas of the upper room filled his senses. In the vision he felt himself being watched and, looking up, a jolt of electricity went up his spine at the sight of the face that was turned towards him.

Joseph wrenched his eyes open in shock, physically shaken by the power of the experience. He glanced up involuntarily at the small congregation to see if they had noticed his discomfort, but all had their eyes closed or heads bowed in prayer. Except for Leola, whose gaze was fixed upon him, filled with wonder and reassurance. He took a deep breath to pull himself together and gently lowered the paten onto the altar. Slowly, he then raised the chalice of wine and held it before him as he continued with the story of Jesus' last night.

"Then Jesus took a cup of wine.
After giving thanks to God, he said:
this is my blood which I will shed for you.
When you drink it in the future, remember me."

Joseph paused again to emphasize the words, but kept his eyes open this time, still shaken by his vision of only a few moments before. He then lowered the chalice and placed it back on the altar. He turned his attention to the paten and broke the bread into pieces. As he did so, his dream from the previous night came back and he saw in his mind's eye the senior monk doing exactly the same thing by the graveside.

He took a piece of the bread and put it in his mouth. He risked closing his eyes. Without warning, something in his mind gave way and he felt time disappear. Suddenly there was only now, but it was a multi-layered "now", a single diamond with countless facets. The past and the present were in that moment absolutely alive and real, together in the same place. He could feel the awesome presence of the being known as Jesus, alongside the monks he had met in his dream only a few hours before. This was not memory, it was living reality. And there was something else present as well, something that could not be discerned, that was fog-like, but which pressed in his mind with great urgency and importance. It was the future. It too was present in the eternal "now". The past, the now and the future, fully present in the same moment.

The ancient Greeks possessed a wonderful word for this collapse of time. They called it "anamnesis". There was no equivalent English word.

Joseph knew in that moment of anamnesis that something with roots deep in the past was coming to fruition, through the present, into the future and that he was at the center of what ever it was. For a few seconds the sense of hidden purpose to his life felt overwhelming.

He jerked his eyes open, almost in panic. He swallowed the piece of bread and then lifted the chalice to his lips. As he sipped the wine, he glanced over the top of the vessel at the congregation. This time they were looking at him and were clearly beginning to suspect that something strange was happening. He focused hard on what he was doing and, with great determination, performed the rest of the service with an air of normality. The only moment of struggle came as he was distributing the bread and wine to the congregation at the altar rail and flashes of his dream from the previous night started to fill his mind. He managed to suppress them and behave as was expected. It was a relief when the service was over and he could stand at the door saying goodbye to people. He was slightly puzzled that everyone seemed to be treating him with obvious sympathy, until it dawned that they must have assumed that his disorientation at the altar was due to his continued grieving. He realized that even the darkest cloud had a silver lining somewhere. It was now mid-morning and as people disappeared through the door, Joseph could see that outside was a beautifully crisp, cold winter's day, with a brilliant sun shining in a clear blue sky. For a few moments the weight that seemed to hang constantly on his mind cleared and a feeling of joy at being alive on such a day filled him. It had been a long time since he had felt like this. He instantly decided that he would take the rest of the day off and go for a long walk. His daydreaming was broken by a figure standing in front of him.

"I'll be clearing up the church, Father, and then come across to the rectory and get the cleaning done if that's O.K. with you," Leola said. Since Clare's death, she had helped Joseph keep the rectory in a reasonable state. The bishop had diplomatically suggested that he get someone to do this after one of her visits. "Why don't you just go and have a quiet sit down somewhere and gather your thoughts."

Joseph, slightly startled, looked down at the old woman in front of him, who steadily returned his gaze. Before he could reply, she spoke again.

"I don't know what was going on at the altar this morning, Father, but I ain't ever felt such power around a person before. You alright?"

Joseph's chin fell slightly onto his chest as the weight returned. He suddenly knew that he had to confide in Leola.

"I don't know what's happening either, Leola. I had an extra-ordinary dream last night and today is so ... strange. It's like reality isn't right. Something is happening to my mind. I keep ... seeing things and ... feeling things. Do you understand?"

Leola leaned back a little, clearly satisfied with his response. Joseph realized that she had been inviting him to open up.

"Aye, Father Joseph, I understand." She hesitated for a few moments before continuing, apparently weighing-up how much she should say. When she spoke, it was with a nervous edge to her voice. "I also sees things and hears things in ways that not all in the church would like. But I don't worry about that. One thing I see is light around people. Sometimes beautiful, sometimes not so good. Father, this morning the light around you was like what I ain't never seen before. Like golden, but with many layers. Like in the autumn when you would never think that there could be so many different kinds of red. Like that, but golden. And there's an air around you, like something about to happen." She hesitated once more, clearly not sure whether to continue. "And there be something else. Like you've got ... company. Do you know what I mean Father?"

Joseph stared at Leola, as she revealed another extraordinary aspect.

"Er ... yes ... I know exactly ... what you mean."

Leola looked enormously relieved by his response. He remembered once more how difficult it was for her to speak to a priest about that side of her life. This was already a day full of marvels. His mind raced as he sought for some more words, but before he could say anything Leola grabbed his arm and looked at him intently.

"Your beautiful Clare, we spoke, spent time together in the woods, you know?" Joseph just nodded his head, tensing himself for what might be about to come next. "Well, she were an ... unusual ... person, like yourself, and we spoke much. I just want you to know that I'm here if you need me. You understand Father?"

Joseph nodded his head once more, not quite sure what to say. His confusion was saved by someone coming back in through the church door. It was Agnes, one of the old ladies who had been at the Mass. Her eyes fixed upon Leola's hand, which still gripped Joseph's arm. Agnes' mind clearly raced with curiosity at the sight. Joseph sighed inwardly. He hoped that he was not about to be assailed by another installment of the petty politics that so many of the congregation confused with religion.

"Excuse me Father. Hope I'm not interrupting anything." She paused as though to make some point that only she understood. "Something's happened. It's on the news, on the radio in the car. It's all a bit strange and I just had a feeling that I should tell you."

"Oh ... right Agnes," Joseph replied, as he felt Leola's grip leave his forearm. "What's happened?"

"Well, Father, it's all, as I say, rather ... strange."

Chapter 7

Mackenzie Jones had completely forgotten to check her make-up and hair. Never before in her career had she failed to do so before going on air. Male or female, appearance was everything for a television presenter. But what had happened over the last hour, together with the sight that met her eyes when she finally reached the top of the Skylon Tower, had blown everything else from her mind.

It was 6.00 am and still dark in Niagara. The rainbow colored illumination of the Falls was still switched on, twenty-one xenon lights painting the crashing waters in misty pastels. Normally at this time of year the illumination would have been turned off at 10.00 pm the previous evening, but it had been left on for her benefit, or, to be more precise, for the television documentary on Niagara that she was fronting. The producer had wanted to do a piece on "Niagara at Night", particularly focusing on the casinos, restaurants and nightclubs on both sides of the border. The Canadian and American authorities had been only too pleased to cooperate with anything that might be good for business.

A little while earlier she and the crew had been outside getting some background shots of the illuminated Falls from the Canadian side. Nearest to them had been the Horseshoe Falls, separated from the more distant American Falls by the darkened shape of Goat Island. Mackenzie had been doing a piece to camera with her back to the cascading water, struggling to make herself heard above the roar. Then odd things had started to happen. First, she noticed that the small, rather drunk, but thankfully good-natured crowd that inevitably gathered on a late night / early morning shoot in an entertainment district, had began to point upwards over her head. Then, as she tried to ignore the distraction, the film crew started to do the same. She had been tired, damp and in no mood for being messed around. She had not even bothered to say anything, but had just walked off camera in mid-sentence heading straight for the assistant producer. His boss had generously let Bobby take charge of that particular shoot while he found a good reason to visit a nearby casino. It was the first time she had worked with Bobby and his youthful confidence and abrupt way of speaking had been riling her all night. Now he was going to get it. She had been in the business much longer than he and, even if her career had stalled over the last few years, she was not going to take any crap from someone like him.

"Can we have some concentration here Bobby," she had demanded, putting her face a few inches from his, "You know, like, some professionalism?"

"Er, yeah, right Mac ... of course," had been Bobby's stumbling reply, as his eyes remained locked onto a point somewhere above her right shoulder. Then, as though pulling his thoughts together with great effort, his gaze had drifted back to her. But the far-away look in his eyes had remained. "I ... I think you'd better look over there. What is it?"

Angrily, she had whipped around, ready to tear him off another strip for wasting her time.

It was then that she had seen it. She had immediately known what it was, without any doubt. Or perhaps it would be more accurate to say that she knew what it was not. It was definitively, absolutely, shockingly not of the world she knew. And this was too much, so her mind fought against acknowledging the thought. It was a thought that was world shattering. Yet it was a thought that could not be denied, so it hovered on the edge of her attention, awaiting its moment to be invited in.

Hanging absolutely motionless over the Falls had been the most extraordinary sight she had ever seen. It was a deep ellipse of incredibly brilliant light, continually fluxing and changing in intensity across its surface, hinting at subtle colors that blinked in and out of existence. Within moments she had been staring upwards like everyone else, the piece to camera completely forgotten. As she had looked closer, she had noticed that within the pulsating light were suggestions of structure, of something curling its way inwards. It had then occurred to her that she might be looking at a spiral, slightly tilted towards her. There was something about the shape within the light that triggered a memory, that reminded her of something, but it would not come to mind. The reporter in her tried to estimate the size of the object, but as she did not know its distance or altitude, no judgment was possible.

Then something happened that looking back afterwards she could not quite remember clearly. Mackenzie found herself becoming totally absorbed in the object, as would a child with a shiny pebble or pretty flower. It felt almost as though it reached out to her. The pulsating light became, for a while, her whole universe. It was not only its sheer strangeness that held her, but the sublime sense of beauty that it evoked within. It made her want to cry. She wanted to shed the kind of tears that came from a sense of relief, of home-coming, of joy at hugging a long-absent loved one, from realizing that there is still wonder in the world after all. It was a feeling that surged out of her depths for no obvious reason. She had felt a tear run down her cheek, as she lost track of time.

The interruption when it came had been sudden and brutal. Mackenzie had been wrenched back to the world by the shouting of the producer as he ran towards them from the direction of the casino.

"Why aren't you getting it?" he had yelled. "What's the matter with you guys? Get the camera on that thing before I fire all of you."

Mackenzie had come back to earth with a jolt and had surreptitiously wiped the tears from her face with her sleeve, while a poor disorientated Bobby was on the receiving end of his boss's rage. She had felt very shaken inside, but had pulled herself together for the producer's benefit, as much as she had been able.

Once the camera had been directed onto the pulsing object, the producer had taken her to one side and looked at her quizzically. They had worked together many times over the years and had developed a mutually respectful, if wary relationship.

"What's going on Mac? I can understand that bozo getting frozen to the spot at the sight of some fancy hot air balloon, but not you."

His words had shocked Mackenzie out of what remained of her confusion. She had stared at him in disbelief. She had not been able to understand how he could say such a stupid thing. But then she had looked in his eyes and had known in that instant that there was no room in his mind for the unknown. For him everything was nailed down, explained and classified. She had found herself talking softly to him.

"That's no hot air balloon Danny."

Her tone and steady gaze had made Danny hesitate for a few moments before the instant, reassuring explanations won out again.

"Aw, come on Mac. What else could it be? It's those illuminations guys or some kids pulling a stunt. It's just the fancy colored lights being reflected off a balloon."

She had continued to eye him steadily. "Danny," she had said gently, "Just look at it."

Danny had shrugged his shoulders and looked once more at the swirling patch of brilliant light. After a few moments she could tell that his confidence was shaken. It was too much and too powerful. It penetrated the mind too deeply to be dismissed with such ease. Danny still tried, but his voice no longer carried the surety it had.

"Hey," he had said with all the nonchalance he could muster, "Perhaps it's kind of like laser beams being fired at some low clouds, or maybe it's the air force doing something."

Mackenzie had just stared at him, but Danny had not got where he was through being intimidated so easily. He had begun to rally.

"Anyway, what matters is that we get plenty of shots of this thing. It'll go down a treat on those crazy UFO shows that the cable channels love."

As he had said this, she knew that she had finally to say the words out loud.

"The problem is, Danny, it is a UFO and it's not crazy."

As soon as she had said the words she had felt liberated and embarrassed at the same time. Danny's face had been a picture of mixed emotions as he had struggled to embrace what was before his eyes. Then the cynic had won out again and a look of derision had started to form. Mackenzie had felt her temper rising, but before she could say anything Danny's mobile phone had started to ring. He had pulled it out of his pocket with obvious relief and had wandered off with it pressed against his ear. She had watched, feeling utterly frustrated, as he had walked across the grass towards the Falls. She had not known why, but it really mattered to her that someone else acknowledged what to her was obvious. It was then that Bobby, clearly still struggling to get his mind in order, had whispered in her ear.

"It's wonderful isn't it? It's like ... it's like ... a healing. I don't want to call it a UFO, 'cause that sounds cheap. But it is, isn't it?"

Startled by his presence, she had jumped around to look at him. That had been all she needed. There had been something shining out of his eyes that told her that she was not alone. She had smiled at him and he had sheepishly grinned back. She had then decided that Bobby was the greatest person in the world. At that moment Danny had wandered back over looking very agitated, but it had not stopped him staring at the two of them curiously.

"Er ... right ... O.K. ... it seems ... er ... that things may not be as simple as I thought."

Mackenzie had peered at him intently. She could tell that something had changed.

"What do you mean?" she had demanded, the gentleness in her voice being a thing of the past.

"Well that was ... the boss ... the big boss herself." He paused to let the gravity of that piece of information sink in. "It seems that something ... odd ... has been tracked flying to Niagara. I've just been told ... in no uncertain terms ... to get the best position we can before we go live."

"Live?" Mackenzie had gasped. "We're here recording a documentary."

Danny had suddenly looked worried.

"Yeah, I know Mac, but this is big, really big and we're on the spot."

They had then gone silent and looked at one another. It had dawned on both of them that this was one of those moments that all news people prayed for, and secretly dreaded. A great story had fallen into their laps. Would they be good enough?

Mackenzie had been the first to react.

"Right," she had said looking around, "Where are we going to get the best pictures?"

It had only taken a few seconds for them to realize that it was actually a silly question. There, just a little way inshore, looming over them, was the answer.

"Bobby, go and sort it with the manager," Danny had ordered without lowering his gaze.

"Yeah ... right boss," Bobby had replied as he headed off, obviously still more than a little spaced-out.

Mackenzie had watched him depart and then made to go and collect her stuff, but had stopped as a thought occurred to her.

"Hey Danny, you said that thing has been tracked here?"

"Yeah, that's right."

"So where's it come from then?"

Danny had hesitated before answering, swallowing a couple of times. Then he had just said, very matter-of-factly, "Oh, the moon."

So now she stood on the observation deck of the Skylon Tower, 500 hundred feet above street level and nearly 800 feet above the bottom of the Falls. It was a monument to 1960s concrete and taste, resembling to her mind a tapering car axle stuck upright in the ground with a wheel on top. In daytime the view was magnificent and it was possible to see the whole length of the Falls. Standing there, she remembered going up the tower as a child with her parents. She had not thought about it in years and, for some reason, started to feel emotional again. She fought to get control. She was on air in five minutes and needed to be focused. This could be the greatest opportunity of her life. She was determined not to waste it. Around her the crew were frantically setting up their equipment, all the while glancing up at the incredible sight that remained motionless out in the night, with the Falls still tumbling and swirling below in their garish colors.

Mackenzie took a few deep calming breaths and stared out at the object. She started to become absorbed by it once more and found that, as she did so, a deep stillness began to fill her. And from the stillness, from nowhere, a thought appeared in her mind, one of those rare thoughts that are so powerful that it completely changes our experience of the world. It slowly dawned that she was in the middle of something that dwarfed her, something so vast in its implications that her life was just a spark dancing around the edge of a mighty fire. It was a thought that brought with it profound peace, for it put her own story into a new perspective, in which her worries about her career and other personal dramas fell away. They suddenly seemed so small. It was as though she had been looking at this marvelous moment through the wrong end of a telescope. It was like waking from an intense dream. She turned away from the window and looked back at all the scurrying and tension. A few moments before she had been caught up in that shared consciousness, now it just struck her as bizarre. She knew in that instant that she did not have to worry about the broadcast. From the sense of vastness that she now felt in her mind, everything would flow perfectly.

Then another thought came as if from nowhere. It simply reminded her that life itself was wondrous and utterly mysterious, and the appearance of the object was just something that was happening against this even greater backdrop. It asked what would happen if every day she could be aware of this greatest of all mysteries? What would happen if she could rediscover her child-like wonder in the midst of the world? Mackenzie sensed that if she could, her life would never be the same again.

She shook herself inwardly and turned once more to look at the shimmering ellipse of light. More strongly now, she sensed that it was not passive. That as she joined with it, it was reaching back. It was, somehow, behind the incredible thoughts that were flowing through her mind. The realization sent a shiver down her spine and her mind began to struggle as its model of reality, which had shaped her thoughts all her adult life, began to be shaken at the roots. She looked over her shoulder at the tension-filled chaos and wondered if they sensed it too. She could instantly tell that some of them did, but not others. The first group, of whom Bobby was clearly one, had an air of slight confusion about them, as if they could not quite think straight and whenever they glanced at the object something happened to their faces. It was almost as though they looked younger for a few moments. The second group was different. There was a self-absorption and intensity to them that almost repulsed her – yet she knew that only a little while before she would have appeared the same.

She looked out again towards the object. From the top of the tower she could see that it was slightly below her, over towards the US side of the Falls. She estimated that it must be about a thousand yards from where she stood and maybe about a hundred feet across, but in the dark it was still difficult to judge. It struck her as odd that it was off-center. Coming up in one of the elevators, she had been briefed by the crew's researcher on what little was known about the object. All the researcher had was the little she had been able to glean over a mobile phone. It seemed that the object had first been observed on or near the moon by astronomers, before being detected in other ways. To Mackenzie's forensic mind one thing was clear. Everything the object had done demonstrated purpose, so she knew in her bones that there had to be a reason for its very precise positioning.

As she looked down she noticed once more the spiral structure on the object. Although still obscured by the shape-shifting tidal flows of light across its surface, the pattern was much clearer from above than it had been from ground level. She could now see that the spiral was closely segmented as it turned inwards. She loved how it looked. It felt very natural for a reason that she could not at first pin down, before she finally remembered what it reminded her of. Once more she was taken back to childhood and to a beach she had visited with her parents. She remembered the thrill as she had turned over a broken piece of stone and seen this very shape. Her father had explained that it was a fossil, the remains of a creature that had swum in the sea millions of years before. Her mind had been too young to fully understand, but at a visceral level it had filled her with wonder and joy. When she got home, she had looked up the shape in a book. It was called an ammonite and had been a creature that had lived in a spiral shell one hundred and sixty million years before. She could not really envisage such a number, but it had felt very, very old. In that moment her child-like absorption in "now" had been blown apart as she had contemplated such a span of time. The shape itself had also fired her imagination and she had tried to picture what it would be like to live at the center of such a spiral. To the mind of a child it had felt very safe. Years later she had seen a Nautilus in a sea aquarium and had fleetingly tasted once more the vastness of existence, before the attentions of the boy she had been with had proved too distracting. And now, all these years later, in extraordinary circumstances, here it was again. As she gazed out it felt even safer this time.

The thought broke her reverie and the reporter in her suddenly woke up. It wondered whether most people would find the object reassuring, or would it be just a few like her? Shouldn't she feel threatened by it? Then the obvious question dawned on her. Where were the military? Surely they should be swarming all over a strange, unidentified object in North American airspace? And there had been no statement from the two governments as yet, the researcher had told her in the elevator, despite their being under siege from the news agencies. This in its own way was as extraordinary as the object itself. Once more, Mackenzie had a feeling that the world was changing and would never be the same again.

Bobby came over and, as he approached, Mackenzie noticed that a kind of calm had now descended. The equipment was in place and everyone was ready.

"One minute Mac."

"O.K. Bobby. Just one thing. Anyone know the place that the object is over? It looks to me like it's off-center to the Falls."

Bobby smiled at her.

"Oh yeah. I noticed that and made some enquiries. It's over a small piece of land between the Falls. It happens to be called Luna Island."

Chapter 8

For a couple of hours Joseph sat, transfixed, in front of the television.

From the moment the screen had burst into life he had realized that the world he had known, which had formed and shaped him from birth, was gone forever. It had been destroyed.

As soon as he saw the object he had no doubt what it was. It was too alien. It was not of this world. The object was from outside the boundaries of the human psyche, which was the human world. He did not need the commentator's recounting of its journey from the lunar surface to tell him this.

And he knew that this was mind-shattering.

There are moments in life when something fundamental changes forever, is ripped away, and when there is no going back to how things were before. The past has gone and will never return. When this happens the foundations of what we believe life to be, what gives it meaning and purpose, what gives us an illusion of security amidst the unfathomable mystery of existence, can crack open. It leaves our minds desperately grasping for firm handholds. Perhaps we find ways to shore up the sub-structures of our mental world with new building blocks, or maybe the whole edifice has to collapse before something new can be built. We prefer and strive for the former, but in our wiser and more courageous moments suspect that the latter allows something better to rise from the ashes, something new with deeper roots. But there are times when we are given no choice, when the psychological earthquake is so powerful that complete breakdown is unavoidable.

Joseph had no doubt that he was now, suddenly, without warning, living in such a time. He knew with complete certainty that this was a mind-shatterer that would impact the whole human race. Overnight their mental world had gone, leaving only a vast unknown. It was a collective nervous breakdown. This was new, uncharted territory.

It frightened him.

As Joseph watched the television this thought would not leave his mind. He found it ironic that he should be more concerned about how humanity would react than the intentions of the alien visitor. It was another sign of the low opinion he held of the rest of his species. It was not something of which he was proud.

He had tasted the truth of breakdown for himself with Clare's death and still did not know where his path lay. It was too soon. As a priest he had also seen such breakdowns impact the lives of other people, but they at least had benefitted from the anchor of the rest of the human mind-world, with its rhythms and seeming certainties. Joseph could barely imagine what would happen with a collective breakdown, where the rock of a shared sense of normality had been swept away.

As he contemplated the object it brought home to him the power of a symbol, for that is all it was at the moment. It was doing nothing except simply being present for all to see. Yet what it told humankind about itself was more powerful than any super-weapon. Without speaking, it told human beings that they had no idea what was happening, that they were fragile and vulnerable, that all their certainties were false and that the future was now an unimaginable land. Above all, it told them that they were still children - and this is the last thing that children want to hear.

Then Joseph remembered something, but it was far from reassuring. Years before, he had read about the early encounters between European explorers and the indigenous people they had come across. For the remote tribes it had been just as world-shattering as what was now happening to the human race as a whole. Societies had broken down and with them the lives of individuals. The shock of meeting a race so different and superior had been too much. In more recent times, explorers had taken on board this hard lesson and contact had been managed with great care. Joseph wanted to believe that whoever sat in the light vessel would follow the same path.

Joseph began to experience the shock himself. He found himself needing to turn the sound down on the television and divert his eyes for a while. He looked around the room in which he sat. The familiarity helped. Like most of the rooms in the rectory it was large, rectangular, with a high ceiling. Joseph was slouched in his favorite, battered armchair. To his left was an equally battered sofa on which Clare had liked to sit. Although both chairs were in poor condition, they were enhanced by having exotic oriental cloths draped over which Clare had bought from secondhand shops. He smiled to himself as he remembered that the cloths had been a source of occasional friction between them. He had always acknowledged that they looked wonderful, but had been irritated by their habit of sliding off every time someone sat down. This was for him an unnecessary complication in life. Clare had been content to simply reposition them until the next time. He had suggested fixing them in place but Clare had baulked at such practicality.

Since her death it would not have occurred to Joseph to do anything other than leave them as they were.

Clare had possessed a gift for arranging rooms. It had nothing to do with style or fashion, but with something deeper. Her rooms changed consciousness. The walls of this room were plain, an unpatterned wallpaper painted a delicate shade of magnolia. Four pictures were spaced out around the room. The first was an extraordinary Japanese painting of a vast mountain range, with a small figure standing in the foreground on a small rocky outcrop, gazing at the majestic vision. Another showed a mysterious river glade, with innumerable shades of green blending into the light blue of the water. So subtly did the colors shade into each other that it was impossible to discern with any precision where one ended and the next started. Then there was a painting of a small garden bench, with a bright green lawn stretching away in front and, behind, a wall of flowering red rhododendron bushes. Finally, there was an impressionistic painting of a mysterious hooded figure in a white robe that appeared to be walking across a sea of waves. This was the image that affected Joseph the most, but he had never worked out why this was. All of the pictures seduced the mind, while refusing to succumb to easy interpretation. He had once asked Clare why she had chosen these particular pictures, but she had been unable to explain. They just seemed to speak to her. The experience of the room was completed by a variety of carefully positioned potted plants.

There was something about the simple order, clarity and subtle blending of color and image that worked magic in the mind. It had taken a while for Joseph to realize the gift that Clare possessed, but as he had visited many different homes in the course of his ministry it had gradually dawned on him. Clare's rooms were a contemplation. They were an outward expression of the depths of her mind. During their shared spiritual quest, they had spent time exploring Zen Buddhism and Joseph had realized that somehow, without any conscious effort, Clare had been able to capture the atmosphere of Zen in the spaces she created.

It was also during this Zen period that he had learned how to meditate. Except that it had not really been like learning, but more as though he was discovering something for which he had a natural aptitude. He had found that his mind could sink into deep stillness without effort. The practice felt familiar and the stillness a place he knew well. This had fascinated Clare, but since her death he had avoided the stillness, anxious that it would be filled with thoughts of her.

Joseph then noticed something strange. He was thinking about Clare with clarity, without dissolving. He looked back at the object on the silent screen in front of him. Perhaps its disturbing presence brought unsuspected gifts.

Joseph looked out through the large sash windows that gave a magnificent view of the rear garden. He could see all the way to the end, where the ground dropped away towards the town far below. He could not see the town from where he sat, but its memory resurrected thoughts about how humanity would cope with the shock of the object at Niagara. It occurred to him that he might be too negative, too influenced by his despair of people. It was possible that it would bring human beings together as new and inspirational horizons opened up. As the infinitely greater context of human life was revealed, perhaps its divisions and rivalries would appear ridiculous – and even dangerous if what the object represented were to be seen as threatening.

He wanted to believe this. He thought of the young Hawaiian girl, an astronomer, who he had seen interviewed on the television. She had been one of the first to see the object during the lunar eclipse and witness its strange dance. It had clearly inspired her. Though obviously a committed scientist, the dreamy far-away look in her eyes had left a profound impression. Then there had been the television reporter at Niagara who, with the object clearly visible over her shoulder, had almost glowed in harmony with its light. Her whole being had shared its stillness.

Yet he could not get away from the thought that, for most, contact would have the opposite effect. The shock of the encounter could demolish people's commitment to the structures that held societies together, possibly reducing their sense of belonging to family and those immediately around. Developed societies and their complex economic support systems were anchored in an ephemeral quality called "confidence". It was shared beliefs, ideals and trust that glued them together. Joseph foresaw great problems if these began to unravel. He particularly feared for societies and communities built around fundamentalist religious beliefs. He wondered about their reaction once the initial shock diminished. How long would it be before words like "satan" and "demon" were heard? Only time would tell, but Joseph had no doubt that governments around the world would be making nervous preparations for the worst.

Yet for a while Joseph was sure there would be only numbness. It would be like the numbness he had felt in the days immediately following Clare's death, when his mind had been unable to come to terms with the fact of her absence. Everything had been too sudden, too quick. Even when he had identified her body in the mortuary, his mind had insisted that her chest was rising and falling with the rhythm of breath. As with the smell of coffee earlier that morning, he had known that it could not be so, but his mind had been unable to conceive of a non-breathing Clare. In the days and weeks that followed he had felt as though he was in the middle of a dream. Life had seemed unreal. There had been emotion, raw and powerful, but it had only been later, as the numbness wore off and his mind began to acknowledge its new reality, that a deeper, chronic grieving had emerged. Joseph wondered how long humanity's collective numbness would last. He hoped that it would be a long time.

Earlier in the day there had, of course, been the inevitable government statements desperately reassuring shell-shocked populations that there was nothing to fear. The authorities had obviously decided that complete openness was the only way to encourage calm. A succession of eminent figures had taken to the screen, two of which had made a particular impression on Joseph. The first had been an irritable scientist from a lunar ranging facility who described how the object had interfered with his laser beam. The second had been a Canadian NORAD general who had recounted how the object had been tracked from the moon all the way to the Earth's surface. He had also described odd maneuvers that the vessel had performed while floating above the Earth. The general had been so impassive that he could have been describing the weather, rather than the most extraordinary event in human history. British television had also carried a live broadcast by the American President. Although he shared little common ground with the President's politics or religion, Joseph had felt great sympathy for him as he tried to cope with the unthinkable. Joseph had also been grateful for his honesty. The President had confirmed that the object clearly displayed intelligent behavior and a desire to attract attention. He had then also confirmed, trying to make it sound like the most natural thing in the world, that the object was being treated as extraterrestrial. The honesty had been wise and necessary. Joseph was sure that any attempt to prevaricate, to deny the obvious, would only have stirred suspicion and discontent among badly shaken populations. He had then said something else that needed to be heard – that the object had shown no aggressive signs and, indeed, appeared to be demonstrating great caution in revealing itself. The President had leaned forward deliberately at that point and looked straight into the camera. He had then stated his conviction that the object came with peaceful intentions and that he looked forward immensely to pursuing this momentous encounter. He had concluded by saying that he was, of course, in touch with other world leaders and that the United Nations Security Council would be meeting later that day.

Once the President had finished, the news program had reverted to the inevitable panel of experts discussing what had been said. Joseph was not sure how anyone could be expert in anything like this. He had turned the sound down (something he often did – which had annoyed Clare immensely) and had sat with his thoughts. The first thing that had struck him about the President's statement had been what was unsaid – that is, where he was speaking from. The background in the picture did not look like the White House. Joseph guessed that he was in a secure location. It did not say much about the President's faith in the object's peaceful intentions. He had also wondered how the

President must be feeling personally about the arrival of the light vessel. Although he had always been coy about the subject in public, he was known to hold fundamentalist Christian beliefs. It was suspected that he was a creationist, who believed that the earth was only 8000 years old and that he also rejected evolution. In Joseph's experience this nearly always went side by side with a strong belief in the devil and all his demons. He wondered what would eventually emerge from the mix when the President had been able to process the extraordinary events of the last few hours. Then the live pictures of the object had reappeared on the screen and he had turned the sound back up.

Now, hours later, he sat in silence still trying to absorb what had happened. He looked back at the television, at the object hanging silently above the crashing waters of Niagara and realized that there was something else that he had been avoiding since he had first set eyes on it.

It had a connection with him.

He knew that this is what the dream and the Teacher had been preparing him for, and why the Mystery had reached out to him so powerfully that morning at Mass. Yet he did not want to think about this. One voice in his mind told him unequivocally that the feeling of connection was just his ego at work and that he was making a link where none existed. He wanted to believe this voice for the possibility of such a connection was disturbing, even frightening in what it might ask of him. It also seemed absurd. He was nobody, an insignificant parish priest in a small market town in England. It was fanciful to think for even an instant that he could have any part to play in such a global drama. But the voice sounded desperate, for it was failing to drown out a deeper and, paradoxically, quieter voice that simply told him to trust what he knew. The problem was that he did trust this deeper knowing and its implications sent a shiver up his spine.

It was time to break the mood. He picked up the remote

control and turned the television off. He became aware that he was hungry and looked at his watch. Lunchtime was long gone. He stood up and made for the kitchen, wondering what scraps might be left. He was not good at going to the shops. He walked in across the flagstone floor and opened the fridge. It was not a happy sight. At that moment he heard the front door open and Leola's unmistakable footsteps.

Chapter 9

It had not been easy persuading Leola to share a sandwich with him while he went back to watching the television. Such informality with the rector obviously made her uncomfortable. It was with clear reluctance that she inched her way into the living room and perched on the edge of the sofa. It struck Joseph that she was the first person to sit there since Clare. It actually felt good, as if something had been released.

Then Leola caught sight of the object that remained motionless above Niagara. She leaned forward, transfixed by what she saw, embarrassment forgotten.

The news station seemed to have abandoned what had been a near constant flow of comment and round-table discussion. It was now just showing the pulsating light vessel in its magnificent setting for long uninterrupted periods. This made the experience even more powerful, impossible though this would have seemed to Joseph a little while earlier. The view of the Falls was in itself breath-taking, with the line of cascading, white-foamed waters being broken by the green and brown mass of Goat Island. A little further along was the much smaller Luna Island, above which the extraordinary object hung. Nearest the camera the concave Horseshoe Falls on the Canadian side were partially lost behind a veil of white misty spray. Set against a bright blue winter sky, the sight was magnificent.

Bringing the picture to life were the distant sounds that the TV microphones were picking up. In the background, so constant that through familiarity it became unnoticed, was the never-ending roar of the tumbling waters. But there were also distinctly human sounds of distant traffic and, particularly, the faint babble of voices. The camera would occasionally sweep down from the light object and give a brief view of the land around the Falls on the Canadian side. The source of the voices would then come into view, as crowds of people could be seen on every available surface, watching and waiting. Joseph noticed that the crowds were further forward than they had been earlier in the day, when they had seemed to feel the need to keep a distance between themselves and the object. The people appeared bolder now, the object's long period of inactivity having engendered a degree of confidence. Joseph suspected, however, that this was a fragile courage, which would be easily shattered if anything happened.

Joseph actually found the very ordinariness of the traffic sounds and human voices to be disturbing. The soundscape for the incredible object that sat above Luna Island should have been eerie electronic music, he thought, or the ascending harmonies of a great choir.

The sense of disturbance reminded him of an experience as a young man. He had been persuaded to go to a soccer match between England and Germany. As the English flag had been raised, the German national anthem had been played by mistake. Even though his intellect had dismissed the incident as unimportant, it had disturbed him for days afterwards. The incongruity, even at such a trivial level, had shaken something in his mind. But the experience of his youth was nothing compared to his feelings as he watched and listened to the TV broadcast. The juxtaposition of the ordinary and extraordinary at Niagara was far more unsettling. It was almost unreal. Leola did not say anything for a while and just sat, eyes fixed on the screen, ignoring her cheese sandwich. Gradually, Joseph became as interested in watching her as the television. He sensed that something deep was happening, that she was seeing the object in a different way to him. Then she spoke.

"There's been stories. People like me who say they've met ... strangers ... who've come in balls of light."

Joseph was taken back by the suddenness of Leola's words and by their implications. He grappled for a few moments with how to reply.

"What do you mean ... 'people like me'?"

Leola turned from the TV and her eyes fixed on his. She now looked even more uncomfortable than when she had entered the room. She spoke slowly, in her broad rustic accent, obviously picking words with great care.

"Well, Father Joseph, I think that you know the answer to that question. I loves the Church, though I often wonder why given the nonsense that goes on, and I loves Jesus. But I'm part of something else as well. Something much older, something ... natural ... which don't need big buildings, just a clearing in a wood or a hilltop. Those in the country who know might call me wise woman, but others would call me 'witch'. It is a ... way ... that's passed down from mother to daughter, since before any can remember. We feel ... we see ... life ... as it flows through all things and we use this knowing to help others. That's what I be, Father, as I thinks you know."

When Leola finished speaking, her eyes searched Joseph for some reaction.

"Although Clare would never tell me about your ... conversations ... I kind of realized that this was the case," he said in a deliberately gentle voice. "It's fine by me. I know that my way is just one face of the great mystery of life. I don't have a problem with any other way that seeks to do good."

Leola looked relieved and relaxed a little.

"I suppose I know that really, but in the past there have been ... problems ... with priests and church people and it's made me ... nervous. Silly, given what your Clare told me about you, but the scars are deep for me and my kind."

Joseph wondered, not for the first time, what Clare may have told Leola about him. But then something else that Leola had said came back. He suddenly saw that she might have been hinting at something. He had to know. He spoke hesitantly.

"Leola, you said that the ... old way ... is passed from mother to daughter. I don't think you have any children. Who will you pass it to?"

Leola looked at him with compassion in her eyes.

"I think you know the answer to that too, Father. Or rather, who I were going to pass it to. You lost a dear wife and I ... I lost the daughter I never had."

They both regarded one another in silence for a few moments, before Leola looked down and carefully wiped some moisture from her eye. Joseph did not know what to say. He knew that in the last year of her life Clare had spent a lot of time with Leola, but now realized that he had not seen just how close they had become. Perhaps he had been too absorbed in his own life to see. He now understood, with a twinge of guilt, that in being so wrapped up in his own loss, he had not seen how others around might be grieving too. He continued to look at Leola with her chin resting on her chest, dabbing at her eyes. He remembered all the kindness and patience that she had shown him over the last few months, despite the sadness she must have been feeling. Then he found some words coming to mind. They were the right words to say because they were the truth.

"Leola, that's such a beautiful thing. I think it's wonderful that you felt about Clare in that way."

Leola raised her head, relief showing in her eyes.

"You mean that, Father? I didn't know how you'd feel about it." She paused and took a deep breath before continuing. "The old man and me, well, we could never have little ones. It were a big sadness for us. Over the years I tried to show ... things ... to girls I knew, but they didn't have it in them. I'd given up by the time you and Clare came. But as soon as I met her, I knew she was, well, like me, but didn't know it. It were something about her. Something about the way life flowed through her. The way her eyes shone." Leola paused and smiled shyly. "It were a bit of a shock, though, that she were the rector's good lady." She paused again before continuing, clearly hesitant about saying the next thing. "But there was more to Clare than what's in me. She had something else that I'd never seen before. There was a different kind of flow in her to what I was used to seeing."

Joseph was fascinated.

"What do you mean?"

"It's not easy to explain," Leola replied, her face screwing-up slightly as she struggled to find the words she needed. "It's a bit like ... it's a bit like ... when you go to one of them fancy food stores in town and they've got all that strange fruit and vegetables from other countries. You kind of know what it is – fruit and veg – but it's different to anything you've seen before. You just get a feeling that it's from somewhere very different to here ... to what you know. That's what I felt with Clare. The life force was strong in her, but some of it was ... well ... kind of foreign ... if you know what I mean." At this point Leola looked back at the television and pointed to the object that still hung immobile over Niagara. "And that's the same. But much more so. I feel it. It be ... well," she said giggling, " ... a whole lot more foreign."

Joseph could not help himself and burst out laughing at Leola's wonderful description. Her face broke into a broad grin.

"That's the first time I've heard you laugh for a while, Father."

"You do have a wonderful way of putting things sometimes," Joseph replied trying to get control of himself, while marveling at the almost forgotten feeling of laughter.

Leola stared at him for a few moments and, to Joseph, it seemed as though something changed about her that he could not quite pin down. Then she spoke again.

"And you're the same, Father."

"Sorry, what do you mean?"

"There's a great ... energy ... in and around you. Just like darling Clare. But it's far more ... focused ... concentrated. It's like my nephew when he was a little boy. He'd get a magnifying glass and shine the sun through it onto a piece of paper to set it afire. And there's something else. There's lots of ... flows ...

weaved into yours that ain't you, if you know what I mean."

Joseph felt himself go slightly hot and tried hard to keep his voice calm.

"Ah, you may need to, er, explain that."

Leola paused before continuing.

"It's like that," she said pointing at the television once more. "It's like them amazing water falls. Kind of complicated, but still one flow. But when I look at you, it's like there's more than one river flowing and that they're all wrapped around each other." She leaned towards him. "But again I think you really know what I'm talking about."

Joseph was getting even hotter. He paused before speaking. Once more there was something he had to know.

"Did Clare tell you about … what's been happening to me?"

Leola reached out and held his hand.

"Aye, lad, she did. We were very close towards … the end. She had to share it with someone who might understand. Do you mind? Don't be cross with her."

Joseph felt tears come to his eyes. He marveled once more, but this time at how easily tears could follow laughter. He also noticed that Leola had called him "lad" again.

"No, no, I could never be cross with her." He took a deep breath. "Anyway, it actually feels good not to be alone with it all."

Leola gripped his hand even tighter. Joseph could feel her old leathery skin against his.

"Father, you've got to understand that I've seen all this around you before, but only in glimpses, sometimes. It's overflowing now. It's ripe. And it's all to do with him." With her other hand she pointed at the object on the TV screen. "I saw it around you this morning in the churchyard, but now I know it's about that. You're as much at the center of today as that thing. You've got to understand this."

She released his hand and sat back on the sofa.

Once more Joseph did not know what to say. Her words had penetrated deep into his psyche. He knew, as he had earlier, that what she said was true. But once more the realization brought fear in its wake. His mind baulked at what might be required of him. Finally he spoke.

"I know," was all he could say. Then he looked over at Leola and tried to smile. "But at least now I also know that I'm not alone."

Leola just looked at him for a few moments, her eyes piercing his. Then something seemed to leave her and she appeared to diminish slightly. She looked back at the screen. She changed the subject without warning.

"It's not chance that he's over such powerful water," she said pointing at the screen.

"Er, no," Joseph replied, trying to catch up with her abrupt change of direction. "They said earlier that the Falls might be symbolic. That the ... visitor ... chose that place because it's where two countries have learned to cooperate. Also, because something over the Falls can't be hidden. Everyone can see the object."

"Aye, that may all be true," Leola said dismissively, "But he likes the water that one. I can sense it. In the old way, water has great power; that touches the soul. I know this to be true. I feel it myself and work with it. And he feels it too." She looked at Joseph. "This is telling you something about him that you may need to know."

"Oh, right," was all Joseph could find to say. Then a thought occurred to him. "It's odd how we're both talking as if we know that there's only one ... being ... aboard the vessel. There could be many."

Leola just stared at him enigmatically for a few moments and then went back to watching the television. Her reaction left Joseph unsettled, as though he had missed something but could not figure out what it was.

After a while, something else began to nag at Joseph, something unfinished, but it took him a couple of minutes to remember what it was.

"Leola, you mentioned a while ago about people who say they've met … visitors … like that, who've come in balls of light. People like you."

Leola did not reply for a few moments, but continued to contemplate the television. Then she turned to look at him once more.

"As I said, there are stories. Old stories, passed down, about meetings with strange beings, garbled in the retelling. In some, the beings are called fairy or elves, or some other name. How much truth is in them, I don't know. But there are people still living who claim things like it. It seems to me, though, listening to them, that what happened was on another … level. That they had travelled … in their soul … to inner worlds. I don't think it was like this," she said pointing at the TV. "This is different. This is … solid." She paused for a few moments. "Perhaps, Father, this is a meeting of worlds in more ways than we realize."

Leola went back to the television, leaving Joseph gasping in her wake. For many people Leola would appear almost simple, with her seemingly slow mind and ponderous way of speaking. Yet she had just pulled together in one sentence the inner and outer threads of what was unfolding in his life. He seemed to be at the fulcrum of a meeting of worlds. The world of the mind with the world of matter. He found himself becoming very still inside, the kind of stillness that comes from having glimpsed something fundamental.

He became aware that Leola had stood up and was collecting the plates from their late lunch.

"Oh, right, thanks," he managed to blurt out as she headed for the kitchen.

He got up and followed her out, determined that she should not have to wash the dishes. But as he walked past the door to his study, something flashed in the corner of his eye. He leaned around the door and saw that the red light on the telephone answering machine was blinking on and off. He remembered, guiltily, that he had earlier disabled the telephone ringer so that he could watch the television in peace. He tended to do this a lot, at any excuse. He did not like ringing telephones. He went over to replay the message, but before he could press the button his hand stopped in mid-air. It was not just one message. The display was telling him that the machine's memory was full. This astonished him. He had deliberately bought a machine with extra memory because of the large number of calls he got. He had never known it to be even half full before – and only then when he had been away for a few days. He sat down in the chair in front of the desk, his good intentions about the dishes forgotten, and began to listen to the messages. As he quickly skimmed through, he found them to be basically the same. All kinds of people, most completely unknown to him, wanted to know if the church was open. Many also wanted to know if there would be any special services because of what was "happening", as most people seemed to prefer to obliquely describe the events at Niagara. As the last recording finished he stared at the telephone in amazement, unable to understand why he was suddenly so popular.

"You shouldn't be surprised," Leola said from the doorway.

Joseph turned around in the chair.

"But I am," he replied in a perplexed voice. "Why this sudden interest in religion just because of what's happening at Niagara?"

Leola stared at the carpet for a few moments, obviously gathering her thoughts.

"It's not to do with religion, Father. Well, not as you and I understand it. It's to do with fear."

"Fear?"

"All they know ... all that makes them feel safe, is gone."

Joseph's mind went back to his earlier thoughts about the

effect the visitor's arrival might have on people.

"I can understand that, Leola, but why should so many turn to religion?"

"It's more a turning to the Church, Father, not religion. People today ... well ... they're rather like trees who try to pretend they ain't got roots. But it's the roots that stop the tree falling over when the storm blows. And the Church, it's part of our soul as a people, part of our deep old roots. It's like instinct in an animal. The biggest storm of all is blowing from that Niagara place and people are reaching for what they know."

Joseph was once more astonished by Leola's insight and her ability to explain the profound in such homely terms. She had not finished.

"But it's also more than that. It's like ... well ...when folks wake up from the dream that they know what life is, as well as being frightened, something in them opens up. It's like they've been skimming across the surface and, suddenly, they have to stop and they feel the depths beneath ... or perhaps it's better to say within. Likely it's only felt dimly, but it's felt nevertheless. And many sense something looking back at them. And the Church for most in this country is the only place they know where they can go with this feeling. It's the place where they sense it will be accepted ... even if nothing is said. It's the place ... where ... where ... the feeling is ... well .... warmed and fed." Leola started to look embarrassed. "I just wish I was better with words so I could explain."

Joseph smiled to himself. She had no idea of her astonishing clarity.

"You explain it all beautifully. I think I understand now. I've encountered this around funerals. Being close to death opens people. You can see it in their eyes. The certainty has gone and the unknownness of existence surrounds them. They don't know what anything means. They look to me and the Church to hold them until they can walk back into the world they know and forget the scary deeps. But a few don't walk back. They stay and plunge into the chasm to see what ... or who ... is there."

"Aye, Father, and today when we turned our televisions on, everything we knew died. And people want to come to the Church for the funeral, so that they can then adjust and move on."

Joseph tried to think out what to do, but Leola was ahead of him once more.

"I tell you what, Father, why don't you just go and sit in the church. I'm thinking that there's probably some there already who wouldn't mind having a word."

"Oh, right, good idea."

"And I'll get some people over and we'll ring all those folks and tell'm what's going on. Why don't we say there'll be some kind of service tonight, at eight o'clock?"

"Er, yes, O.K."

"And I'll ring young Rosalind. You know, Frank and Betty's daughter. She works at that local radio station that people seem to listen to. I'll get her to have the details given out."

Joseph felt like laughing again.

"Great idea. I'm glad I thought of it," he said with a grin on his face.

Leola stared at him suspiciously for a few moments and then tried to hide a smile.

"Some people think I'm bossy, Father."

"I'm not complaining."

Joseph headed towards the door and then stopped as a thought struck him.

"Of course, I've got absolutely no idea what to say to people. I'm just as lost as they are."

Leola looked hard at him.

"No you ain't, Father. Trust what you know. Trust those that are with you. The rest will take care of itself."

Joseph paused as her words sunk in. Then he turned and walked out of the room.

He sensed that it was time to move.

When he arrived on this magnificent world he could not be sure how events would unfold, only that the path would become clear one step at a time. The great currents that surged from the hidden heart of existence had carried him to this place, their probable course suggesting what was to be. And the ripples that spread from the primary flow could also be discerned to some extent. Yet there was always that wonderful, exciting element of the unknown at work. The response of conscious awareness could never be predicted with certainty. It was here that new creation could erupt at any moment, as freewill exerted its dominion.

So he had waited and watched, sensitized to the subtle shifts in the texture of existence as it wound its way. Now he sensed a moment approaching which required that he be elsewhere.

It was time to move towards the encroaching darkness, across waters of a different quality. He anticipated with pleasure the crossing of the ocean, so different in character to the mighty, crashing river below. He would journey slowly, for there was no rush. He knew where he was going and what was likely to happen when he arrived.

In his mind he reached out to the presence that was his companion. Tendrils of thought touched and then intertwined. Intention melded with readiness. Gradually the light that surrounded him began to subtly change in color and intensity, as its kaleidoscopic swirling accelerated. The strong sense of the pounding waters below started to fade as the vessel set out on its new journey.

The initial impetus given, he lessened the connection with his companion and, as he did so, another sensation impinged upon his consciousness. It was the bitter taste of fear. After all the beauty of the last few hours it stung and he took a few moments to adjust. In his mind he viewed the intruder and its source was instantly revealed. Below him he sensed small, hard-walled minds reeling and seeking escape. He regretted this, but could do nothing. Their fear arose from ignorance, nurtured by self-absorbed consciousness.

But perhaps, over time, his arrival and the hidden story yet to be revealed would bring healing to some, and maybe to many.

Chapter 10

There is something very moving about watching someone light a candle.

It is something about the purity of the flame and the act of simple concentration required. It is, in the same moment, childlike and profound. It says something that can never be expressed in words and thereby says far more.

To watch several hundred people light candles, each in their turn, having waited patiently and silently for a long time, is special indeed. Joseph found the sight powerful and mysterious, but it was a gentle power that spoke of the best of what it is to be human.

He sat to one side of the altar where earlier in the day he had celebrated Mass. It was difficult to believe that only that morning the events at Niagara had not been a part of his life. Now they dominated. Everything had been stood on its head and would never be the same again. Looking back twenty-four hours was like seeing another country, in another age. And it was not just in the outer world. He was aware that within him something unnamable was growing. It was as if he was becoming hypersensitized to the fullness of each moment. He had tasted periods of illumination before when his experience of existence had burst into a glorious technicolor and the unity of all things had become self-evident. But it had never possessed the strength that it now had. For a fleeting moment, he wondered if it was connected with the departure of the Teacher.

He was in the chair on which he always sat, yet tonight it was as though he was experiencing it for the first time. It was a dark oak medieval priest's chair, beautifully made by some long dead craftsman. It had become so familiar that usually he barely noticed it, but tonight it set his senses on fire. He was acutely aware of the hardness of the wood, the smoothness of its polish, the brown of its coloring and the intricate shape of its many carvings. He felt as though he could spend the rest of his life utterly fulfilled, simply experiencing what the chair had to offer. And it was more than just the chair. Everything to which he gave attention offered the same wonderful absorption. Yet it was the sight of the people, young and old, single or in families, quietly and reverently lighting candles a few yards away that most fascinated his expanded consciousness. The quiet dignified dance of their actions possessed a grace that contrasted so sharply with what Joseph observed as he went around a world usually filled with noise, argument and an ever-increasing search for excess. This was a side of humanity that he could love. He wondered why it was so rarely revealed.

In front of him, slightly to the right, was the altar with its embroidered green and gold frontal, which sparkled in the yellowy-white light of the candles that filled the church. It was dark outside and the church felt almost subterranean, like a fantastic cavern in the bowels of the earth. To his left, running along the edge of the sanctuary in which the altar stood, a few feet from his chair, was the waist-high altar rail. It was carved from the same wood as the priest's chair, probably by the same unknown craftsman. Going away from him, on his left, towards the main body of the church was a broad aisle with empty choir stalls on either side. On the continuous lectern that ran along the front of the stalls, a line of candles was lit on both sides creating a pathway of light to the altar. It was here that the people waited their turn to light a candle and place it in the troughs of sand that Joseph had placed along the altar rail. With his back to the wall, off to one side, he was out of the direct line of sight and so could watch without being noticed.

And still they came forward, seemingly without end, soft unobtrusive organ music providing a meditative accompaniment. The evocative aroma of incense hung in the air.

Before the service the churchwarden had told him that every

seat was taken and many people remained outside. A rudimentary sound system had been quickly rigged to include those outside, although Joseph had doubted that they would wait around in such freezing cold. Yet the numbers coming forward suggested otherwise. And it was not only the number of people that was so impressive; it was what he saw in their eyes. Occasionally in his career there had been very large congregations for the funeral of some notable personage, but there had been a different feeling than was the case tonight. At funerals most of the people were present out of a sense of duty. They were going through the motions. Tonight, however, there was a focus, a reverence and, above all, a humility that he had only rarely encountered. He knew that the thoughts accompanying this simple ritual would be varied and that many would not reflect the ethos of the building in which everything was happening. But for Joseph this was not important. What mattered was that they were deep thoughts that came from the heart. That was true prayer, whatever belief system shaped their form and content. It was strange to think that one of the first effects of the strange visitor that hung over Niagara was to bring people to the indefinable experience called prayer, even if that was a term most of them would never use.

He watched a family come forward. The mother was obviously putting on a brave face for the children, a boy and a girl, as they crowded around her, excited at the prospect of lighting their candle. Joseph remembered the family. He had baptized the children a few years before, but their names escaped him. The children, wide-eyed at being allowed to light a candle and resisting all attempts to guide their hands, solemnly held the wick in the flame and, dripping wax everywhere, carefully pushed their candle into the sand that lined one of the troughs. When each had finished they stood back to admire their handiwork, the little girl biting her bottom lip with pleasure. Then their mother moved forward and Joseph noticed that her hand was shaking slightly as she picked up her candle and lit it. She paused and stood very still with her eyes closed for a few moments, before placing it next to those of her children. Then it was the father's turn. As he approached, Joseph recalled more details of the baptism and remembered how off-hand, almost dismissive the man had been. He had wanted Joseph to know that he thought it was all unnecessary nonsense. But now everything had changed. As Joseph watched his face in the candle-light, all he could see was confusion and uncertainty. The man looked at the pile of candles for a few moments before carefully selecting one. Joseph noticed the exaggerated care he took in choosing and lighting it. He had seen this kind of behavior before with people trying to get an illusory sense of control in a situation that that was beyond them. Joseph suspected that this was a man who was used to being in control, for whom the arrival of the uncontrollable would be particularly difficult. The man hesitated, not knowing where to place his candle. Then, from behind, his wife gently guided his hand to the group of three already placed by the family and pushed his into the center. In that moment he looked both grateful and terribly lost. Joseph continued to watch as the woman led her husband away, clutching his hand fiercely. The children followed, oblivious to their father's distress, excitedly discussing in loud whispers which of them had the best candle.

The candles had been a flash of inspiration that afternoon when Joseph had been struggling to put together a service that would help people for whom church and Christianity were a foreign land. His worries had taken on a new dimension when Leola had informed him that "young Rosalind" no longer worked at the local radio station, but for the regional television news who were very keen to send a camera crew to record the service. They were doing a piece on local responses to the extra-ordinary events of the day. He had agreed with a heavy heart.

He had sat in the church all afternoon having a succession of conversations with people who seemed to feel the need to spend some time in the grandeur of the building. He found that he had to say very little. Joseph watched as the simple act of speaking aloud about fears and worries to someone who was really listening, enabled them to find some peace. Their body language would change as they spoke. At first, everything about their posture and face would be tense and clenched. Then, as they spoke, the stress would slowly drain.

Most of the people he met were unknown to Joseph. This reinforced his feeling that whatever he did that evening would somehow have to touch people in a way that transcended ideas or beliefs. He had pondered this between encounters without making much progress until, his gaze wandering aimlessly around the church, he spotted the stands that were used to support the coffin during a funeral. Leola's words from a few hours before had suddenly come to mind. She had said that the world everyone knew had died and they needed a funeral so they could adjust and move on. It had got him thinking about his experiences with funerals and around death, about what really seemed to help people. It was then that he thought of the candles. Once a year, on All Souls' Day, two days after Halloween, he would hold an evening service to which he invited the relatives of the people for whom he had led funerals since arriving in the parish. It was a time to remember and to grieve, but also to give thanks for the gift of a life. It seemed to meet a need. Many came. He had noticed that the service itself often appeared to go over people's heads. Partly this was due to its unfamiliarity for most of those present, but mainly it was because the occasion caused them to go deep within. What really connected was a small ritual at the end, when he invited everyone to light a candle in memory of the person who had died. It was this simple act that brought the tears and the silent prayers. It was what people remembered when he met them in the street months later. It was what they said had really helped.

Once Joseph had remembered this, he knew exactly what to do. He had planned the service that evening so that it climaxed with the lighting of candles, except this time it would be for a collective bereavement. He had arranged the rest of the service to lead up to this experience by taking people out of their everyday minds, out of the whirl of thoughts in which they usually lived, into the depths of the present moment. He had used music, bells, incense, light and gentle theatre to create an experience that all could dissolve into, that would open consciousness to the mystery of existence. He wanted people to feel, rather than think. He wanted to give space and permission for emotion to be experienced.

There had to be some words, for feeling and emotion need channels down which to flow, and he had chosen a few brief readings from the sacred writings of several spiritual traditions. Leola had read some beautiful words from a Native American teacher. And this is where he had intended to leave it. He had considered saying something himself, but had shied away on the basis that the last thing people wanted was a sermon. Yet he knew inside this was an excuse. The reality was that he had no idea what to say. He had soothed himself with the thought that it was an excuse that had some truth in it. As the service progressed, however, the feeling grew inside that he had to speak. For one thing, he could sense that people were looking to him to say something, to put the extraordinary events of the day into some kind of context. They expected it of him. They wanted it. But, also, deep within, something was waiting to be said. He did not know what it was and its pressure was relentless. Only saying the as yet unknown words would bring relief.

Now, a little later on, as he sat watching people light their candles, his thoughts returned to what he had said. The words had come from nowhere. They had simply appeared in his mind and he had spoken them. He had been as much a listener as the congregation. As the last of the readings had ended, he had slowly walked over to stand in front of the congregation, his long ornate robes rustling quietly as he moved. He had felt every eye on him in a church silent with expectation. Yet he had felt no trepidation. He had known that the words would flow.

He had stood quietly for a few moments before speaking, looking at the faces, making contact and entering into relationship.

"Today all of us have had an unimaginable shock. Like all of you I am reeling. It is difficult to know what to say at a time like this. All I can do tonight is share my feelings and the thoughts they give rise to. I hope this will be of help."

He had paused at this point to allow people to absorb what he had said.

"When I was a boy I was fascinated by space and the thought of alien life being out there, somewhere. I devoured every science fiction book that I could lay my hands on and spent hours imagining myself among the stars, having all kinds of strange encounters. Nothing excited me more." Joseph had paused for effect before continuing. "But also, when I was lying awake at four o'clock in the morning, nothing frightened me more, as every creak in the house became the footsteps of some monstrous alien creature and the wind blowing outside my window a UFO landing to kidnap me." A few chuckles had gone around the congregation at this point. "In my thoughtful moments, which were few and far between at that age, I had to admit that were the unthinkable ever to occur, fear would almost certainly be my most likely reaction rather than wide-eyed excitement. Of course, I never really expected that I would find out if this was true."

Joseph had paused once more, looking around the faces and making brief eye contact wherever he could. He could see that he had them hooked. Everyone was listening intently.

"The first thing I feel tonight is a visceral, almost animal fear. It's four o'clock in the morning again. My mind can barely take in the prospect of an encounter with something truly alien. This fear is multiplied many times over as my imagination runs wild, trying to picture what sits in the object at Niagara and its intentions. Every horror film I have ever seen keeps playing in my mind."

"As well as fear, there's massive confusion, or perhaps I should say disorientation. It's like my mind can't quite take in what has happened, can't accept that this is real. I feel as though I'm caught in a dream and will wake up at any moment." He bowed his head for a few moments and then looked up again. "It reminds me of when my wife died ... was killed. For weeks afterwards I kept forgetting she was gone. My mind would play tricks and, for a split second, I would think that I saw her out of the corner of my eye or would hear her voice in the distance. She was at the center of my world for so long that something in me even now can't quite accept that she's no longer here. In the same way, with the arrival of our strange visitor (or maybe visitors) everything that structured life for all of us, gave it meaning and a sense of security, has been shattered."

Joseph paused for effect before continuing, his eyes searching the rapt faces that looked back.

"Yet at least this time I am not alone, for we are in this together. We are all frightened and confused, but we can support each other. We must make sure that what has happened today brings us closer, rather than pushes us apart. We must make sure that this is a time when our first thought is to help our neighbor before ourselves. This experience must bring out the best in us, not the worst."

A murmur of agreement had gone around the church and Joseph had seen a few heads nodding. Perhaps his worries of earlier in the afternoon would prove unfounded. He had then allowed the congregation to become still once more before continuing.

"But there are also other thoughts going around my head tonight that are not fearful or confused. I don't know where they come from and they feel like deeper, more powerful thoughts. I keep thinking about how astonishing it is that anything exists at all. I keep thinking about the unimaginable vastness of the universe. I keep thinking about the mystery of time as it stretches into the unfathomable past and the unforeseeable future. I keep thinking about the ever-unfolding creative impulse of which I am as much a part as the greatest star. Above all, I keep thinking about the amazing fact of life and consciousness. My body is made out of the same stuff that lies in the ground beneath our feet, yet it stands before you alive and aware. And when I think like this, I see what is happening in a new and infinitely greater way. I experience a strong feeling that this is just one more element of the marvelous unfolding of creation. I begin to feel incredibly grateful to be alive at this extraordinary moment in time." He had paused once more for effect. "But I am also still fearful and confused." This had produced a few smiles.

Joseph had then stood in silence allowing his words to be absorbed, before finishing.

"There's one more thing, very personal, which burns in me tonight. Ever since I can first remember, I have sensed a deep meaning to existence. That it is going somewhere. That it has a purpose. That behind this purpose there lies an inconceivable intelligence and will. That everything that arises in existence is an expression of this presence. I happen to call this presence "God" and relate to it in a particular way, but others find different words and concepts to be helpful. Tonight, I have an almost overwhelming sense of this presence and that whatever resides in that strange vessel of light is as much its child as you and I. And this gives me an inexplicable faith that, whilst times ahead may be very challenging, all is ultimately well."

He had then brought his talk to a conclusion.

"So those are my thoughts tonight. They are rambling, fearful and confused. But also they are inspired and full of hope. I offer them in case they are of help."

Joseph had stopped at this point and remained in silence for a couple of minutes, standing before the congregation. It felt like the right way to end. To share the inward journey together, as his words were pondered. He had then nodded to the churchwarden and the lights had been turned off, to be replaced by a mass of lit candles, previously positioned in any nook and cranny he had been able to find. Most important of all, the candlelit path to the high altar had been revealed. He had then invited people to come forward and light a candle as an expression of their fears and hopes. He had turned and been the first to walk along the path, taking his time, before lighting his and placing it in the sand. He had then taken his seat next to the altar and had watched the graceful, dignified procession of people follow him.

Joseph's thoughts were brought back to the present by the churchwarden quietly signaling. He looked around and saw that the procession was finally coming to an end. He watched, fascinated, as the warden, last in line, lit the final candle and held it in front of him. He bowed to the altar as his lips moved in silent prayer, before carefully placing it in the sand. Joseph's relationship with him had always been difficult. He was a man in whom Joseph had always struggled to detect any great spiritual impulse, yet his actions spoke of hidden currents. Joseph was humbled by the sight.

As the warden found his way back down the path of light, Joseph stood and walked in front of the altar, turning to face the congregation. The silence in the church was palpable. In front of him the sand boxes were alive with flickering light. He then looked down the parallel rows of candles that burned brightly along the choir stalls and, as he did so, caught a momentary, very delicate whiff of incense. As he looked more carefully, he could just see tendrils of the aromatic smoke winding slowly through the semi-darkened atmosphere. It was deeply evocative. He became aware, once more, of being the center of intense attention. A mass of faces watched him from the candle-lit church. He brought the service to an end.

"I hope that what we have experienced here together this evening has helped in some way. The church will remain open all night and you are welcome to stay, to talk quietly or to go home. This is your house tonight, if you wish to make it so. May the peace of God be with you all."

Joseph began to walk down from the altar along the candle-lit path. He planned to position himself by the door of the church so that he could say goodbye to people as they left.

It was then that he became aware of something happening.

It was to do with the light in the building.

At first it was very subtle and Joseph wondered if it was a symptom of his hypersensitized state. But then the congregation started to notice it as well. People began to look around and peer into the cavernous, darkened roof space above their heads.

The light in the building was turning blue. Not a strong blue, but a delicate shade that seemed to weave itself into the flickering candlelight. Joseph stopped in his tracks, just before the first row of people. The blue was now very evident, throwing strange shadows onto the ancient stone of the church. There was something about it that stirred dim, elusive memories that hung, tantalizingly, at the edge of consciousness. He closed his eyes for a few moments and became aware of a distant vibration, only just discernable. He could not be sure whether it was in the world or coming from deep inside him. He knew that it was growing, or rather getting closer. He was vaguely aware that people around him were beginning to get disturbed. Voices were being raised, soon to be followed by the first scream. But he was becoming too absorbed to be affected. He simply stood, absolutely still, with eyes closed, as around him a mass exodus started towards the doors. Had he been paying attention, he would have been relieved to see that, although very scared, most people did not panic. Acting quickly, with heroic good sense, the churchwarden quickly had all of the various doors opened, allowing everyone to stream out.

Then Joseph felt the invitation.

There were no words; just a compelling idea that he should leave the church, for something awaited him outside.

His eyes snapped open and he drew in a gasping breath. As he did so, those nearest to him looked around and Joseph saw their eyes widen in astonishment. He looked down and was stunned to see that he now stood in an intense beam of blue light. He immediately looked upward to find its source, but all he could see was the dark outline of the vaulted timber roof, eerily illumined by the more general blue tinge that permeated the building. The concentrated beam in which he stood, which pooled onto the floor around him, seemed to have no specific source. It just coalesced around him from the more general hue that filled the church. He lowered his gaze and found that he now stood in a clear space as people pushed backwards to get away from him. The fear he saw in their eyes was unnerving.

The summons came again, even stronger than before. It pushed everything else from his mind and he began to move through the throng towards the nearest door. He wondered how he would make it with everyone packed so tightly, but the blue incandescent beam moved with him and his path cleared as people pushed to get out of his way. For a few seconds he wondered what he must look like and saw a picture in his mind of something unearthly, almost angelic. Yet again the summons was repeated and he went out through the door. He expected to be met by starlit blackness, but instead he found that everything, the walls of the church, the gravestones, the grass and the faces of the people, which were all turned upward for some reason, were bathed in a silvery-white light. He assumed that it must be from the full moon that still hung in the sky, yet there was something not quite right about the light. There was a gentle, barely discernable undulation to it. It seemed to have inner waves that were constantly sweeping through. For a fleeting moment he wondered if the effect was being caused by clouds overhead. There was, though, a sense of relief that the disturbing blue light of a few moments before had gone – until he looked down and saw that he, and only he, still stood in a cone of blue. He jerked his head back to look at whatever had so transfixed everyone else.

There, above the old church, above ancient and sacred land, was the magnificent, utterly alien vessel of light. What had been to Joseph a picture on a television screen only a short time before was now an incredible reality bestriding his world. And it was singling him out. As he stood in its ethereal spotlight he felt something reaching to him, touching his mind, and before he could react he plunged into dreams and the churchyard faded instantly from awareness. He never saw the people start to run away. He never heard the slamming of car doors, the revving of engines or the sound of wheels spinning on gravel.

In a short time he was completely alone - almost.

The only company he had was the television crew who, summoning all of their courage, stayed to record the footage of a man held in a beam of light that would make their careers. And an old lady, with eyes closed and a huge smile on her face, gently rocking back and forth.

Chapter 11

Joseph was awakened by daylight streaming through thin curtains.

Once more he had the sense of having experienced a powerful dream. Yet it felt different to the previous morning in a way that, in his groggy state, he could not at first pin down. It was as he tried to remember the dream that the truth hit him with terrible force. It was not a dream. The church, the frightened people, the blue light and everything else that was seeping back into consciousness, were real. It had all happened. Joseph jerked bolt upright in bed as events of the previous day began to fill his mind, his heart beating rapidly. In a state of near panic he looked around the strange room trying to work out where he was. A car journey came dimly into awareness, then a very large house and, finally, to his quiet horror, the bishop. Then he knew where he was. He was in one of the many bedrooms of the bishop's home. Remembering that much helped and he started to calm down a little. But he still did not have a complete picture, just jumbled pieces. And some pieces were missing. He knew they were there, but they were tantalizingly just out of reach. Also they were different, somehow, to the other memories that he was recovering. They had a different quality. They felt different. They were not so solid, yet paradoxically seemed more real. For a few moments Joseph tried to bring them into focus, but they seemed to dance out of reach just as he thought he had one in his grasp.

He shook his head in frustration and pulled back the quilt to get out of bed. It was then he discovered that he was still dressed. He decided not to look in the mirror on the large old-fashioned wardrobe on the other side of the high-ceilinged room. The last thing he needed was to see the disheveled mess that he undoubtedly must be. He gingerly put his feet onto the thick pile carpet that had seen better days, feeling some gratitude that at least he had not got into bed with his shoes still on. He then had a dim memory of some mysterious man removing them the night before, which he found vaguely embarrassing. It reminded him of an occasion in his youth when he had been very drunk on cider and had to be put to bed by friends. In fact, the way his mind felt this morning had a lot in common with a hangover. He wished with all his heart that it were that mundane.

He tried to get to his feet, but quickly sat down again as a wave of dizziness swept over him. He realized that whatever had happened the night before had left its mark in more ways than one. Joseph steadied himself for a few seconds and, very carefully this time, tried to stand again. He was greatly relieved when, after a few moments of gentle swaying, he found that he could stand and keep a clear head at the same time. This felt like a real achievement. He moved to the window and pulled back the curtains. The light hurt his eyes and he shaded them with his hand while they adjusted. He could feel a monster headache coming on. He took his hand away and was able to see a little better through the window. He found that he was looking down onto the large courtyard at the rear of the bishop's house where, in times gone past, he had parked his own car when attending events. This is something that he had only ever done reluctantly, usually under great pressure from the bishop. Why people wanted to attend such meetings and social events was beyond his comprehension. The courtyard was very secluded and could only be entered along a narrow driveway that ran along one side of the massive Georgian house. It was not unknown for major blockages to occur, as people leaving one event found their way blocked by those arriving for the next. On the far side of the courtyard from Joseph was a long stable block, now converted into garages and storerooms. And enclosing the whole house, its extensive grounds and the stable block was a high wall. Large ornate iron gates controlled the only entrance to the grounds. It was a place where one could be very private if so desired.

Beyond the stable block, on the other side of the wall, Joseph could see a mass of tree tops where the private arboretum that went with the bishop's house was to be found. Although not visible from where he stood, Joseph knew that between the wall and the enclosed arboretum was a public road. It led to an expensive housing estate, constructed years before on land sold off by the Church. The arboretum had been planted when the house was built, long before any road divided the land. In the couple of centuries since, it had matured into something special. Most of the year it was closed to the public. On those occasions when it was open, large crowds streamed in to see the spectacular collection of trees and what had become, due to its isolation, an amazing nature reserve. Joseph had been in there once with Clare on a private visit at the invitation of the Bishop. As he stood at the window he could remember holding her hand as they crossed the road to stand before the solid wooden gate of the arboretum, with the large iron key weighing heavy in his coat pocket. He had never forgotten the experience of entering and closing the gate behind them. They had found themselves on a small rise in the ground, giving a good view of the secluded landscape. As they had stood looking around, he almost felt he had been given a taste of what the world might have been like before the advent of humans. For the first time in his life, he was in a place where that sense of humanity's all-pervading presence was absent. He had felt like a visitor in the deepest sense of the word.

Joseph shifted his gaze to the courtyard and the three cars that were parked there. He presumed that he must have arrived in one of them and tried to work out which. He recognized immediately the large four-wheel drive vehicle. Every priest in the diocese knew it well. The bishop claimed that she needed it for the massive amount of driving she did around her extensive domain, in all seasons and weathers. Most thought that this was a good and sensible reason, but the more ardent environmentalists among the clergy were not impressed. Beside it was an expensive looking bright yellow sports car, which to Joseph's inexpert eye appeared Italian. Joseph had no interest in cars and tended to believe that all flashy sports cars were Italian. It was the third car that brought a frown to Joseph's brow. He felt that he should know to whom it belonged, but like so much that morning he could not bring it to mind. It was an elderly battered wreck that one could imagine being stopped by the police every time it passed their way. For no obvious reason, he had a feeling that this was the car that had brought him here.

Joseph's eyes were starting to hurt again, so he turned away from the window and inspected the room. In the far corner, almost hidden by the wardrobe, he caught sight of a wash basin. It was just what was needed. He walked over and splashed copious amounts of cold water onto his face, astonished that something so simple could feel so good. He cupped his hands under the streaming water and took a long drink, realizing how thirsty he was. He fumbled for the towel and dried his face. As he lowered the towel and opened his eyes, he found himself looking into a small mirror over the basin. He saw an exhausted, red-eyed face, with wildly disheveled hair. His appearance shocked him for a few moments, as the effect of what he had experienced the previous night became even more obvious. He looked around for his jacket and noticed it hanging in the far corner of the room. Below it he saw his missing shoes. The jacket was an old friend that he had worn continuously for many years. Clare had tried to wean him off it, but without success. He searched through the numerous inside pockets and found another old friend. He had bought the metal comb as a teenager, at a time when they had been fashionable. It had been one of his many forlorn attempts to fit in with his peers. They were long-gone, but he still had the comb. He stood in front of the mirror and, with much pulling and tugging, managed to restore his hair to something resembling normality. He sat down on the bed to put on his shoes, then grabbed his jacket and headed in determined fashion to the door. He was not looking forward to going downstairs and the difficult conversations that awaited, so was doing what he often did in difficult situations – plunging in without allowing time for worry.

He paused for a few moments with his hand on the door handle, then opened it and stepped through. He found himself in a long corridor with doors leading off on either side. To his left the corridor came to an abrupt halt a few yards away, so he walked in the opposite direction and soon came to an imposing stairway. He carefully found his way down the stairs, his head still throbbing with some intensity. At the bottom he arrived at a place that he recognized. He was in the grand hallway of the house, which he had passed through several times on his way to a meeting or function. In front of him were the imposing double doors that led to the gravel parking area in front of the house. To their right, the magnificent grandfather clock that he had admired on previous visits loudly ticked its way towards eternity. Joseph stopped and listened for a few moments, but could hear nothing except the clock. He knew that there had to be other people around, but locating them in such a large house might require a little effort. He turned and began to move down the wide, wood-paneled corridor that led away from the entrance, past the staircase, into the main part of the building. On either side were the offices of the bishop and her staff, together with the various meeting rooms that he knew so well. He stopped at each and put his head around the door, but found them all unoccupied. He reached the end of the passageway, where a large window opened onto the rear courtyard that he had looked down upon a short while earlier. He glanced through the window in the hope that he might see someone outside, but all that could be seen were the three cars. For a few moments he thought that he would have to retrace his steps and find a way into another part of the house, but then very faintly he heard voices in the distance. It worried him slightly that the voices seemed to be raised in anger and suspected that this was the only reason he had heard them. He looked around for the source of the sound but was puzzled as there did not seem to be any more doors for him to try. He listened more carefully and was drawn to the last section of paneling on the right-hand corridor wall by the window. He put his ear to it and the voices became more distinct. A thought occurred to him and he stood back to examine the panel carefully. His suspicions were confirmed. The last panel was a disguised door into what originally would have been the kitchen and servants' quarters. This was not unknown in houses of this period, where the owner was keen to eliminate any unnecessary sign of the lower classes from the main body of the house. Joseph now understood that the grand rooms, which would have been the domain of the owner and his family, had been converted into the offices and meeting rooms, while the old servant area had been made into private accommodation for the bishop.

Joseph reached down and turned the disguised handle that opened the panel. He stepped through into a narrower and much less imposing passageway. The voices were now more discernable and he followed the sound until he stood in front of an open doorway, looking into a large and very modern kitchen. Only the worn flagstones that covered the floor revealed its much older origins. Three people were sitting around a circular, solid-looking dining table. In front of each was a half-empty mug of coffee. A heated discussion was obviously in progress. No one immediately noticed Joseph's arrival and he was able to observe the three people for a few moments. Two he knew well, the third he had never met before. All looked flushed and displayed tense body language. The argument seemed to have reached some kind of stalemate and a stony silence had ensued.

Joseph wanted to turn around and walk back the way he had come, but he knew that this was not an option. He stilled his mind and said a quiet prayer, before stepping fully into the room.

"Hello there."

Three heads turned instantly to look in Joseph's direction. He noticed how immediately, in an unspoken conspiracy, they tried to hide what had been happening and force smiles onto their faces. The bishop leapt to her feet, catching the table on her way up and making the coffee left in the mugs slosh dangerously from side to side. She was clearly disconcerted by his sudden appearance. She looked nearly as disheveled as him, with her purple clerical shirt creased and dog collar awry. Her medium length graying hair also needed a good comb – and in a split second of madness Joseph thought of offering to lend his. He had a sense that the three had been up all night.

"Joseph! Good morning. We didn't hear you come down. It's good to see you looking better. You were not ... well ... when you arrived last night."

Joseph looked at her carefully. He had never before seen her in a less than completely controlled state. He had a feeling that it was connected with more than just him.

"Good morning Jennifer. I don't remember very much about how I got here, but thanks for looking after me." Joseph turned to take in the other two people present. "Actually, I suspect that I need to thank all of you from the few threads I can remember about last night." He turned to the other woman present. "I take it that you drove me here Leola."

"Aye Father, that I did, although you were not very complimentary about my driving or my car," Leola replied with an air of hurt innocence, before staring at him intently. "But I needed to get you away and here was all I could think of."

"You needed to get me away? Er, right," said Joseph not really understanding what she meant. But he would leave such questions for a while until he had got his bearings. He turned to the third person at the table, who was regarding him with great interest.

"I'm afraid that I can't remember you name sir."

"That would probably be because we have never met before, Father Joseph," the man replied in good English, but with what sounded like a Mediterranean accent. "Unless, that is, you count my carrying you up stairs and putting you to bed as some kind of introduction."

"That was very kind of you. I do have a vague memory of something like that happening."

The man stood up and turned to face Joseph fully. Joseph could now see that he had a brown, thickset face with dark curly hair receding from the forehead. Although not much taller than Joseph, he was powerfully built and clearly would have had no problem carrying someone up a flight of stairs. A strong-looking hand was held out for Joseph to shake. Joseph stepped forward and gripped it, wincing as he felt the bones of his hand being unintentionally crushed.

"I am Alexander ... Alex ... from Greece. I am an old ... friend ... of Jennifer's."

Joseph glanced in the bishop's direction and saw her face go slightly red. He knew all he needed to. He had always imagined her as someone completely focused on her career, allowing no distractions. After all, she made no secret of her ambition to rise as high as possible within the Church. Joseph was pleased to discover her more human side, yet it should not perhaps have come as a surprise. He realized now that her compassion and sensitivity around Clare's death must have had its roots in experiences of her own.

"Good to meet you Alex. It was good luck you being around."

For a moment Alex's face darkened and he glanced at the Bishop in silent reproach.

"Indeed, although I have hoped to be around more but it has not proved possible." There was an icy silence for a few moments, before Alex's face relaxed and broke into a philosophical grin. "But I am here now at the center of everything that matters, with the famous Father Joseph Williams, ready to be of service."

"Famous? I don't understand," Joseph replied in a shocked voice.

Alex was about to respond when the bishop interrupted.

"Alex, I think that Joseph may still be confused about last night and certainly has no idea as to ... subsequent events. I think that we need to give him time to adjust and gather himself."

Alex looked at her, as though about to argue, then relaxed once more and nodded. Joseph got the impression that the initial impulse to object came from deep habit rather than reasoned disagreement. He had known some relationships to be like that.

They were all startled when Leola spoke up. In the intensity of the exchange, the three of them had almost forgotten that she was there.

"Why don't I make Father a bit of breakfast and we can tell him everything that happened. And he," she said very pointedly, "can tell us his side of things."

The bishop looked crossly at Leola, who returned her stare without flinching. The tension between the two women was palpable. Joseph had no idea as to its cause.

"Good idea, Leola," the bishop managed to get out with great effort. "I'll give you a hand."

For a moment Leola looked as though she might object to the offer of help, but then nodded her head. Joseph sensed it might be a good idea to leave them alone for a while. He looked over at Alex, who seemed to be thinking along similar lines.

"Alex, is that your amazing sports car outside. Any chance of a quick look before breakfast?"

"No problem," Alex replied, while raising an eye brow humorously. "Walk this way."

Joseph followed him out through the door. Behind him, all he could hear was the opening of cupboards and the clink of plates. There was no conversation. Alex turned confidently to the right and led Joseph further down the narrow corridor, past more windows that looked out onto the courtyard. It was obvious that Alex knew his way around the house. He opened a door and they emerged into the morning light. Joseph shivered as the cold hit him. Alex, dressed in a short-sleeved shirt, seemed oblivious to the temperature despite coming from warmer climes. They strolled out of the shadow of the house into the sunshine and Joseph felt a little less chilled. They meandered their way towards where the cars were parked.

"So, you are interested in cars then Father Joseph?"

"Actually Alex, not in the slightest. I just thought it might be a good idea to allow the bishop and Leola a little space. The atmosphere between them was colder than out here".

Alex chuckled. "Ah, yes, two powerful people trying to inhabit the same territory. Don't worry. They have good souls and will work it out in time."

"I don't understand. What territory are they fighting over?"

"Why, you of course my friend."

"What, me?" Joseph replied, looking both startled and worried in the same moment.

"What else?" Alex tried his best to look serious, but he was obviously enjoying Joseph's discomfort. He stopped and put his hand on Joseph's shoulder in conspiratorial fashion. "It is not what you think, understandable though that would be. It is that they both feel ... responsible ... for you." Alex's humor dropped away and he became very serious. "The loss of your beautiful wife affected them both deeply and their hearts went out to you. Perhaps without realizing they have become a little possessive as a result. When each was in her own sphere it was fine. Now they occupy the same space and they must ... adjust. I'm sure they will".

Alex turned and ambled towards the cars, leaving Joseph staring at the ground thinking hard about what he had just heard. It was actually obvious and he was shocked that it had not occurred to him before. But then, as with Leola the previous day, he saw that he had been too wrapped up in his own world of hurt to consider the effect of Clare's death on others. He may have been at the center, but the event had sent out powerful ripples that he was only just beginning to see. Yet as he thought about what Alex had said, he had the feeling that this was not the whole explanation for what was happening between the bishop and Leola. He looked up and saw that Alex had reached the cars and was waiting for him. Joseph wandered over to the yellow sports car.

"So this is yours?"

"Ah, beautiful isn't she," Alex beamed as he moved to stand on the other side of the hood from Joseph. "Do you like Ferrari's?"

"Is that Italian?"

"Oh yes," Alex laughed. "I can see that you do not lie. You really don't know much about cars."

"A big, yellow Italian sports car sounds excellent to me. I'm sure it's very fast."

Alex looked suddenly grumpy. His ability to change mood almost instantly was beginning to unsettle Joseph.

"Too fast, maybe, at least in the eyes of your wonderful police."

"Had some difficulties then I take it?"

"Indeed. But perhaps I am old enough to know better," Alex replied, his good humor starting to return. Joseph grabbed his opportunity to get back to the subject he really wanted to talk about.

"Alex, what else is going on between the bish ... Jennifer ... and Leola?"

"Ah, you do not miss much do you Father Joseph?"

"Well, I don't know about that. But I do know that I would be more comfortable if you would call me Joe."

"But I would not be more comfortable. I was raised in the

Greek Orthodox Church which is still in my blood and we call our priests 'Father'. So you will have to put up with it, as you say in English."

Joseph felt mischievous. "So do you call Jennifer, 'Bishop', in all ... circumstances?"

Alex smiled shyly. "How do you say again in English? Oh, I know – none of your damn business." He then roared with laughter and Joseph found himself joining in. A bit of his mind noted that he seemed to be laughing a lot now. He decided to pursue the subject while the iron was still hot.

"So how did you and Jennifer meet?"

Alex stared into space for a few moments and then looked relieved at the opportunity to talk. Joseph got the impression that he had a lot bottled up inside.

"It was many years ago when we were both students. I was over here for a year studying English religious art. It is what I do. I am an artist. I paint modern ... spiritual ... pictures, inspired by the great icons of the Orthodox Church. In Greece now, I am well known in certain ... circles ... where my images sell for a lot of money, enough to buy Ferrari's. Jennifer was studying theology and we found ourselves at some of the same lectures. It was very strange, for we were ... are ... such opposites, yet the attraction was so strong it was almost overwhelming. I swept her off her feet – and she swept me off mine."

"In what way are you opposites?"

Alex grinned from the other side of the bright yellow car.

"Isn't it obvious? Jennifer is, well, very conventional. She believes in order and authority, whether in religion, politics or life in general. She likes everything controlled. Me? I am anarchical by nature. I love spontaneity, I resist authority and I love the unknown." Alex lowered his voice slightly. "Actually, I will tell you something. When I met Jennifer all those years ago I was in England hiding. Or perhaps as the Hollywood movies would say, lying low until the heat wore off. In Greece then, I was into radical politics. I was very left wing. I had … done things … that made it a good idea for me to get out of the country for a while." Alex grinned across at Joseph. "Can you imagine Jennifer with such a revolutionary?"

Joseph just smiled back. Indeed, it was a remarkable thought. Alex stared upwards at the sky for a few moments before continuing.

"So right from the beginning we have loved and fought. We have tried to be with each other and failed. We have tried to split-up and failed. I have tried other relationships, but they are not Jennifer and so they fail also. So for twenty years we live this half-life, neither one thing nor the other. But last year I say to her that this cannot continue. I say that we must marry and commit ourselves. Despite the difficulties, I am sure that it is what God wants."

Joseph could not hide his fascination with this revelation.

"And what did she say?"

Alex sighed and looked sad. "At first she said no. That she would have to be sure that the marriage would work before doing it. Then I get angry and say that nothing in life is certain. That she must be prepared for adventure and risk. Then she says that I am irresponsible, and so on. We argue and argue, as we have for years."

Joseph felt genuinely sad for the two of them. "I'm sorry it didn't work out."

To his surprise, Alex brightened up.

"Ah, but maybe it will. Something changed a couple of weeks ago. One night, without warning, I get a call from Jennifer saying that she has been thinking about my proposal and wants to talk some more. It was interesting, for her voice was different to normal. It was not so certain. It almost seemed as if she had been crying. So I say that I will come over straight away. I jump in my car and drive across Europe, thinking that finally my dream will happen. But when I get to England, first I am stopped by your police for speeding and then, when I finally get here, Jennifer is back to how she used to be. So we argue again." Alex paused. "Yet this time is different. I can feel it. And I know why."

Alex looked over at Joseph's puzzled face.

"I think that what happened to your beautiful wife has affected my Jennifer. I think that it has made her understand that she and I, well, we only have so much time."

Once more it was brought home to Joseph that Clare's life and death had sent ripples out into the universe in all directions. He wondered what other changes she had wrought that he would never be aware of. Despite the sadness that Alex's words evoked, Joseph was glad for him.

"So this time there is real hope?"

"Yes, I think this is so and my heart sings with joy." Then Alex's face clouded a little. "But there is still one obstacle, which for Jennifer is very difficult."

Joseph was intrigued. "What's that?"

Alex looked at him for a while without speaking. Joseph started to feel uncomfortable and was relieved when his Greek friend finally broke the silence.

"This is something, Father Joseph, that it is not easy to talk about. Indeed, I am not sure whether I should." He paused again, reached down and opened the door to the car. "Sit in the passenger seat and I will show you the marvels of Italian engineering."

Joseph was thrown for a few moments by Alex's sudden change of tack. He hesitated before opening the door and sliding into the most comfortable car seat he had ever encountered. The next ten minutes were something of a trial for Joseph, as Alex showed him in great detail the vast array of electronic marvels that the car boasted. Joseph discovered that enthusiasm is not always catching. Yet all the while Joseph sensed another train of thought at work in Alex, that beneath the outer bonhomie a decision was being made. When he ran out of gadgets to demonstrate, Alex started the engine. The roar was astonishing and, Joseph had to admit, viscerally satisfying. Something primal found the almost animal-like rumble deeply attractive. Then without warning the roar was cut off. It took Joseph's senses a few moments to readjust to normal background sounds. He found Alex looking at him from the other side of the futuristic cockpit.

"Father, I was not completely honest when I said I am an artist. That word does not really convey the … full flavor … of what I do. But most of the time I find it convenient to describe myself this way when dealing with people."

"Oh, right," was all Joseph could think of to say. It did not matter, however, because Alex was already moving on.

"It is not easy to explain, but let's say that I have a deep … and practical … interest in the relationship between the material world and the mind. And that the images I paint, whilst still being what most people would see as normal pictures, also contain hidden patterns, symbolism if you like, that may be an aid to exploring that relationship. The images can … stimulate … that connection and are at the same time inspired by what it reveals."

Light began to dawn in Joseph's mind as to what Alex was trying to explain, but he let him continue for a while. Also, in a way that he could not understand, he knew that what he was hearing was of the utmost importance. That, in some way, it was an insight, a link, into what was happening and how the future might unfold.

"You see, Father, I explore … with others of a like mind … the possibility that this world, this level of existence, is only an effect of a deeper cause. And by following the sacred road of awareness back into the depths of our own consciousness, which must be a product of that deeper cause, we may begin to … shape … those causal elements to bring about blessings to this world."

Joseph decided that it was time to put Alex out of his misery.

"Alex, are you talking about the practice of magic?"

Alex's face froze in astonishment for a few moments, his mouth half open as though about to speak. Then he sat back in his chair, resting his hands on the top of the steering wheel and began to laugh quietly.

"I can see, Father, that I made the right choice in telling you. It is usually my ... our ... way to keep this part of our lives secret, but I had a feeling that this was something that needed to be shared with you."

"Clare, my wife, and I explored many beliefs and philosophies. The deep magical writings were of interest to me. They shed possible light on some ... experiences ... of my own."

Alex turned to look at Joseph, his eyes shining with fascination.

"Ah, perhaps I am getting a glimpse of why our strange friend has such an interest in you. I think you could tell me much more, but perhaps this is not the time." He laughed again as Joseph struggled to hide his relief at these last words. His laughter then faded. "But as I am sure you can see, Father, for Jennifer this is very difficult. I am a member of a fellowship who, although all Orthodox Christians like me, practice what she regards as heresy and perhaps even evil. She is very conventional and biblical in her views. She will not accept that this way is an ancient, although long hidden path in the Christian heritage. Were it not for her love, which I do not doubt, I am sure she would have nothing to do with me."

Joseph gazed at Alex with compassion. He could see how torn the Bishop must be. He imagined what it would have been like if he and Clare had encountered some similar obstacle in their relationship. It would have been a living hell.

"Everything is changing, Alex, all of the time. I have no doubt that love will win in the end."

Alex looked away from him, out of the side window of the car.

Joseph had a suspicion that there were the beginnings of tears in his eyes. He decided that it was time to change the subject. Fortunately, the original topic of their conversation came back to mind.

"Er, right, anyway. So what else do you reckon is going on between Jennifer and Leola?"

Alex looked surprised, then relieved at the change of subject. He thought for a few moments before replying.

"They are ... anathema ... to each other. Do you understand this word?"

"Yes. I think so. It is an old Greek word which means to denounce or to be in abhorrence of someone or something". Joseph paused, frowning before he continued. "But surely you can't be suggesting that Jennifer and Leola feel this way about each other. They are two of the most decent people I know"

"Ah, but you see Father Joseph, that is part of the problem. They are truly good people, but each represents what repels the other. And because of their goodness, their feelings spoon a large dose of guilt into the mixture."

"So why are they anathema to each other?"

"To some extent it is similar to how it is between Jennifer and me. As we have already discovered, Jennifer is a very conventional Christian, for whom the Bible is everything, and who struggles to live with other spiritual paths. Leola is a priestess of nature, who connects with the primal currents of life in all its forms. Jennifer's beliefs cannot embrace the old ways that Leola practices, and so she is disturbed at Leola's involvement with the Church and her friendship with you. From Leola's point of view, she and her kind have suffered much at the hands of people like Jennifer in times gone by and this is difficult for her to forget. But also there is something else about how they relate to ... let's call it 'truth'. For Jennifer, the truth is intellectual, a set of ideas, and in this she finds a sense of security. Whereas for Leola truth is an experience in the moment, beyond words, that may only be tasted, for whom Jennifer's way feels stifling, if not dead. And all of this gives them different reactions to our strange visitor. Jennifer is disturbed and threatened that her very ... controlling ... view of reality has been shattered. Also, her beliefs lead her to doubt the ... goodness ... of the visitor. But for Leola, the visitor is wonderful and just another part of the mystery of life."

Alex paused for breath before continuing.

"So they argue about what happened to you last night and the best way forward. I get involved and say that they must trust and follow yourself, as it is you who have been chosen. Then all our personal stuff gets mixed up in the argument, which goes on all night until you walk in."

Joseph was disturbed by what he had just heard. But it was not because of the personal stuff. It was Alex's use of the word "chosen" that echoed through his mind, refusing to fade away. It was a powerful and frightening word, with unspoken implications that stirred below the surface. His thoughts were interrupted by Alex.

"But you know, Father Joseph, the problems between Jennifer and Leola will resolve. Once they discover each other as human beings rather than ... concepts ... everything will change."

Joseph struggled to get his mind back to the present.

"Er, yes, Alex, I'm sure that's right."

Alex stared at him thoughtfully for a few moments, clearly aware that Joseph was suddenly troubled.

"Ah, I think it is time that we went back in. Breakfast must be ready by now."

Joseph just nodded and they got out of the car and made their way across the courtyard towards the kitchen.

Chapter 12

They were greeted by the aroma of coffee, toast and eggs. Joseph realized how hungry he was. The events of the previous night seemed to have drained his body as much as his mind. They all sat down around the table and began to eat. Joseph immediately noticed that the atmosphere between the bishop and Leola had changed. The air of unspoken conflict had drained away and left a kind of peace. Perhaps, Joseph thought, their sharing of a common mundane task, which had taken them out of the intensity of their minds, had helped.

At first the conversation was sporadic as they tucked into the food, restricted to polite requests for someone to pass the salt or remarks on the weather. But Joseph felt a tension rising within that could be resisted no longer. It had been good to walk with Alex, have breakfast and focus on something reasonably normal for a while. Now, though, the events of the previous night filled his mind and would allow no rest. He slowly put down his knife and fork, and then looked around the table. The others watched him, knowing what it meant. It was almost as though they had been dreading this moment, but knew it had to come.

"We need to talk about last night."

There was silence for a few seconds, as though each was waiting for another to speak first. Then the bishop made as if to reply, but suddenly something in Joseph knew that he had to take charge. That from this first moment there must be no doubt as to his authority. He cut the bishop off just as she was about to speak, ignoring her look of pained surprise.

"First of all I need you to tell me the whole story of what happened. From the end of the service onwards. Up to that moment I can basically remember what was going on, but after that it all gets less ... tangible." He was gratified to see that his leadership seemed to have been accepted, at least for the time being. He had a suspicion that something about his voice had changed, but could not be sure. He briefly wondered about this before continuing. "Leola, why don't you go first."

Leola nodded and drew in her breath, obviously gathering her thoughts.

"I'll just tell it as I saw it. At the end of the service, when you were walking down towards the back of the church, everything started to turn blue. The very air itself kind of changed color."

"Yes, I remember that. It was barely noticeable at first and then it got stronger."

"Aye, that's right. But there's something else, as well. I heard something in the distance, like a hum, getting closer. I don't think anyone else heard."

Recollection began to flood back into Joseph's mind.

"Yes, I remember that too now! It was like something was approaching, something powerful and then it … invited … me." As Joseph spoke he felt the shock rise up inside. He leaned back in the chair and found himself breathing heavily. He looked at the others. Their focus upon him was intense. The bishop appeared very disturbed.

"Aye, Father, that it did. I heard it too, but only as like I was listening to someone else's conversation in the distance. It were not meant for me." She paused before continuing. "And that be when you went all … strange."

"What do you mean 'strange'?" the bishop interjected with some force, her face a picture of concern.

"Well," Leola replied obviously trying to stay calm, "Father Joseph began to look … absorbed … like he were kind of in a … trance."

The bishop said nothing, but her look of worry deepened even further at Leola's description. Joseph felt it necessary to reassure her.

"Nothing to worry about Jennifer. It may have looked like a trance from the outside, but I was just listening … very intently. I could feel something trying to reach out to me and I was responding as best I could."

Joseph knew that this was not the full truth, but hoped it would placate the bishop. His hope was in vain. She looked at him for a few moments and then spoke, obviously choosing her words carefully. He knew that he was about to get involved in the latest installment of the conversation that had been going on all night.

"Joseph, you know that I try to be as open as I can about experiences that are, shall we say, beyond my own background and knowledge. You know as well that I have always honored your very different ... approach ... to spiritual questions. But I must also be true to myself and my beliefs. And I must also be a ... critical friend ... to you. It is certainly part of my faith that evil walks this world, seeking to deceive and corrupt. How can you know that this ... summons ... was not from that source?"

Joseph was grateful for the care and respect with which the bishop had phrased her question, especially given that she was obviously very uneasy about what had happened. But an inner wisdom told him that he had to draw a line in the sand now. This kind of conversation had to be stopped in its tracks. He looked straight into the bishop's eyes.

"Jennifer, I completely understand your worries and I know that they come from a genuine concern for me. All I can do is assure you that the ... presence ... who reached out emanated nothing but goodwill. I trust it totally."

As he spoke, he could sense the authority in his voice strengthen. He suddenly knew with absolute clarity that the strange authority he was exuding was a different expression of the illumined state that he had experienced while sitting by the altar the evening before. It was something emerging from the depths of what he was, manifesting in a new form. It was a very strange sensation. It was as though the "authority" was him, and yet also not him. Part of Joseph was separate to it and watched it at work. Yet it was also who he was. For a few moments he tried to remember if he had experienced this feeling before, but nothing came to mind. Once again he wondered if the Teacher's departure had unleashed something within that had been dormant.

The bishop appeared a little shaken by the force of his reply, but was made of stern stuff.

"But Joseph, how can you be sure that you are not being deceived? How can you take such a risk?"

Joseph could see that this was not going to be easy. The authority in his voice grew stronger and seemed to almost have a life of its own. The words poured out.

"Because life is risky. We are constantly stepping into the unknown, whether or not we are prepared to acknowledge this fact. Putting aside whether I share your view of the nature of evil, I take a risk every time I deal with another sentient being. I will not be crippled by fear or the need for a sense of control." He saw the bishop flinch slightly at these words. "I will not turn away from this awesome moment because I am trapped in under-standings that may have served humanity in the past but are now inadequate. Let's face it, Jennifer, the Church has been very good at doing this and has made itself look pretty stupid. We mustn't go back to the equivalent of arguing that the sun goes around the Earth. More than anything else, though, I have touched that which lives in the light vessel and I have ... tasted ... its nature."

The force of Joseph's words hung in the air after he had spoken. He continued to gaze steadily into the bishop's eyes feeling the power stream from him. After a few moments her nerve broke and she dropped her gaze. He felt a sudden pang of guilt at what he had done and leaned forward in his chair. His voice softened, but did not lose its edge of authority.

"But I need you to keep asking the question. I desperately need you to keep being my critical friend. Will you do that for me?"

His words softened the atmosphere and she tried to smile and nodded her head. Joseph looked around the table, the deep presence within him needing to know that his authority was now established. Alex was looking back at him with a mixture of awe and anger. The demolition of Jennifer must have been hard for him to take, but Joseph's gaze did not waver. Alex started to appear uncomfortable and turned his head to stare out of the window. Joseph noticed that Leola was looking at the bishop with concern.

"So, what happened next, Leola," he asked, the authority in his voice still palpable.

Leola looked slightly aggrieved that she was also being subjected to it.

"Well, Father, then the blue light around you started to ... thicken. It was like you were in a spotlight, only blue. Then people began to notice that you were not ... normal ... and began to move away from you. And then you moved towards the side door, with everyone clearing a path."

As Leola spoke, the details flooded back into Joseph's mind. They had always been there, but had been scrambled. Now they were rediscovering their true order. He could feel himself moving towards the door, see the people backing away and feel the cold outside air hitting his face.

"I knew I had to follow you," Leola continued, "So I pushed through the crowd and managed to get outside just a bit after you." She paused and looked a little embarrassed before continuing. "I ... I ... knew that you mustn't be ... alone."

Out of the corner of his eye Joseph saw the bishop look sharply at Leola, her head on one side, as though seeing something for the first time. He deliberately softened his voice further.

"What happened then?"

"Well, when I got outside it were all, like ... silver ... and then there was you, just like standing there, in this amazing beam of blue light. I could barely see you it was so bright. But I could see that your arms were held out a bit from your sides and you were just staring upward into the light." She paused, clearly having to gather herself for what came next. "And when I looked up along the blue light, there it was. That thing from them Falls, that object, just hanging over the churchyard with this blue light shining on you." She paused again, looking down at her hands. "And I was hearing it even stronger. Like it were speaking to you, but not in words. I couldn't understand what was being said but it was so ... so ... wonderful ... it was like music." Leola looked emotional as she remembered the evening. There was silence for a few moments and then she looked up at him.

"What did you hear, Father. What did it say to you?"

Joseph's mind was already there, trying to relive his time in the light, but all he got were glimpses of incomplete images and incoherent thoughts. The more he tried to pull them together, the more frustrating it became.

"I don't know, Leola. It's all very confused in my mind."

He paused, allowing the images and sensations to pour in, but they were still just jumbled fragments, jostling against each other. He felt very disturbed, as though a part of him was missing. But then there came reassurance, rising up from the depths, from the same source as the authority with which he had spoken. He would remember when the time was right. He tried to believe this intuition.

"Please, go on. What happened next?"

Leola looked a bit annoyed that Joseph would not share what he had experienced. She stared at him for a few moments before continuing.

"Well," she said with an edge to her voice, "There's not much to tell after that. All the people, they got away as soon as they could." She started chuckling, her good humor restored. "It seems that they were a bit shocked at seeing the rector being held in a blue light from an alien space ship. Some people, they just don't have any imagination." Leola's way of saying this brought genuine smiles around the table and eased the tension a bit further. "I just stood and watched. It was such a privilege. And I was listening and feeling too. It was like ... being swept up in sparking water. Like being washed clean." She looked deliberately at the bishop. "It was beautiful and wonderful."

"And how long did all this last," Joseph interjected quickly, not wanting a confrontation between Leola and the bishop.

"Well, at the time I couldn't really have said. I was too lost in what was happening, but now I know that it was about half an hour or so."

Joseph looked puzzled.

"How do you know that now, when you didn't at the time?"

Leola looked surprised by the question.

"Why, because it's on the television of course."

Joseph stared at her in stunned silence for a few moments, not quite being able to believe what he had just heard. Then he managed to get a few words out.

"On the television! You can't be serious. How?"

"Why, Father, you must remember. Because of young Rosalind."

Joseph's mind was blank for a few moments, before he remembered the crew from the regional news program.

"So not everyone ran away then," he commented half to himself, in quiet horror.

"Oh no, Father, just them stayed and me. But I didn't know they was there till afterwards and you collapsed when the blue light turned off. As I were helping you to stand up, I saw them still filming. I didn't think much of that and I gave them a piece of my mind I can tell you. Filming a man when he's not well – that's unkind."

Joseph stared at her for a few moments, the enormity of what he had just heard slowly sinking in. For the event to have been witnessed by several hundred people was bad enough, but for it also to have been filmed by a television crew was calamitous. His mind raced to catch-up with the implications. He began to grasp at straws.

"Well … I suppose … it was only local TV," but his words trailed off as he realized their futility. In the age of instant worldwide communication, he had no doubt that the images were already spread far and wide. He now understood what Alex had meant when he had referred to the "famous" Father Joseph Williams. He sat in silence for a couple of minutes trying to think things through. The others did not disturb him, sensing that he needed this time. Finally, he looked at the bishop.

"How bad's the damage?"

"Joseph, the most famous person in the world is currently sitting in my kitchen eating my eggs."

For the second time in twenty four hours Joseph's mind had to take in a new, infinitely different reality. Only a short time ago, humanity had been alone in the universe, except in its imagination, and he had been an obscure, introvert priest in a little corner of England. The transformation of the first reality, he was getting used to. The demolition of the second, he could barely grasp. In many ways it was the most difficult to take in. He found himself shaking his head slowly. The others looked on in sympathy. He tried to pull his thoughts together.

"I suppose the pictures are being shown endlessly on all the news channels?"

"Absolutely," Alex chipped in. "But they are extraordinary to see. I found myself just watching them over and over again." He paused and looked at Joseph intently. "You will have to see them for yourself, Father Joseph."

Joseph recoiled at the thought and was relieved when the bishop immediately leapt to his defense.

"No, Alex, absolutely not. Only if and when he is ready."

Alex suddenly became very passionate.

"Jennifer, he must. It may be the key to understanding … to

remembering ... what happened. We may not have time for caution."

Alex and the bishop began to argue. It was clear that they were well practiced. Yet Joseph barely heard them as he sank into thought about what Alex had said. He did not want to accept it, but in his heart he knew that Alex was right. He knew deep down that the object was waiting for a response and that it might not wait forever. An invitation had been issued, but delay could well be seen as refusal, or maybe unreadiness, for what was on offer. Also, what of the reaction of the rest of humanity to what they were seeing on their television screens? What might occur once the initial shock wore off? Joseph's primal distrust of his fellow human beings left him with a very uneasy feeling. He knew what he had to do. He must plunge in. He interrupted the argument, which was beginning to run out of steam anyway.

"I need to see it now," he said without warning, silencing both of them. Even Alex looked a little shocked.

"Now, Father? Should you not rest a little more? It is quite ... powerful ... if you have not seen it before."

"I have to see it now, so that I can grasp it better, as something that really happened."

Joseph made as if to stand up, his determination obvious to all. The bishop hurriedly waved him back to his seat, seeing clearly that she had no choice in the matter.

"It's O.K., Joseph, there's a TV in here. I'll turn it on."

She walked over to one of the wall cupboards, opened the doors and revealed a very modern-looking television. She switched it on and stood back with the remote control in her hand.

"The pictures have been repeated all night, so it shouldn't be too difficult to find a station that's still showing them." There was a slight pause as she flicked through the channels. "Ah, here we are. Just beginning it seems."

For about half an hour, Joseph sat mesmerized as extraordinary images filled the screen. Had he not known, he would have assumed that it must be something from a science fiction movie. Yet in another way it could not be, for it was not sufficiently dramatic. It was, in fact, the lack of drama that gave what he was seeing astonishing impact. The screen simply showed a beautiful, flowing stream of blue surrounding a barely discernable figure that, whilst still touching the ground, also gave the impression of floating. In the background was the shadowy outline of the large church, with a delicate silvery tinge that seemed to shine on it from above. Occasionally the camera would pan vertically, when the blue-hued figure would be replaced by the now more familiar image of the light vessel. Then it would pan downwards again to show the silent, still figure that, Joseph had to keep reminding himself, was him. Joseph was grateful that there was no commentary being imposed on the pictures. The only sounds were the gentle breathing of the camera operator and an occasional, inaudible comment from whoever was present.

Joseph became oblivious to time as he watched, lulled into a kind of peace. The peace was shattered as the light extinguished without warning and the figure fell to the floor. The silence suddenly became shouts of alarm from the camera crew. The last thing Joseph noticed was a figure ambling from the shadows of the church towards the prone figure on the ground. He turned away and, without being asked, the bishop muted the sound on the TV. Behind his back, the pictures started to run again from the beginning.

Joseph did not know what he felt, only that something deep within had been shaken and stirred. He knew that memories were now closer to the surface, ready to coalesce when the time was right. He tried to get his mind working normally again.

"Is the light vessel still there, over the church?"

It was Leola who answered. "Aye, Father, that it is. It hasn't moved. It's waiting."

Joseph was about to ask what she meant by "waiting", but he knew the answer before he spoke. It was waiting for him. It was waiting for him to respond to whatever had been placed in his mind. He made himself breathe slowly and tried to think systematically. An obvious question suddenly occurred to him.

"But why aren't they here?" he demanded.

The bishop, obviously flustered, struggled to take in what Joseph had said.

"Sorry Joseph, I don't understand. Who are you talking about?"

"The press, the television cameras, everything like that. Why are we sitting here peacefully around a breakfast table, when the telephone ought to be ringing and reporters should be banging on the door?"

Leola replied to his question. "Because as soon as I saw them TV people I knew that I had to get you away. Find somewhere for you to hide. So I wracked my poor brain and thought of here. Had a real job finding it in the dark. And you didn't help much, being so out of it. Didn't stop you commenting on my driving though, you cheeky devil. Or my lovely car. But get here we did eventually and no one knows where you are. But they're going frantic trying to find you."

Joseph stared at Leola in frank admiration. She was truly an extraordinary person.

"Leola, all I can do is thank you from the bottom of my heart."

Leola looked very embarrassed that the rector should speak to her in this way. She started to absent-mindedly spread marmalade on a piece of toast. Joseph continued to watch her in mild amazement.

"And I also apologize for anything I said about your driving and your most excellent car."

Leola stopped spreading the marmalade and smiled shyly.

"Oh, don't you be worrying about that, Father Joseph, I'm better at driving tractors and my old girl has seen better days."

"Leola, what state was I in? I can't remember anything about the journey."

Leola thought for a few moments and then replied in a quiet voice, "Well, you were a bit like my old man, just before he passed away. Your eyes were open and you were kind of here, but also not here. I could talk to you and sometimes I thought that you heard, but then I could see that you were like in another world. You didn't seem to be seeing me, but something else." Leola paused, obviously remembering more. "Come to think of it, my nephew used to sleep walk and it was much the same as you last night. You could talk to him and he kind of heard you, but also he wasn't there."

Joseph thought about what she had said and then looked at Alex and the bishop.

"This is what I was like when I arrived?"

They looked at one another and there was an unspoken agreement that Alex should speak.

"There was a banging on the door, after midnight, and I insisted on answering it myself. I did not think it right that Jennifer should at that time of night." The bishop looked annoyed as he said this. "When I opened it, there you were, being held upright by Leola. She told us what had happened and we could barely believe it, but then the pictures came onto the television and we understood. By this time you seemed to be on the edge of collapse, so I took you upstairs. We did not know whether to call a doctor, but thought it would be too risky. Anyway, you did not seem ill. More like just exhausted, so we just kept watch all night - between cups of coffee and big arguments."

Joseph looked at the three of them as he began to understand what they had done for him.

"You've been good friends to me. I am very fortunate."

Alex and the bishop looked as embarrassed as Leola had been a few moments before. They both reached for the marmalade jar. Another thought struck Joseph.

"I came here along the corridor where your offices are, but the rooms were empty. Where's your secretary, Sandy, and Michael, your chaplain?" Joseph looked up at the clock on the far wall of the kitchen. "It's mid-morning. They should be here."

"Michael, fortunately for him, is away on a training course," the bishop replied. "I rang Sandy early this morning and invented a job for her to do somewhere else. I wanted as few people as possible to know you were here until we thought out how to handle things. But it can only be a matter of time before people realize where you are. I'm already getting phone calls. I don't like having to lie."

Joseph smiled wryly. "You've got to hand it to the media. They are very good at finding people who don't want to be found."

The bishop leaned forward, a stern look on her face. "Joseph, it's not only the media who are after you."

Joseph looked puzzled. "What do you mean?"

The bishop sighed. "With all due respect, Joseph, you are sometimes very naïve. Not only are you now the most famous person on Earth, you are also the most important. People only have to turn on their televisions to see that you have been singled out by our alien visitor and, quite obviously, had some message communicated to you. I think it's safe to assume that you are of intense interest to the governments of this world."

Joseph sat stunned, gazing at the wall beyond the bishop's shoulder. The enormity of what had happened to him revealed itself a little more. The bishop gave him no respite.

"I've already had a call from the Prime Minister himself, in person, asking if I know where you are. He happened to mention that he had already received calls about you from other world leaders. I enjoyed lying to him even less than deceiving the press." She looked over pointedly at Alex, who stared back defiantly. "But I was persuaded, against my better judgment, that it was essential that you had time to sort things out in your mind. That this was more important than the truth." She looked down at her hands. "Lying isn't something bishops are supposed to do, especially to the person who appoints them."

Despite his continuing shock at what had been said, Joseph looked at the bishop thoughtfully. He could not help but appreciate what she had done for him and the sacrifice that it might entail. But then the situation stated to overwhelm him. There was a limit to what he could handle and he had gone far beyond it. He felt the indefinable sense of authority that had filled him, rapidly begin to fade. Nothing in his life had prepared him for anything remotely like this. A real sense of panic began to take hold. He closed his eyes and tried to breathe as evenly as he could. Then he felt his hand being gently taken by Leola, who simply held it without saying anything. Then his other hand was taken in a much stronger grip, as Alex reached over. His mind slipped into surrender, recoiling from the unbelievable and seemingly insurmountable. He lay in helpless desolation.

And in that place, at the very roots of his mind, something saw its opportunity and began to expand.

A space began to unveil itself, within which another quality of authority arose, that brought with it a new kind of knowing. The texture of his mind began to change. The jagged, rock-strewn wilderness that had been his mental landscape was transformed into a velvety, perfectly still pool, from which emerged thoughts that were not of him. Or rather they were not of the being that walked in the world and knew itself as Joseph, but of that essence that illumined, that lay behind the very temporary corporeal being. As Joseph opened his eyes, he found himself marveling at the sun-lit kitchen and the incredible beings that looked at him with such concern. The despair was gone, as though it had never been. He had a sense of being two people. One had a name and history, the other was timeless and had never been born. Yet they were also one. Joseph swam in the sense of bliss that this brought and noted that it did not feel the same as when the Teacher had been present. He wondered why he had never tasted such a state before, and for a fleeting second was convinced that, in fact, he had, but could not pin down where and when this might have been. Then, from the pool of knowing another insight surfaced. It told him quietly and with absolute certainty that what he was experiencing was the true state of human existence, not something to be regarded as special. Then the thought sank back again, leaving gentle ripples in its wake.

Joseph began to look around the room, oblivious to those who held his hands. They looked at one another, sensing that something extraordinary was happening. In a part of his mind, Joseph recognized that he was experiencing yet another facet of the same illumined consciousness that he had tasted the previous evening by the altar, and which had been the source of the authority with which he had spoken only a short while earlier. But this time it was immeasurably deeper and more vast. His eyes rested on the clock once more and he felt, in his soul, the dual truth of the movement of time within the enfoldment of the eternal now. Yet it was also the ticking of the clock that brought him back and the world of drama, story and events once more began to impinge on his mind. The pool of knowing and the deeper, unnameable sense of identity did not evaporate, however, but slowly moved into the background, still present but less tangible. He found himself letting out a deep sigh and the memories of his situation returned, but now in a greater context. He released the hands that held his and looked around at his friends.

"Thank you," he said quietly, but they were not sure whether he was addressing them or someone else. There were a few moments of silence as Joseph brought back into focus what he had been told minutes earlier. As he did so, from that deep velvety place within, came absolute clarity.

"There can be no contact with governments."

There was a brief silence as the others absorbed what he had said. Inevitably, it was the bishop who responded first, clearly very concerned.

"Joseph, of course there must be. It is only ... right ... that this matter be handled by the proper authorities, who have a greater perspective and proper resources to call upon. When you're ready you must hand yourself over and help them all you can."

He watched the bishop as she spoke and could see that she had no doubt about what she was saying. Joseph's stark declaration had shocked her view of the world, where everything had its place and was handled in an orderly manner by the proper agencies. In her world everything was under control. But Joseph knew that the Visitor wanted them to understand that very little was under humanity's control. This was the first lesson.

"No Jennifer. If our strange friend had wanted to involve governments he would have approached them directly or perhaps the United Nations." Joseph paused to allow the still pool of knowing to influence his words. "This is about a direct encounter with all of humanity, through, at least at this time, one individual. It's not clear to me, but it's something about the outer connection allowing something deeper to happen. The encounter must not happen through the veils and smoky mirrors of governments. I know this."

The bishop looked genuinely disturbed by what he was saying. She had clearly never countenanced such a response.

"How do you know this?" she demanded irritably. "How can you be so certain?"

"I just know, but not in the usual way that I know things," he replied with a quiet intensity.

The bishop stared at him as the implication of his words sank in. Her eyes turned back to the television screen and the figure held in the blue stream of light.

"Oh," was all she managed to say.

Joseph was not sure whether his current illumined state was directly connected with the events that were unfolding, yet again, on the screen. But he was grateful that the bishop's connection of the two prevented the need for further explanation.

"There's something else that you can help me with, if you are willing?"

The bishop, now very disconcerted, nodded her head hurriedly.

"Of course, Joseph, anything I can do."

"I want you to arrange a press conference for me. Today. As soon as possible."

The import of his words took a few moments to sink in. The other three people around the table looked quietly shocked at what he had said. Alex leaned forward in his chair.

"Father, are you certain this is a good idea. Just a little while ago you were appalled by the publicity." Alex paused, clearly choosing his words carefully. "After all, and I say this with much respect, you do not give the impression of one who will be comfortable in such a situation."

Joseph found himself smiling at Alex's attempted diplomacy.

"Alex, the very prospect fills me with dread, but I know what I must do. I'm not really sure why, but it's something about connecting with people. Somehow, through the outer connection, something hidden will begin to develop."

Alex's eyes drifted to the television screen and without saying any more he just nodded his head slowly.

There was silence for a few moments, before the bishop leapt to her feet, once more catching the table on the way up and rocking the remaining contents of their mugs. The thought of having something practical to do was clearly a great relief to her.

"Right then. Things to do. Best to keep this in-house. I'll get Marge, my press officer, over here straight away. We'll set something up in the large banqueting room. For late this afternoon. Can seat over a hundred in there. Maybe more. Yes, that's what I'll do." She suddenly stopped in full flow. "Joseph, I ... we ... must tell the ... authorities ... that we're doing this.

They can't just find out like everyone else."

"Yes they can," was Joseph's only reply.

The bishop looked ready to argue, but then once more her gaze took in the television.

"Of course," was all she said, as she left the kitchen looking very disturbed.

Joseph turned to Alex, but found his Greek friend's eyes still fixed on the now empty doorway.

"Isn't she magnificent!" the bear of a man exclaimed to no one in particular, letting out a long sigh in the process. Joseph did not know what to say, having never thought about his bishop in that way before.

"Er, right, yes, absolutely." He pulled himself together. "Alex, there's something that you can help me with too."

Alex looked delighted.

"Anything, Father Joseph, anything."

"What we talked about earlier. Your … experience … with images and the mind. I need you to help me remember what I … saw … last night. I need you to help me understand."

Alex looked very serious.

"I would be honored, Father." He thought for a few moments. "We will need somewhere, a place with a special atmosphere." He paused again, obviously searching his memory. Then he smiled. "Ah, yes, I know just the place, that perhaps has been waiting for this very moment. But it will take me a while to get it ready."

Leola's voice made them jump. They had almost forgotten that she was there.

"And I'll be there too," she stated in a voice that brooked no argument.

Alex looked slightly disconcerted, but then conceded gracefully with a nod of his head. He looked thoughtfully at her for a few moments.

"Actually, I think that would be a good idea indeed. You are very close to this. Closer than me. You must be there, most certainly." He paused and continued to stare at her. "Also I think you bring a different ... perspective ... which matters."

Leola looked very pleased. Joseph's eyes took in the breakfast table and the rest of the kitchen.

"And while you're sorting out the room, Alex, I'll set about the washing the dishes."

Leola looked at him doubtfully. "And I'd better be helping you, Father."

"No need to worry, dear lady," Alex interjected quickly. "There is a dishwasher."

Leola looked around in disdain.

"I really don't think we'll be needing one of those."

He watched as the sun rose over the horizon. He had done this many times, on many worlds, yet it never failed to move him. He did not really understand why this was. It was something to do with the sense of new creation, of purity and of the hidden becoming manifest. Also, its sheer power touched something deep within. But these were just threads of a larger tapestry that he could not see.

He continued to watch as the shadows retreated from the plateau beneath and the church and its surrounding land were revealed. He had felt the power of this place from the moment of arrival the previous evening and the coming of sunlight connected him with it in a new way. It was difficult to describe, but he had a sense of being on the edge of a vortex, a whirlpool, except that, somehow, mysteriously, the maelstrom was multidirectional. It was a revolving door that could turn in opposite directions at the same time. This was not a new experience for him, but this place had a particular and unique quality that fascinated him. He understood better now why Joseph had been drawn here.

It was a place where time and space turned inwardly on themselves.

It was a place where the shell of outward reality was thin, and the inner worlds and the cyclical ripples of time might be more easily encountered. For most on this world this would be an unsought, uncontrolled and frightening meeting. Fortunately, most were too desensitized to be vulnerable. For a few, who were to some extent open, it could be a womb in which a new species might be born.

He went within himself and sought the currents of time that permeated this special place. He sensed the ripples that went out, to return empowered and transformed, and then to go out again in their spiral of manifestation. He felt the presence of living minds, long dead to this plane of reality, which over millennia had sought deeper relationship with existence in this place. The outer form would have differed beyond description, yet the yearning was the same.

He focused and sent out a specific greeting. It was not only Joseph that he had come to this place to meet. There was a pause before his greeting was returned and swimming out of the depths of time came the fellowship of the forest. They had touched before as plans had been laid, but the power of this place amplified the connection, giving it far greater taste and texture. They shared silence for a while, nurturing the new closeness. Then they and he began to teach what each needed to learn from the other. This was necessary if they were to work together, as they must.

After a timeless while, all had been said and farewells were exchanged. The fellowship sank back into the depths of time and his awareness returned to the sunlit plateau. He found his thoughts returning to the being called Joseph. In so doing, he encountered the land beneath in a new way and felt the sadness of loss. He knew from where this sprang and remembered well the time when it had erupted into his brother's mind. He had longed to sooth the pain. Not to remove it, for that would have been unnatural. But to help his brother see it in a greater light.

It had not been easy to do nothing, to hold back and concentrate on what must be done.

There was only so much time, for the inner tides would move on and the moment when their balance might be tilted would pass.

Chapter 13

Joseph was surprised when Alex led them out of the back of the house and across the courtyard. Strangely, Leola seemed to be almost expecting it. The two men were forced to walk slowly as she ambled along, taking long looks upward at the sky. Joseph wondered if she was expecting the light vessel to appear overhead and, as he thought about it, it occurred to him that this might be a distinct possibility. The Visitor clearly had a great interest in him and could easily feel the need to follow Joseph to his new location. But then Leola spoke and it was clear that other matters were on her mind.

"It's nearly noon, a good time to contact the inner realms. The energy will be nicely balanced."

Alex looked at her with great interest.

"Indeed, dear lady. You clearly have some learning in these matters."

Leola looked up at him. "No, not learning, but years of experience that makes me ... sensitive ... to the flows of life. Books have never been my way."

"And who is to say that your way is not better, more natural. I sometimes think that I have filled my head with too many ideas."

"No, Mr. Alex, your learning's very important. Mine is the old way, which yours is building upon and improving." She grabbed his arm and stopped him in his tracks. "But my way must not be forgotten, for it's the root of everything."

Alex looked down at her from his greater height and patted her hand. "Do not fear, my friend, I know that only too well." They both started walking again, with Joseph trailing behind, fascinated by what he was hearing.

Alex addressed Leola again. "And what does your inner vision say about what we are about to do?"

"It tells me that the old house would be no good for this. That the ... atmosphere ... would not be helpful. That we need somewhere more ... natural. So I'm not surprised that we're going out into the grounds."

Alex smiled. "I have the perfect place, just beyond those trees and bushes over there."

Intrigued though he was by the exchange, Joseph was now starting to feel a bit worried by whatever Alex had in mind for him. The expanded consciousness he had experienced earlier had been slowly fading and was now in the far background. The "usual" Joseph was firmly in the driving seat. He shuffled behind the other two with increasing reluctance. They reached the far end of the courtyard and headed off across the lawn, on the far side of which were the trees that Alex had indicated. The grass beneath their feet was wet, the morning frost having been melted by the sun that hung low in the sky to the south. Joseph felt some of the freezing moisture seep into his shoes, chilling his feet. As he looked down, about to feel sorry for himself, he noticed that Leola wore only sandals yet was clearly oblivious to the damp cold. Alex was walking along in an open-necked shirt. Joseph decided that he needed to be a bit tougher. The trees towards which they walked were evergreens and their low branches, together with the bushes and brambles that surrounded their base, obscured whatever lay beyond. The barrier appeared so dense that Joseph wondered how they were going to get through. When they reached the end of the lawn Alex began to speak.

"I found it a few years ago when I was staying with Jennifer. It was just a lump in the ground that had been there so long that nobody noticed it anymore. And because it was up against the wall, out of the way, it was just left to become overgrown. But I am Greek and in my country every lump in the ground is potentially interesting. So one afternoon, when I was bored, I pushed my way through the bushes to have a look. I think you will be as entranced as I was. I came out earlier and made some preparations, while you two were clearing up."

Joseph and Leola, who had no idea what he was talking about, watched as Alex carefully drew a length of wood from behind a tree and used it to part a seemingly impenetrable area of bush and bramble. As he did so, a path through the thicket was revealed. Alex held the wood in place while Joseph and Leola carefully found their way through the gap. They waited while he eased the foliage back so that the path would remain invisible from the outside. Alex noticed their curious looks.

"The gardeners no longer work in this area of the grounds. I persuaded Jennifer to tell them that it was to be left wild, as a nature reserve, so that my little discovery would remain a secret. She was not very happy, but succumbed to my charm. I think, though, she is a bit worried about what I get up to out here. She only came here once and now prefers to remain in ignorance."

As Alex walked off, Joseph and Leola looked at one another with some amusement. They were also, by this stage, very curious to find out what Alex's great discovery had been. They followed him down the narrow path between trees and bushes, the ground beneath their feet crunching, still frozen in the absence of direct sunlight. After a couple of minutes they came to a small clearing. Directly in front of them was a large wall, beyond which Joseph knew must be the road. It had been built when the new estate had been constructed about a mile away, but the stone was already so weathered that it looked ancient. And there, about fifteen feet in front of it, was the lump in the ground that so excited Alex. Calling it a lump, though, did not do it justice. It was an oval-shaped rise in the ground, about twenty feet across and six feet high at its apex.

"When I first found it, it was covered in thick bushes and brambles that had not been touched in many years. It was when I cleared them that I made my great discovery." Alex stood in front of them beaming, as though they should by now know what he was talking about.

Joseph spoke for both of them. "Alex, what exactly was it that you found?"

Alex looked at him bemused for a few moments and then burst out laughing. "I am a fool. I get so excited every time I come here that I cannot think straight." He strode off towards the lump in the ground, beckoning to them as he went. "Come, come and I will show you."

Joseph and Leola followed more slowly and when they caught up with Alex he was standing in front of an old, very battered-looking wooden door that was cut into the southern side of the hummock. Three worn and slippery-looking stone steps led down to it. The door was made of large planks of wood that were held together by robust, ornate cast iron brackets. It gave the impression of being very old and neglected. The lengths of wood were warped and the metal fittings covered in rust, although it appeared that some attempt had been made to ameliorate the worst effects. The door fascinated Joseph. It felt like the entrance to another world.

"So, what do you think?" Alex boomed.

"What is it?" was all Joseph could think of in reply.

"I will show you," Alex declared, looking very pleased with himself. He went down the three steps, apparently oblivious to their ankle-breaking potential, and turned the large iron door-catch. The catch resisted for a few moments and then gave way with a clunk. Alex leaned his weight against the door and with a loud squeak it opened. As it did so both Joseph and Leola bent their knees to see what lay beyond Alex's bulky frame, but the inside was too dark.

"Wait there a moment, while I light some candles," Alex instructed as he disappeared through the open doorway.

Joseph and Leola did as requested and within a few moments were rewarded as a flicker of light appeared in the subterranean darkness. Within seconds it was joined by several others and they were able to glimpse what looked like a stone-slabbed floor, with the shadowy outline of a hearth towards the center of the room. Then they heard Alex's voice summon them from inside. Joseph offered Leola his arm and, with great care, they descended the steps and made their way into the underground room. The sight that greeted them was like something out of a fairy tale. In the middle of a roughly circular room was the hearth that they had spotted from outside. It, too, was circular and constructed from curved pieces of stone placed on top of the ground layer. Joseph inspected the ceiling and could just make out where a narrow chimney pipe must once have gone through to the outside. On the left-hand wall was a stone built platform, which Joseph surmised must have served as a bed. It was now covered by a modern-looking inflatable mattress, with a number of cushions randomly strewn on top. Against the far wall from the doorway, on the floor, was a small selection of antique porcelain pots of various shapes and sizes. They were very dirty and looked as though they had been there since the chamber was constructed. There was also a mysterious cardboard box with Greek writing on the side. Against the wall to their right were a few folding wooden chairs of more recent origin. The candles that provided a flickering, slightly eerie light were situated in various nooks and crannies that were cut into the walls. Yet there was something about the chamber that puzzled Joseph, that did not seem quite right, and it took him a little while to work it out. The chamber felt remarkably dry. It should have been damp, probably with trickles of water running down the walls. It was underground and it was winter. But the whole room felt dry and welcoming. He realized that whoever had created it had known what they were doing. Then he noticed something else in the shadows of the far wall. It was another door, almost identical to the first, and sealed shut. It added even more intrigue to the chamber.

"Is that another entrance over there?" he asked, as Alex, having finished with the candles, turned to greet them. Alex looked cagey.

"In a way, but for another time perhaps."

Joseph took the hint. "Oh, right, of course. So what is this place then? It's amazing."

Alex clearly wanted to stretch out the game a bit longer.

"And what about you, dear lady, any ideas?"

"Can't say that I have, Mr. Alex, but I love the feel of it. Mother Earth's very close in here. And it feels like a ... gentle ... place."

Alex looked even more pleased. "So, shall I tell you then?"

Joseph could not help but laugh at his friend's boyish enthusiasm. "Go on then, before you burst."

Alex paused for a few moments to build dramatic tension and then announced, "It's a hermit's cell."

Joseph stared at him in surprise, his mind working overtime. Religious hermits had been quite common in medieval England, but had all but disappeared after Henry VIII's break with the Roman Church in the sixteenth century. He looked around the cell once more, not being able to quite believe what he was hearing.

"Alex, I know this is old, but it's not that old. There haven't really been hermits since the Middle Ages. Are you sure it's what you think it is?"

"Oh yes, Father Joseph, for I have managed to trace the history of the cell from historical records. But perhaps this marvelous place isn't what *you* think it is," Alex came back mischievously.

Joseph was thrown by this rejoinder and his puzzlement must have shown on his face.

"Let me clear up any confusion you may have," Alex said, looking satisfied with himself. "It is the cell of an *ornamental* hermit."

It took a few moments for the words to register, but then a big smile appeared on Joseph's face. Alex grinned back. Leola, however, did not share the joke.

"And what's an ornamental hermit, if I may ask? Sounds very strange to me."

Alex put his arm around her shoulders. "It is indeed strange, dear lady. When I first read about them, I struggled to believe the words on the page. I do not know whether any other nations had them, but it would come as no great surprise if it were only the mad English - with all due respect. Perhaps Father Joseph would like to explain?"

Joseph dragged the details out of his memory. "It was a fashion craze among the rich landed gentry of the late eighteenth and early nineteenth centuries. It's a long story, but basically it involved paying someone to live as a hermit in the grounds of your estate so that you could show them off to your fashionable friends. Usually the individual was required to live in pretty primitive conditions, have very little social contact with anyone, not cut their nails, hair or beard and so on. If they managed to put up with the deprivation for a set number of years they were allowed to go back to normal life with a nice lump sum of cash. From the stories I've read, though, most gave up long before that."

Leola looked at each of them in turn, as if to check that she was not the butt of some joke. Then she said to Alex, "Blimey. You're right, Mr. Alex, we truly are mad as hatters."

Joseph allowed his eyes to scan the cell. "So an ornamental hermit lived here then," he said half to himself.

"Several, actually, over a period of about forty years," Alex interjected. "Most gave it up quite quickly, but the last one - a man called William Stokes - seemed to get a taste for the life and declined to leave when his time was up. He became something of a local celebrity and was held in high regard. It seems that he developed into something of a holy man in these parts and there was much sadness when he died. From the records it appears that people did not think it right that he be replaced because of the esteem in which he was held, so the cell fell into disuse and was forgotten."

"I like that story," Leola said quietly and for a minute or so they just stood looking around, their thoughts occupied by William Stokes. It was Alex that broke the silence.

"And now, two centuries later, it will again be used for a holy purpose."

Joseph's nervousness began to return. "Ah, yes, and what exactly have you in mind Alex?"

Alex looked at him for a few moments, as if seeing for the first time Joseph's reservations.

"Nothing to concern yourself about, my friend," he said gently. "As you have asked, I am just going to help you connect with your deeper mind, in a conscious manner as an act of deliberate will, so that what our Visitor has placed there may be brought to this level of awareness." He paused, considering his next words carefully. "But I must warn you that deep consciousness often does not speak in the way we are used to, so we may have to be patient with what is revealed." Before either of them could respond to this enigmatic pronouncement, he turned, walked to the far wall and picked up the mysterious cardboard box. He carried it back and placed it on the floor beside the hearth. He looked up at Joseph and Leola.

"Father, perhaps you could get a couple of those fold-up chairs and place one at each end of the bed, facing each other."

"Oh, yes, right," Joseph replied, making his way over to the other side of the chamber.

By the time he had finished the task, Alex had taken a dark purple cloth from the box and spread it over the hearth. As Joseph watched, he placed a large, solid-looking candle at the center of the cloth and applied a flame. It was what he did next, once the candle was alight, that caused something within Joseph to stir. From the box, Alex extracted a beautiful blue glass tube that he carefully lowered over the candle. Immediately the chamber took on a blue tinge. Of their own volition, fragmentary memories of the previous evening started to flicker through Joseph's mind. He tried to dampen them down. Whatever was going to happen, he wanted to be controlled, not random. To pull his mind in another direction he asked Alex a question.

"Where did you get that glass tube? It's a very odd shape to have just lying around."

"No, Father, you are wrong. It was not just lying around, as you say, for it is part of … the tools of my trade. I have many such … accessories … that I use in my work. Color can be a particularly powerful means of evoking a different quality of consciousness." Alex then began to take command. "Father, please lie down on the bed with your head on the pillow. And remove your shoes first."

Joseph was taken by surprise by the sudden instructions, but quickly moved over to the bed. In a way, he was glad that Alex was not giving him time to think. He noticed that Leola was already seated on the chair at the foot of the bed, with her eyes closed. She was gently rocking from side to side and gave the impression of listening very intently to something. Joseph perched on the edge of the bed and unlaced his shoes. Out of the corner of his eye he continued to watch Alex make his preparations. From the box came a small incense burner, which was soon alight and giving out a delicate, yet evocative fragrance. With that the preparations seemed to be complete and Alex looked up from his work. Joseph took the hint and lay down on the mattress, resting his head on one of the cushions. He found himself looking at the ceiling of the chamber which, due to the slope of the roof, was no more than a couple of feet from his face. He heard Alex moving around and wondered what he was doing. It did not take long to find out. One by one, Alex went around the room blowing out the candles in the wall niches. As each was extinguished, the light in the room metamorphosed into an ever-stronger blue. After the last one was done, Joseph heard him sit in the vacant chair to the left of his head. He could not see Alex, but knew from the sound of his breathing that he was very close. There was silence for a while and Joseph found himself beginning to sink into a trance-like consciousness, lulled by the wavering blue light and the aroma of incense. Random memories of the previous evening began to return again. As though sensing this, Alex spoke.

"Now we start. There is nothing to worry about, Father Joseph. We are simply going to help you take your awareness, fully under control, into the deeper layers of your mind where, last night, you encountered a being of another world. It is only there, perhaps, that such an encounter may at first take place, as it is there that we come closer to our common source. I have arranged the outer conditions so that they may assist with this journey, so now I would ask that you absorb the blue light of this room into your awareness and then close your eyes."

Joseph did as he was asked and as his eyes closed he found himself floating in a sea of undulating blue, which in places seemed to shift imperceptibly into a subtle mauve. It was a good place to be and he was content to float and await whatever Alex would ask of him. He noticed that his mind was now very alert. He was completely in control and could have snapped back into the outer world at any moment. He was experiencing a state rare among humans - deep relaxation combined with profound awareness. Alex then addressed Leola.

"Good lady, it would be an honor if you were to grace us with some words before we dive into deeper waters."

Joseph was surprised by Alex's request, but it did not disturb his mind. He simply waited to hear what Leola would say. There was silence for a short while and then Leola stirred. Except it was not quite Leola. Leola was there in the voice that Joseph heard, but entwined in something else. Something that was primal, elemental and not quite human. And she did not speak, but chanted with a slow, primitive pulsating rhythm.

"Hail to thee, my Lady Arianrhod, princess of the stars and of the silver wheel. Hail to thee, my Lord Gwyddion, prince of the skies and the word of power. May your blessings be upon us and the traveler who brings words of power from your realms. May the Awen that illumines his song shine forth so we may dance and sing together, that the new may be born. Blessed be. Blessed be. Blessed be."

Then there was silence again, but everything had changed. The atmosphere had thickened and become almost dreamlike. Behind Joseph's closed eyes, the blue and mauve ocean of consciousness now swirled kaleidoscopically, astonishing and beautiful to watch. Joseph sensed that something was trying to emerge, to take form out of the energized color. He began to wonder if he should allow this impulse to have its way, when his thoughts were interrupted by Alex's voice.

"Eis to onoma tou Patros kai tou Huiou kai tou Hagiou Pneumatos."

In the name of the Father and of the Son and of the Holy Spirit - the ancient words echoed through Joseph's mind and sank into the depths. They connected with his soul in a way that Leola's invocation, beautiful though it was, never could. They were an expression of who he was. That part of himself that existed before he had choice as to identity. They were words to be laid alongside Leola's, as different themes in the same symphony.

"Amen," he found himself saying, surprised to find Leola's voice joining with his. For a few moments there was silence, and then Alex spoke again.

"Now we are ready. Father Joseph, it is time to remember. I need you to see in your mind the blue beam of light in which you were held last night. Do not force anything; simply allow it to arise, to emerge into awareness."

The effect of Alex's words was instant. As they were being said, the interwoven blue and mauve field of consciousness in Joseph's mind started to coalesce and take shape. Within a few moments all he could see was the brilliant, mesmerizing beam of blue light that he had beheld the previous evening. It was there in his mind's eye, against a background of velvet blackness. Its reality was absolute. Joseph knew that this was more than a memory. The beam was separate to him, even though it was in his mind. Whatever he was at this moment "stood" before the beam, able to choose whether to step into its silky embrace. He waited for Alex to speak again.

"Now, Father, I ask that you step into the cascade of blue. Allow it to wash over you, to cleanse and to purify. Allow it to become one with you, and you with it."

Again, Alex's words triggered an immediate response and, without effort, Joseph found himself moving forward into the beam. As he did so, just for a moment, he had a fleeting impression of something in the background, just outside the area of illumination. It was something that surrounded both him and the beam of light. For an instant, Joseph thought he glimpsed a circle of robed figures, but could not be sure. Then he was in the light and felt himself dissolving. Yet he was still present. He realized that he had not disappeared, but in some indefinable way had transformed into another state of being. He suddenly knew that this was necessary so that he might connect with what was being communicated to him. From far away came Alex's voice.

"Father, now you must, as an act of will, recall your time in the blue light from last night. If you hold this thought, this command, the light will respond."

Joseph, or rather the presence that still knew itself by that name, emanated this desire from his being. A wave of intent left him and instantly the blue universe which he inhabited responded. Images began to form, one after the other, their shape and texture metamorphosing as each emerged in turn. First he saw an ocean, a real ocean of white-capped waves in startling sunlight. Then he was in the ocean, surging through its life-giving water, twisting, turning and leaping out in great arcs before plunging back once more. Yet he was also watching himself at play, or rather what he seemed to have become. From this other perspective, he saw a large, powerful, shiny-skinned dolphin powering its way across open water with clear, yet undefined purpose. It was extraordinary to watch something so perfectly designed for its environment express itself so completely. So absorbed was Joseph in the dual experience and image, that to search for its meaning never occurred to him. It was life itself, overflowing in exuberance. So it was a shock when the image changed without warning and a bright, silvery, strangely-textured sheet of light impacted his eyes, blinding him for a few moments. The transformation was so sudden and complete that he was disorientated. Then the image resolved itself and Joseph realized that he was looking at a mountainside of sheer cliffs, reflecting the brilliant sunlight. He stared at the cliffs for an indefinable time, with a feeling that he knew them, but could not bring to mind the details. Then, again without warning, something in the image began to change in a way that made no sense. Above the illumined cliffs, the clear, almost blinding disc of the sun appeared, moving in a slow curve against the vault of the sky. It jarred with Joseph because he did not understand how the cliffs could still shine with such ferocity when the sun was rising behind them. Then something in his mind told him that this is how it was in dreams. He was about to protest that this was not a dream, that its feeling of reality was far too intense, when everything transfigured yet again. His heart leapt in shock as he was plunged into darkness and a face appeared, no more than a few inches from his. It was not a comforting face. It was a woman with wildly disheveled hair and eyes that seemed to stare into the distance, from irises that were no more than pinpricks. Around the face, tendrils of strange smoke wafted upwards as the woman's mouth moved, yet emitted no sound. It was a profoundly disturbing vision and

Joseph struggled to move away from the woman. It was a great relief when the face was replaced by a new image. This time he was once more outside in bright sunshine, his eyes adjusting to the glare. After a few moments he began to make out where he was. He was standing at the center of a large open space and in front of him were the tiered ranks of hundreds of stone seats, curving around him on both sides. He was in an amphitheatre, but as this thought came the image disappeared instantly, leaving a deep nothingness. It was such a complete nothingness that Joseph could barely stand it and a sense of panic began to grip him. But then it, too, was gone and he was once more in the extraordinary blue light, being bathed and cleansed by its purity. The relief was immense and Joseph allowed himself to float in the soothing waters for a while. It was Alex's voice that brought him back.

"Father Joseph, you have traveled and now you must return. Please step outside the blue light and become centered once more in your body, in this place, at this time."

It took Joseph a few moments to recognize the voice. He seemed to know it from a long time ago, from another life. Then recognition impacted on his consciousness and with it memories of the material world. He knew that he had a choice. He could return or stay in this place for as long as he wished. He was in charge, yet he could not say with surety anymore who or what he actually was. But then, from even deeper, an impulse rose up that said gently, yet forcefully that he must now return. It mattered. He found himself beginning to separate from the blue light. He was still in it, but no longer was it. His normal sense of time began to return. He had a sudden sense that what he had experienced as a journey of just a few minutes had in the outer world been much longer. Alex's voice sounded again, more urgent this time.

"Father, you must leave the light now, without further delay."

Joseph wondered how Alex knew that he was still in it, but

the concern in his voice was obvious and Joseph summoned the will to leave the blue universe. He stepped out into the velvety darkness in which it was wrapped. As he did so, he once more glimpsed the circle of robed figures, but in moments they were gone. Yet still he lingered, reluctant to leave such extraordinary beauty.

"Joseph, you must open your eyes now."

This time it was Leola's voice and it carried a force of command that permitted no opposition. Joseph's eyes snapped open. He heard quiet sighs of relief close by and sounds of movement. Almost immediately the blue-tinged light in the chamber changed to a flickering yellowy-white and in his still woozy mind he guessed that Alex must have removed the blue glass sleeve from the hearth candle. As he lay trying to reconnect with the normal world, he heard more movement and gradually the light brightened further as more candles were lit. Joseph took a few deep breaths and caught the fading aroma of incense. The fact that the incense had burned away reinforced his feeling that he had been absent for some time. The sound of one of the wooden chairs being unfolded and positioned gave him the impetus he needed to sit up. Only at the last moment did he remember how close the sloping roof was to his head and avoid a nasty collision between flesh and stone. He sat on the edge of the bed and looked around. Leola was repositioning the fold-up chairs where they could form a rough circle and Alex was bending over three cups, pouring into each a hot steaming liquid. He looked-up as Joseph stirred.

"Ah, Father, it is good to have you back. We were getting a bit worried there for a while." Joseph noted that although Alex's words seemed light-hearted, his face appeared strained. "Come, have a cup of tea, the English answer to the problems of the world - and other worlds for that matter." Alex was obviously amused by his joke and his face relaxed a little.

Joseph slid off the bed and cautiously stood up. He felt rather shaky, but was determined not to betray this fact to his companions. "Hope you've got biscuits as well," he joked back to Alex as he made his way cautiously to where Leola was sitting. Her eye caught his and he immediately knew that there was no fooling her.

"I think you'd better sit down, Father," she instructed firmly.

Joseph gratefully lowered himself onto the rickety chair next to her. Alex made his way over clutching three steaming mugs and handed them out, putting his own on the hearth next to where he would be sitting.

"You've certainly come well prepared", Joseph mused.

"Even better than you think, Father," Alex grinned, going back to his box and producing a plastic container of cakes. "But, seriously, food is a good way of coming back down to earth after such ... journeys ... which are also draining in themselves."

He came over and offered the cakes around. Joseph found that he was ravenous and grabbed two of them.

"How long was I gone? It seemed like only a few minutes to me."

"A long time," was all Leola would say, while looking at him intently. Out of the corner of his eye, Joseph saw Alex hide a grin.

"It was, indeed, much longer than I expected, Father. I have much knowledge in these matters and have rarely encountered such ... depth ... of traveling." He looked at Joseph with great interest. "Such ... ability ... can only be the result of considerable experience. Once again I begin to see why our strange visitor is drawn to you."

Joseph felt slightly embarrassed. "I'm afraid that whilst I've practiced with ways of going deeper into the mind, it is nowhere near enough to explain what's just happened."

Alex was not put off. "Or perhaps, Father Joseph, you brought the experience with you into this life."

Their eyes met and in that moment a deeper Joseph knew the truth of what Alex was saying. The spell was broken by Leola.

"Father, time be moving on and we must know what was said to you last night. What did you see?"

Joseph took a long drink of his tea, ate some cake while he focused his thoughts and then described everything. When he had finished there was silence, as Alex and Leola pondered what they had heard. Joseph took the opportunity to help himself to some more tea and another cake. Leola spoke first.

"Our friend, he's trying to draw something out of us. Something we know already."

"It is often the way, dear lady," Alex replied absent-mindedly. "Those who move with good intent on the inner planes will often nurture our ability to see for ourselves, rather than give easy answers. Also, pictures can convey many shades of understanding. They can be like a well to which we may often return. Mere words can be so limited." He paused, before speaking again with more focus. "But I have some ... thoughts ... as to what these images may mean. Yet those thoughts trouble me."

"They trouble you?" Joseph asked. "I am left with nothing but good feelings about what I saw - even about the strange woman. There is something amazing and exciting at the heart of the images, even though I can't yet pin down what it is."

"Do not misunderstand me, Father. I too share that sense of excitement. But if I am right, it means ... that whatever rests in the vessel above your church has vision of unimaginable breadth."

"And why's that, Mr. Alex?" Leola interjected, looking intensely interested in what she was hearing.

"Because, very simply dear lady, our visitor must have known that Father Joseph would be meeting me."

Leola and Joseph stared at Alex for a few moments, as the import of his words sank in. Neither could think of anything to say. Alex looked back at both of them and then stood up.

"I think it is time that we returned to the house. Jennifer must be wondering where we are." He started to blow out the candles.

Chapter 14

Joseph was hiding.

He had been since returning with Leola and Alex from the hermit cell a couple of hours before. As soon as they had emerged from the underground chamber it was clear that their secret was out. The first thing they heard was the metallic squawk of police radios on the other side of the wall, followed by a heated discussion between an officer and a local resident about the closure of the road. The bishop had clearly been busy in their absence and the announcement of the press conference had triggered a vigorous response from the authorities. They had looked at each other without speaking and then Alex had shrugged his shoulders with an air of resignation. Joseph's stomach had tightened as the shocking transformation of his life was confirmed. Leola had set a slow pace as they found their way back to the house. They had only just got into the servants' corridor that led to the kitchen, when they saw a procession of large four-wheel drive vehicles, with dark tinted windows, pull into the courtyard. Joseph had looked at Alex.

"I'm not going to speak to anyone before the conference," was all he had said.

Alex had nodded and rushed him through the kitchen into a private sitting room beyond. The room had a window that looked out onto a small enclosed vegetable garden.

"I will stay in the kitchen and make sure you are left alone," Alex had reassured him.

"And I'll be staying in there too, in case you're needing anything, Father," Leola had joined in, appearing through the doorway.

"Thanks," Joseph had replied. "I just know that it's very important not to have dealings with anyone in authority. I don't really understand, but it's something to do with ... purity ... with a ... fresh beginning. It's about touching everyone directly."

Alex had nodded. "In this of all situations, we must follow our deeper guidance, even if it does not make complete sense." He had then sighed. "But I fear this will make life very difficult for Jennifer."

The two of them had then left him alone and he had explored the room. The small garden on the other side of the window was just bare earth at this time of year, but he had been able to imagine its summer abundance. The high wall that enclosed it looked original and its flaking mortar and brickwork suggested that it was not in the best of condition. Next to the window was a television and, with a heavy heart, Joseph had known that soon he must turn it on. He needed to update himself on what was happening in a world changed extraordinarily in less than two days. He needed to know how people were responding. On the other side of the fireplace he had discovered a door that led, to his delight, to a small bathroom with a shower. He had immediately made use of its facilities and had stood under the streaming water for some time, feeling refreshed with every passing moment. When he had eventually emerged he had found a plate of sandwiches and a pot of tea on a low table at the center of the room, and had settled down to watch the television while he munched through the food.

The first image that had filled the screen had almost made him jump out of the chair. It had been the bishop's house, viewed from the front, its imposing visage making a powerful statement about history and stability. The picture had then switched to show a large elegant room. Rows of seats were positioned before a long table, which was covered with a beautifully embroidered red and blue cloth. Gold tassels hung down to the floor. Behind the table were three ornate, royal blue padded dining chairs and, on the wall, a massive oil painting of a man wearing bishop's finery. Joseph knew the room well. It was not far from where he sat and his stomach had knotted itself as he realized that in a short time he would be sitting behind that table, on one of those chairs, talking to the world. He had put down the sandwich he had been eating and concentrated on breathing slowly. Then the sound of his name had jerked his attention back to the screen. It was the moment when it finally felt completely real. The program had started doing a piece on him, having pasted together whatever biographical facts they had been able to discover at such short notice. For a brief moment, Joseph had felt sorry for the researchers who had been ordered to find out all they could about such an insignificant person as himself. The program-makers had also been out in his parish interviewing people who knew him. Joseph had needed to hear what was said. He had to understand how people were reacting to what had happened to him.

He had been gratified to hear people talking about him with some affection, as someone who seemed to care when he baptized, married or buried them. He had found it less reassuring when most had then paused, looked slightly guilty, before leaning forward and describing him as also being slightly strange, as had been his lovely wife before her tragic death. They had then gone on, as English people do when they have said something not completely complimentary, to reassure the interviewer that Joseph was a very decent chap. Of course, the program had soon zoomed in on the death of Clare, which Joseph had been quietly dreading. Yet, to his surprise, he had been able to watch with more of a feeling of poignancy than the devastating sadness that had previously been the case. He tried to imagine what Clare would have made of all this, but struggled to have any clear thoughts. What was happening was too far beyond anything they had gone through together. In a powerful moment, Joseph had realized that their lives were moving apart. He was now experiencing things separately, on his own, and his shared life with Clare was slowly diminishing within his consciousness. This was a bitter-sweet feeling. It was an inevitable part of the grieving process. Clare was becoming history, as she must. For reasons he did not understand, the events of the last two days had helped him to start accepting this fact, although there was still a long way to go. As he sat listening to the story of her death, his sadness was increasingly tempered by gratitude that he had been blessed with such a love.

Then the program had spoken to people about the events of the night before. The mood had changed completely. Thoughts of Clare had been swept from his mind by what he had seen on the screen. It was not what was said that so disturbed him, but the look on the faces, in the eyes of the people as they talked about what they had watched on their television screens. He had seen fear and uncertainty, barely under control in some. Their mental world had been shattered, and was still being shattered. All feelings of security and meaning were under threat. He knew that sooner or later, if nothing happened to salve such powerful emotions, there would have to be an outlet. His understanding of human psychology, and of the history that it produces, had told him that a scapegoat would be needed. He had known that his singling out by the light vessel had made him a figure of disturbing mystery. It would also take little for this to become hostility.

This unease had been multiplied tenfold as the program had gone on to show reactions around the world to the television images of him being held in the blue beam of light. He had seen the same fear, already being amplified into anger in some places, as the pictures were interpreted through cultural and religious sensibilities. In some parts of the world, demagogues with shaking fists were asking why a Christian, with a white skin, from a former colonial power had been chosen. They asked what this said about the intentions of the Visitor. In other places, Christian demagogues with white skins spoke of the Book of Revelation and how it foretold that before the second coming of Christ, the Devil would hold sway over the world. At the moment as far as Joseph could judge, the extremists were listened to by few, but he knew that this could quickly change. And all the while, stock markets plunged and the price of commodities soared. Joseph wished that he could have a higher opinion of humanity, but something in him was profoundly frightened of people en masse.

As he thought about this, he had begun to wonder where such powerful fear might be rooted. He could see that certain life experiences might account for it to some extent. It had not been easy being an introvert orphan, who from childhood had never quite fitted and so been a figure of fun for those who did. Who now despaired every time he turned on the television and whose wife had been killed by mindless, drunken youths. Yet he had also known love in all its glory. He had met good people, like those who surrounded him now. A suspicion had started to grow that something else must be at work, something deeper and more ancient. He startled himself by the last thought. How could such a fear be "ancient"? Yet this insight refused to go away. It held its ground. To get away from the disturbance it triggered, Joseph tried to go back to the original train of thought.

He had remembered what the bishop had said earlier about his being naïve. He had then known one more thing. Governments would be deeply worried by economic collapse, unstable masses of people and the potential for social breakdown that this brought. When the delicate psychological scaffolding that held societies together was shaken, disorder in all its forms was not far behind. Those in power would feel the need to take control, and to be seen to be in control. And that would mean taking control of him.

Joseph had then turned off the television and had been sitting thinking ever since. At first he had tried to work out what he should say at the press conference to ease people's fears. But this had just left his mind confused. It was too complicated. Yet also it did not feel right. As he gave up trying to calculate what he should say, he found a clarity begin to emerge in his mind. The illumined consciousness, the pool of knowing, which he had been increasingly experiencing in its various forms since the arrival of the light vessel, now seemed to be just below the surface. It was ready to make itself known to the extent he was prepared to lay aside his own more worldly thinking. As Alex had said a little earlier, he must now be prepared to follow this deeper guidance. He had then embraced the inner stillness and, without effort, had seen that at this moment in the brief history of humanity, what mattered was that he spoke from this place of profound wakefulness and trusted the words that emerged. There could be no rehearsal or preparation. He would simply have to sit behind that table, in front of the world's television cameras and allow the illumined consciousness that now seemed to be the very background of his mind to express itself. This insight had come as a great relief.

He had then reflected on how his experiences of illumined consciousness and inner guidance had increased dramatically since the arrival of the Visitor. He could not imagine having coped otherwise. He knew that it could not be coincidence. The Teacher had prepared something in him that the light vessel had initiated. Yet the Teacher had then deserted him and Joseph had to admit that he felt hurt by this. Joseph wondered, however, whether if his mentor had remained he would have looked to him for help, rather than tap the resources that had been cultivated in his depths over the previous three years. Perhaps the Teacher's absence was a teaching in itself.

As he had continued to think about this, a great sense of confidence had arisen. He was not alone and had been prepared. Something massive was unfolding of which he was a part. The confidence filled him and he bathed in it. He knew that it would not last; that the pressures of the world would undermine its quiet strength. But in that moment he had been determined to enjoy it.

The feeling that there was a hidden purpose to his life had then gripped him once more. It had occurred to him that he might be on the verge of discovering what lay behind this life-long inner pressure. The thought was both exciting and frightening. Joseph found himself reflecting further on the last two days. As he did so, he became fascinated as more tantalizing associations began to emerge and the apparently random began to reveal a deeper order.

He remembered the dream of the community of monks on the wooded hill and how they had shared communion with him; how he had felt part of them. For no obvious reason, Joseph realized that in his mind he had started to refer to them as his "brothers". It felt right and proper. It also felt good. As he thought about them, he suddenly recalled the circle of hooded figures he had glimpsed as he had stepped in and out of the blue beam of light in his meditation in the hermit's cell. As he remembered this, a vivid spark of connection leapt across his mind. He knew that they were one and the same. He was filled with a feeling of wonder and peace as the threads of his dream and his experience in the blue light wove themselves together. He then remembered seeing his own dead face in the dream. The shock he had felt then returned in dilute form. He wondered about the meaning of this bit of the dream, for he knew that it did have meaning, but could see nothing clearly. Then he remembered Alex's comment, about how he must have brought with him his ability to plunge deeply into the depths of consciousness, and a possible interpretation stirred. Threads once more wanted to embrace each other.

Yet there were also other threads that refused to come together. Freshest in his mind were the cryptic images that he had seen in the blue light. No matter how much he thought about them, a clear message would not emerge. Alex seemed to have an idea what they meant, so perhaps it was only a matter of time before the tapestry took on even more form. But Joseph's mind struggled to get to grips with Alex's extraordinary claim that the Visitor must have known that the two of them would meet. Its implications were awesome.

And the greatest mystery, which dwarfed all others, remained unanswered. What was the Visitor, why had it chosen him and what did the future hold?

Now he sat hiding in his little room, until the time was right. Through the door to the kitchen he could hear occasional movement and muffled conversations. Once, he had heard Alex getting annoyed with someone and Joseph guessed that an unwelcome intruder had met stern resistance. He was absent-mindedly staring through the window at the darkening sky. The daylight was coming to an end, which meant that very soon he would be walking out before the world. Joseph sighed and looked around the room for a clock, but could not see one. The encroaching darkness told him, however, that it would not be long before there was a knock on the door. He was composing himself for what was to come, when another thought came unbidden. He remembered another dream, one that he had experienced many times, that had been swept temporarily out of awareness by the events of the last two days. It was the dream of the great city and the two rivers, and of his meetings with an unknown "someone". As the dream came to mind, he knew it really mattered. It was another thread that, as yet, hung loose.

Before he could take this further, the knock on the door came. It seemed that the moment had arrived. Joseph took a deep breath before replying.

"Come in."

Very slowly the door opened and Alex looked around the edge. He seemed reassured by what he saw and walked in, closing the door behind him. He sat down in a chair and looked closely at Joseph's face, which must have betrayed its expectation.

"We have a little more time, Father, so you can relax for now."

Joseph sat back in the chair, grateful for a few more minutes of peace. He knew that from the moment he walked out of the room, his life would never be the same again.

"How are things out there?"

Alex shook his head slowly. "Not easy. Jennifer is finding things increasingly difficult. She is struggling to keep control of what is happening and I think it is only a matter of time before she is pushed aside." Alex suddenly looked fiercely proud. "She is wonderful and I think only her strength has kept them at bay until now, but their fear is too great and soon ... as you say ... the gloves will be off."

"By 'they' you mean the government?"

"Yes. They just arrived without invitation and walked in. Did you know that there's actually a minister here? He is being quite polite. But with him are others, who seem to be officials and security people. They are impatient and forceful. I have tried to blend into the background and listen to them. It is clear that they want to take control of you, but only their confusion and the speed of events is stopping them. Also, I think you were clever to call the press conference, for it makes them hesitate. The eyes of the world are watching. For now they just look angry, but soon I am sure it will turn to action." Alex paused, his voice dropping theatrically to a whisper. "There are others here too, with American accents. It is not just your own government."

What he heard frightened Joseph. Once more he focused on breathing deeply and found the stillness that lay beneath the fear, patiently waiting for him. His thoughts turned to the bishop.

"I'm sorry for inflicting this on Jennifer. It must be hard for her, especially as she doesn't agree with how I'm doing things."

"She is under great pressure, but I am here for her. She is not alone. But also I think that what she has experienced over the last few hours has helped her to see that maybe you were right to exclude governments. I think that she has been shocked by what has been thrown at her." Alex paused and looked amused. "Who knows, perhaps this will make her into an anarchist like me!"

"I wouldn't count on it."

"But I can hope, surely!"

Joseph found himself laughing. The image of an anarchist Bishop Jennifer was too much. The laughter faded away as he saw Alex's face become serious again.

"Father, what I have heard convinces me that as soon as the press conference is over you must leave immediately. I am sure that if you stay you will lose your freedom. You will no longer be able to walk the path that is before you."

The look on Alex's face was all Joseph needed to trust his judgment. The thought of becoming a pawn in other people's games appalled him. Yet there was also something else, much more important. He knew deep inside that if this were to happen, the Visitor would leave. There would be no more contact. He needed to keep his freedom not only for his sake, but for the sake of the world. But as he thought about how to do this, he felt overwhelmed.

"Alex, I'm sure that you're right, but how am I to escape? How can someone like me evade the power of governments?"

Alex gazed down at his hands for a few moments and then looked Joseph straight in the eye, a decision clearly having been made.

"I can arrange that, if you will trust me."

"You? Alex, these are governments we're talking about. You're just an artist."

"No, Father Joseph, if you recall I am a very special kind of artist, who is in fellowship with a group of people of extraordinary gifts. Some of these people have used their talents in the world and, out of public view, have accumulated great wealth and power. How else could my paintings sell for enough money to buy a Ferrari? I can arrange for you to disappear if you will let me."

Joseph searched Alex's face for any hint of humor, but saw

only deadly seriousness. Then, from nowhere, he remembered Alex's statement that the Visitor must have known that they would meet. More threads came together.

"Alex, I trust you completely. I am in your hands."

Alex did not say anything, but his expression conveyed his pleasure and pride at Joseph's response.

"Where will you take me?"

"That, I will not tell you, Father Joseph. It must remain a secret for now." Alex leaned forward, looking very intense. "But the place will relate to the images you saw in the hermit's cell. I am sure that I understand their meaning. It is marvelous how everything fits together."

Joseph desperately wanted to know the meaning of his vision, but it was clear that Alex had no intention of telling him. Alex seemed to read his thoughts.

"Be patient my friend. It is better this way. Where we are going will help you to … understand … more deeply than if I just gave you words now."

Joseph looked at his friend and, after a few moments, nodded. He found it extraordinary how much he trusted Alex, a man whom he had known for less than a day.

"O.K. Alex. We'll do it your way. How are you going to get me out of here?"

Alex reached into his pocket and pulled out a small electric torch.

"You will need this. When the moment comes, at the end of the press conference, come straight back here. Make sure that you are alone. I will be waiting. We will need to move quickly and decisively."

"Will you be coming with me?"

"Yes, I must."

"What about Leola and Jennifer?"

"They cannot come. There would not be room and also we must move with speed. The fewer people involved the better."

Joseph looked at Alex, weighing his next words carefully.

"Jennifer and Leola must be told we're going."

Alex looked uncomfortable.

"Father, would it not be better if afterwards they can plead innocence with a clear conscience? And is there not the risk that, without meaning to, they might raise suspicions with a chance remark if they knew in advance?"

"That's all very logical, Alex. But this isn't about logic, it is about relationship. The four of us are in this together and that's how it must stay. Anyway, what would it say about the love that you and Jennifer share if you couldn't tell her what we are going to do? And can you really leave without saying goodbye?"

Alex seemed to shrink a little as he pondered Joseph's words.

"You are right, Father. The way that we do this matters." He paused as a new thought occurred to him. "It is something about the Visitor. I can feel it deep down. He requires that we do things in a certain way, which has honesty and love. Nothing else feels comfortable around our strange friend."

"Yes, I think you're right Alex. It's something about the atmosphere, the energy that he creates. What we do must be shaped by … profound relationship … at all levels. Or it will stick in out throats."

They sat in silence for a while, absorbed in the meaning of what had been said.

The loud knock on the door made them both jump. It opened as wide as it could to reveal Leola. For a moment Joseph wondered why she was making such a theatrical entrance, but then saw that hovering behind was someone else. Leola, in her own way, was warning Joseph and Alex that they were not alone.

"It's nearly time, Father. This … lady … is here to collect you." The disdain in her voice was clear.

Leola moved aside to reveal an attractive woman in a smart suit, probably in her early thirties, clutching a clipboard, with a Bluetooth mobile phone headset fitted to one ear. Joseph suspected that her immaculately cut short hair was deliberately shaped to make room for the earpiece. Joseph's first impression was of barely controlled energy. She could hardly keep still. His second impression was disturbing. She had a most dangerous affliction - certainty. He suspected immediately that doubt rarely entered her thoughts. So much of the suffering of the world came from people who carried this disease.

"Father Joseph, I presume." she barked, marching past Leola as though she did not exist. "My name's Jessica Knowles, from the Prime Minister's Communications Unit. I'm in charge of the media event ..." She broke off in mid-sentence as Joseph raised his hand to silence her.

"No you're not, Ms Knowles, I am."

Joseph was as surprised as everyone else at these words. They had just erupted from within. The silence that followed was palpable. Out of the corner of his eye, Joseph saw Leola suppress a smile. The woman was momentarily thrown and did not know how to reply. The possibility of such a response had clearly never occurred to her. He watched as she gathered herself and a steely gleam entered her eye. No one reached her kind of position who was not made of strong stuff.

"Right. Well, let's say that we're working together on this, shall we? After all, the PM is very keen that everything goes well."

Joseph knew that her casual mention of the Prime Minister was meant to intimidate him. He simply looked back at her without saying anything. There was another difficult silence, which was broken by Alex moving towards the door.

"I will leave you to your preparations. I must go and speak to Jen ... the bishop."

The woman moved slightly to one side to let him pass, but did remove her gaze from Joseph. He knew that she was waiting for an invitation to sit down. That would have encouraged a conversation he had no intention of having. After a few moments, she sighed and steamed ahead.

"I need to brief you about the event. I will chair proceedings and the bishop will be there as support. You will make a short statement at the beginning and then some questions will be allowed. The media have been told firmly what the format will be." She stopped, waiting for some reaction. None was forthcoming. She continued, making no attempt to hide the irritation in her voice. "I have made some notes for you on likely questions with some suggested answers." She took a piece of paper from her clipboard and held it out for Joseph to take. He kept his hands by his side and continued looking at her.

"Where's Marge, the bishop's press officer?"

"It was felt that something like this was, well, a bit outside her experience." The woman struggled to keep the condescension out of her voice.

"I think, Ms Knowles, that this situation is outside the experience of us all." He paused to allow the point to sink in. "Unfortunately, I fear that you have wasted a lot of effort. Neither the bishop or yourself will be with me during the press conference. I will be alone. I'm afraid that I will not need your briefing sheet, but it was kind of you to prepare it. As I said a few moments ago, I'm in charge and will do things my own way."

The woman's self-control snapped.

"I think, Father Joseph, that you need a reality check. This is way over the head of someone like you. My instructions are very clear and you will play by our rules. I hope that is understood."

It was obvious from the look on her face that, as far as she was concerned, the debate was over. She held out the briefing sheet again for Joseph to take. He stepped forward and for a moment it looked as though he was going to comply, but then she saw that his arms were still firmly by his sides.

"Jessica, I will say this only once more. I am in charge of this. It will be done my way. Otherwise, this 'media event' as you like to call it will not happen. And if you or your superiors have any doubt as to the source of my authority, I would suggest that you bring to mind what hangs over the Church of St Petroc only a few miles from here, and of the relationship with it that I clearly enjoy."

Joseph did not need to be a mind-reader to know the effect of his words on the super-confident woman who stood in front of him. He knew that in her mind she was seeing him caught in the blue beam of light and all that implied. He saw the confidence drain away as she was reminded that the world had changed, that all the rules of power that had given life meaning and made her feel safe, were no more. She obviously did not know what to say and he began to feel compassion for her. He tried to make his voice as gentle as he could.

"Jessica, why don't you go and make sure everything is ready and, by all means, consult with your bosses if necessary. I need to freshen up. I'll join you outside the banqueting room in a couple of minutes."

She hesitated for a few moments as though about to protest, but then the fire went out of her.

"Oh, right, yes. If that's what you want. I'll see you shortly then."

Joseph watched as she turned and walked away, heals clicking loudly on the stone floor of the kitchen. His shoulders sagged as tension drained out. Leola watched her go.

"Well, you certainly sorted her out, Father."

"That may be so, Leola," Joseph sighed, "But I didn't enjoy it. I almost feel that I'm becoming someone else. Someone much stronger and forceful."

"No, Father, I think that you're wrong there. I'm thinking that you're just remembering who you were born to be, that's all."

Joseph looked at Leola, once more appreciating the profound being that lay behind such an unlikely exterior. She held his gaze.

"I suppose that this is goodbye then."

Joseph was startled. "How did you know?"

"Because I've got eyes to see. You can't stay here. I've been watching our new friends and it's clear what they mean to do as soon as they get brave enough. I know that Mr. Alex has seen it too and will have been laying his plans."

Joseph did not know what to say. Now the moment had come, he realized just how much he was going to miss Leola. He found his eyes starting to moisten. Leola saw it too.

"Now don't you be worrying about anything, laddie. Mr. Alex is a good man. And he's here now because it's meant to be so. You trust him and all will be well."

Joseph struggled to reply. Eventually he could only get two words out.

"Thank you."

It was Leola's turn to feel her eyes dampen.

"Your Clare, she'd be proud of you," was all she said. Then, taking Joseph completely by surprise, she stepped forward and gave him a huge hug. After a few moments she released him. "Now, you'd better be going before that young ... lady ... recovers from her shock and starts being difficult again."

Joseph looked down at her for a few moments, then nodded and turned to walk away. Then a thought occurred to him.

"Don't forget to look after Bishop Jennifer."

He shot out through the door before Leola could throw anything at him.

Chapter 15

Jessica Knowles and the bishop were waiting for Joseph as he emerged onto the main corridor. Walking towards them, he caught a glimpse of himself in a mirror. Something did not feel right.

He stopped and looked at his reflection, trying to work out what it was. Then he reached up and removed the strip of white plastic from his shirt collar that symbolized his priesthood. He immediately felt better and tried to understand why this was. He was not ashamed of what the dog collar stood for, yet something inside had suddenly felt uncomfortable with its display. He reached down into his mind, seeking the root of the unexpected feeling. It took a few moments, but then it was obvious and very simple. He wanted to go before the world as just a human being, not as someone who held a special office or rank, or who represented a particular group. This was a time for people to connect with what they shared, their common humanity. When he turned away from the mirror, he found the bishop staring at him, clearly pained by what she had witnessed.

"You'll have to trust me," was all he said.

He looked at her for a few moments and then smiled. It was a smile that he hoped conveyed his gratitude for all she had done for him. She hesitated for a few moments, before relaxing a little and brushing some hairs off his jacket.

"God be with you ... in everything."

In that moment he knew that Alex had found time to tell her of their plans. He held her gaze for a few moments longer, before turning to her companion.

"In here?" he asked, pointing at an elaborately carved door. Jessica Knowles just nodded her head, evidently still disturbed by their previous encounter. Joseph opened the door and walked through.

So diffident was his entry and so unassuming a figure did he present, that no one at first noticed him. The door was located to one side of the massive room, behind the table with the three chairs that he had seen on the television. Joseph wandered over to the table, hands in his jacket pockets, while the assembled reporters continued to talk among themselves. In one of the pockets he could feel the white strip of plastic that he had just removed. He hoped that he now looked like someone with a taste for black shirts, rather than a priest. In the other pocket he felt the small torch that Alex had given him.

Joseph reached the chairs, pulled out the middle one and sat down. On the table immediately in front of him were banks of microphones. He was pleased to see that the beautiful red and blue table covering was still visible in places. He sat there alone, ready to face the world, except that the world had not noticed him. Joseph found such undeniable proof of his insignificance to be both reassuring and amusing. He leaned forward and spoke in the general direction of the microphones.

"Good evening."

Heads turned nonchalantly in his direction. There was a brief hiatus while recognition dawned, followed by a mad scramble as people turned to face the right way and grabbed notebooks. A few seemed to notice with interest the empty chairs on either side of him.

"In case any of you are wondering, my name is Joseph Williams. I'm the reason you're all here."

There were a few chuckles around the room. The humor seemed to be appreciated. Joseph noted how, quite naturally, he had referred to himself by his given name, without any priestly prefix. The reporters settled quickly, their focus on him intense as they waited for the most extraordinary press conference in human history to begin. But Joseph was not to be rushed. He had spent years standing before groups of people of all kinds and knew that before beginning he must connect with those present.

He allowed his gaze to wander over the expectant faces, finding himself moved by the range of nationalities and ethnic groups that were represented. He was astonished that such a rainbow gathering had come together in so short a time. No doubt many were London correspondents or based in nearby European capitals, a short plane flight away. As he took in the people, he was once more reminded of the countless funerals that he had conducted. What had happened over the last two days was another kind of death. In both situations were people who, without warning, violently, had been taken to the edge of the known and beyond. Yet they had to continue functioning, so carried with them a subtle air of false normality. It was what he sensed in front of him.

Just for a moment, Joseph glimpsed with quiet astonishment how so many aspects of his life had prepared him for what was now happening. He remembered Alex saying that the Visitor must have known that they would meet. He saw with even more clarity that something incredibly deep was playing itself out.

Joseph continued to look around the room and tried to make eye contact wherever he could. He had long ago learned how important this was in dealing with people. He was disturbed to discover, however, that even in this collection of two hundred or so hard-bitten journalists, from all around the globe, there were few who would meet his gaze. It did not take long for him to realize why this was. What had happened the previous evening, before such a cloud of witnesses, had marked him out, separated him from the herd. He was now unspeakably different, beyond the pale, to be treated with suspicion. For most this was not a conscious state of mind, of course, which made it even more powerful and disturbing. Yet there were some, a small number, who did not avert their eyes, but looked back with barely suppressed excitement. These individuals interested him greatly. They gave him hope for humanity.

The tension in the room increased as all waited for Joseph to start proceedings, but he would not be rushed. In an energized silence, he looked over the reporters to the array of TV cameras that lined the back of the room. All were focused on him. He made a point of slowly looking along the line of lenses, making symbolic eye contact with the countless minds that regarded him at that moment, formed and shaped by innumerable cultures, all shaken to their core by the arrival of the Visitor – and by what they had seen happen to him. He knew that this moment of connection with the rest of humanity was vital; that it opened inner doors and freed powerful currents. Whatever happened outwardly over the next hour or so, it was the stirring of these subterranean energies that was important. He felt deeply that this was the intention of the Visitor, expressing itself through him. He suddenly saw with great clarity that his time in the blue light had connected him with the Visitor in ways that he was only just realizing. The images that he had recalled in the hermit cell were only one aspect of what had occurred.

Joseph was aware of an extraordinary stillness pervading his mind. He should have been shaking inside like a leaf, as billions of people waited for him to speak, yet there was only peace. He had no idea what he would say, but it did not matter. He had complete acceptance of the moment, whatever it might bring. He lowered his head and contemplated his hands for a few moments, before looking up.

"I'm sure you have many questions. I would suggest that we just plunge in and see how we get on. Who wants to be first?"

Joseph's eyes roamed across the assembled journalists and he saw that he had taken them by surprise. He was not following the format that Ms Knowles had, no doubt, drilled into them with some force. But it did not take long before hands started to be raised. Joseph picked one at random.

"Why don't we start with you?"

For a while, the questions were general, asking about his background, age, how long he had been a priest and so on. It was almost as though no one wanted to get to the real questions, the ones that they were all there for, that burned in the world mind. Perhaps these questions were so big that they had to be approached circuitously. Finally, however, the moment came as it had to. There was some fumbling as the next journalist grasped one of the microphones that were being passed around. He looked very nervous.

"Father Joseph, we have all seen the amazing television pictures. Could you please tell us in your own words what you experienced last night?"

Joseph noticed that the reporter seemed to have a New Zealand accent. He also realized that his attempt to downplay his priesthood had already been dented. He waited for words to emerge from the stillness that permeated his mind. Then he watched as he retold the story he had shared that morning with the bishop, Alex and Leola. As he spoke, he wondered how much detail he would hear himself describe. He noticed with interest that he recounted the sense of being summoned as he stood in the beam of blue light in the church. The everyday Joseph would have wrestled with the wisdom of sharing such an astonishing claim. He would have debated whether it might undermine his credibility or frighten people. He then watched as he described only vaguely what he had seen while he was held in the light. He did not talk about the mysterious images that he had recovered in the hermit cell. The mundane Joseph would have worried about not telling the full truth, but the Joseph of the depths knew that truth had to be used skillfully, if it was not to become a barrier rather than something which freed. So he watched as he explained that the experience had become evermore dreamlike, to a point where all he had were fragments of memory. He told how he had been left confused, almost in a state of collapse and of how friends had cared for him, giving him time to recover.

He could tell that his reply left the journalists frustrated and on edge, as he knew it would. They spent their lives listening to people's stories and had an instinct for when they were not being told the full truth. So they probed, changing the wording of the questions in an attempt to trick him into revealing more. Joseph watched with amusement as the stillness gently maneuvered around the traps that were laid, but he was also aware of a growing tension in the room as the frustration turned into anger. Finally, one of the journalists leapt to her feet, ignored the proffered microphone and jabbed her finger at Joseph.

"So you expect us to believe that you're summoned to go outside, are then held in a beam of blue light for half an hour, but can't tell us anything about the being that sits in the light vessel?" she demanded in an American accent.

Joseph was expecting another evasive answer to find its way to the surface, but instead he felt the stillness stir and take interest. There was something about the question that it had been waiting for. Or perhaps it was something about the questioner herself.

"Oh, I wouldn't say that," he found himself saying. There was a moment of stunned silence in the room. The woman sat down without realizing she had done so.

"As I said, I have only vague, dreamlike impressions of what went on. The details are a mess. But one feeling I am left with, which is very strong, is that I spent time with ... someone." Joseph paused, sensing how the tension in the room had drained away in a few moments. All that was left was intense interest. He was now talking about what both fascinated and frightened everyone - the nature of the Visitor. As his eyes scanned the faces, he saw that his unexpected response had caused a real humanness to break through many of the journalistic masks.

"We know, instinctively, when we are in the company of another sentient being, even if our understanding of what's happening is confused. I know, without doubt, that last night my mind touched that of the Visitor." The atmosphere in the old and venerable room was now electric. "I sensed certain things about the awesome being that waits for us, but they are difficult to put into words. I sensed a vast intelligence that I could barely comprehend. I suppose it may be what one of the higher primates, like a chimpanzee, feels when it spends time with a person. It can't understand what's happening, so to remember the details afterwards would be difficult. There's no real structure to order the memories. But it knows that it was with an extraordinary being. Maybe that's one way to understand my experience. This is only a picture that may help and it is not to say that the Visitor sees us in this way. Actually, I had the feeling that we are held in the highest regard."

There was silence in the room for a few moments, as Joseph's words were absorbed. Then the woman who had asked the original question reached over and took the previously ignored microphone.

"You said 'someone'. So there is only one ... being ... in the vessel?"

The realization of what he had said stopped Joseph in his tracks. His mind went back to the conversation with Leola the previous day and her enigmatic look when he had commented that they seemed to speak automatically of a single being. But as he thought about the experience in the blue light, he also realized that it was not that simple.

"Yes, I did say that, without being consciously aware of my words. Looking back now, that's certainly what I sensed. There was a single ... center of consciousness. Yet there was something else, an intangible feeling that we were not alone. That in the far distance there were ... others ... but not in the vessel. It's very difficult to explain."

His words brought a profound stillness to the room. The woman reporter looked at him for a few moments before continuing.

"You implied that you sensed other things about the ... being?"

Joseph paused, waiting for the words to come.

"I felt compassion. I sensed a profound understanding of us and that I, personally, was deeply known. I gained a strong impression of age; that this is someone who has seen much. But these words are all I can offer. After that it all gets muddled in my mind."

The woman's aggression was now a thing of the past. Indeed, she was clearly fascinated by what she was hearing. There was no possibility of her surrendering the microphone just yet.

"When it ... touched ... your mind, what did it feel like?"

"Perhaps not so different as you might think. After all, everything is an inner experience, whether we realize this fact or not. You are seeing me now in your mind. I am a perception. The light entering your eye is being converted into electrochemical signals from which a stunningly mysterious phenomenon called 'awareness' is compiling the picture that you believe you 'see'. Maybe I could compare the touch of the Visitor's mind to hearing a voice in the dark, followed by the gentle touch of a hand. There was nothing threatening about it."

"Do you get any idea how this ... telepathy ... works?"

"Not really, only a sense of something natural. It didn't feel new. It was like I was remembering how to do something. But everything is very confused, so I don't really know what was going on." Joseph paused. "I suppose the way the Visitor chose to communicate tells us something else about its nature. It's very much a creature of the mind for whom the depths of consciousness may be its natural habitat. Whereas our focus is on the outer, its may primarily be on the inner."

"And did you sense anything concerning ... its ... intentions?"

As she asked the million dollar question Joseph could almost feel the whole world lean forward to hear the answer. He was rather interested himself. Once more he waited for the words to emerge.

"I got a sense that it's to do with the next stage of our

evolution. It's here to act as midwife and guide to what we may become. By this, I don't mean a continuation of the physical evolution that has brought us over millions of years from holes in the ground, to the treetops and then down onto the ground again. That was merely the outer expression of deeper forces. The real evolution taking place has been in consciousness - the way that we perceive and interact with reality. The Visitor, I sense, offers to lead us to a vaster experience of life."

The female reporter's eyes were now alive with excitement as she formed her next question. Joseph realized that she was one of those who had been prepared to meet his gaze a little earlier. He now understood the cause of her original exasperation and why the stillness was responding. This really mattered to her at a personal level. She was one of those whose wonder and awe at what had happened outweighed her fear. She was inspired by the unknown future that beckoned. He hoped that there were many like this.

"So the Visitor isn't here to stop wars or heal the environment like so many seem to think?"

"Yes it is. But at a causal level - the human mind. This is where everything starts. I feel that it is here to offer us a ... bigger picture ... that will fundamentally change our relationship with existence." Joseph paused as the next words came to mind. He was hesitant to say them, but knew that he must trust what was happening. "But we also have to understand that its ... experience ... of reality is much deeper and multilayered than ours. That it does not only live on the outer surface of physical existence as we do".

Joseph stopped and left the words hanging in the air. No more came. But they were enough to feed any open mind. He was now totally focused on the female reporter and was barely aware of the other people in the room. He watched in silent encouragement as she formed her next question.

"Father, just now you referred to the Visitor as 'waiting' for us. What did you mean?"

"It was a feeling, an intuition, that an offer has been made and we can choose to respond or not. Nothing will be forced on us. Although I am far from sure, I had the sense that the Visitor will leave if we decline the relationship that is offered. Also, there is only limited time."

The woman looked at him intently.

"And that response must surely involve you? After all, it is you that was chosen for contact."

"I don't know why I was chosen. Perhaps the next contact, if there is any, will be with someone else. I may have no further part to play after this evening." The less than truthful answer tasted slightly sour in Joseph's mouth.

The woman continued to stare at him for a few moments. He could tell that she knew his answer was incomplete. He watched her make a decision.

"Thank you, Father," was all she said, handing the microphone back to the attendant. He saw then that she had discovered new loyalties. He had another friend.

His focus on the female reporter was quickly interrupted as a sea of hands shot up. Again he pointed to someone at random and waited while a microphone found its way to a man of, Joseph guessed, Far Eastern origin. The man's body language suggested the tone of the questions might be about to change.

"Mr. Williams, are you not being dangerously naïve? Surely we must assume that the intruder is hostile until we know otherwise? Perhaps you have been tricked or brainwashed in some way?"

The man's words produced a buzz of conversation and a few shouted objections. Joseph smiled inwardly as once more the word "naïve" was used to describe him. It was obviously a theme for the day. As he waited for people to settle, he saw how the question had divided the room. On some of the faces, including the female American reporter, there was outrage. Joseph noted again that these tended to be those who had earlier been willing to meet his gaze. Others showed confusion or indecision. But what disturbed him was the large number, the majority, who clearly had sympathy with the question. He had little doubt that this reaction would be reflected in the watching audience. Joseph waited until he was the center of attention.

"It is a very good question, Sir, and one that must be asked. All I can do is share what I have experienced and leave the world to decide. Perhaps I am not the best judge." He paused while thoughts formed. "It may be that my comfortable Western life, never having known war, spent entirely in a rich and powerful country, has blinded me to the harsher realities of life and leads me to see everything in a positive light. I am very aware of my good fortune and that this has not been the experience of most people in the world." The room was now paying him rapt attention. "But putting to one side my … subjective … experiences of last night, I would offer some thoughts that are, I think, reasonably objective. The first is pretty obvious. If the Visitor's intentions were hostile, would it really choose a nonentity like me as its advance guard? Surely it would have picked a world leader or the general of some great army. Someone like me can be easily dismissed. As I said in answer to the previous question, I have no idea why last night happened to me. But could it be that my very unimportance has something to do with it, as a symbol of the Visitor's intent? Also, why would the Visitor need anybody at all if it wanted to do us harm? Look at the awesome technology. Can you really imagine that we would be capable of any meaningful resistance?" Joseph paused to let his words sink in. "Also, there is something else that may be staring us in the face. Could a warlike, aggressive race have reached the advanced level that the Visitor clearly represents? Would not such a society long ago have destroyed itself by internal conflict, as its capacity for destruction reached the required level? I think a very strong argument can be made that only a civilization that has exorcised its inner demons could have reached such a peak of development."

Joseph focused on the questioner, silently encouraging a response. He knew that the fear behind the question must permeate the watching world. It needed to be brought into the open. The man looked thoughtful and for a few moments said nothing. Then he spoke with icy politeness.

"My people, Mr. Williams, learned over many centuries to distrust visitors who came to our shores claiming good intentions, only to exploit and oppress as the opportunity arose. The peace and plenty that you have enjoyed in your life was built upon such deception as practiced by your forebears. Now the intruder chooses a representative of such a nation. We know to rely only on suspicion backed up by strength. We would recommend this approach to the world in dealing with the intruder. If we lower our guard, we risk losing everything."

He sat down, thrusting the microphone at the attendant. Joseph allowed a few seconds before replying. Then he deliberately leaned forward to emphasize his words.

"And maybe if we don't lower our guard, Sir, we will lose more than everything." He paused to allow the words to resonate around the room. "I would ask you, and everyone else, to imagine what it would feel like if the Visitor made no more contact and simply flew back into space. Perhaps we would all feel safe again and could get on with normal life. But I think that really, underneath, there would be a terrible sense of loss; that an extraordinary opportunity had been spurned. Might this not take the fire out of our collective heart? What would happen to our societies, as our lack of courage eat away at our souls?" He paused again for a few moments. "I believe, Sir, we are built for adventure; that we have some kind of destiny. If you doubt this, look at human history. To deny this impulse at this point may inflict a fatal wound on our collective psyche. Perhaps this is what the Visitor waits for - to see how adventurous we are. To see if we are worthy of what's on offer."

The words had flowed out of Joseph. They had felt like him, and also more than him. It was how he imagined a musician must feel when playing a beautiful piece of music. He could feel the power that expressed itself through the words. He looked around the room. The questioner was shaking his head, while others looked unsure. The American woman and a few others were nodding and smiling. He decided it was time to move on.

"Does anyone else have a question?"

Once more, a sea of hands was raised. Joseph looked around carefully and found himself drawn to a man near the front with a mass of unkempt hair, wearing an expensive suit with an open-necked shirt. He vaguely recognized him as a well known commentator with a British ultra-liberal newspaper.

"Joseph, I notice that you are not wearing your dog collar and that your bishop is not by your side. Has your encounter with the alien cured your belief in God?"

The man sat down looking pleased with himself. His question provoked a few sniggers around the room, but even more intakes of breath and muttered complaints. The question conveyed the usual contempt that a certain kind of Western liberal held for a world view other than their own. It was rooted in an arrogance that made it blind to the offense that such a question would cause to most of those watching. Joseph continued to look at the man while he waited for the stillness to answer. His reply when it came was succinct.

"No."

For a few moments the journalists assumed that this was just the first shot of a longer response and waited expectantly. As it dawned that no more was to come, the laughter started, first sporadically and then spreading to the whole room. The questioner's face lost its look of easy self-confidence, to be replaced by embarrassed anger.

"Anyone else?" Joseph asked as innocently as he could, his

eyes searching the room.

But the questioner was having none of it. He leapt to his feet again.

"Oh no, Joseph, you can't get away with that. You have a responsibility to the world to give a proper reply."

Joseph felt something begin to stir in the stillness, reacting against the man's arrogance and easy manipulation of words. Anger would be the wrong word to describe the feeling. It was more like a determination to oppose something corrupt; to cleanse the air of a pollutant. The American reporter had asked questions from anger a little while earlier, but it had been an honest anger that came from a real desire to know. There was nothing so pure behind this man's words.

"You do not speak for the world, only for yourself." The steel in Joseph's voice cut through the room, producing a cold silence. "You are filled with your own righteousness. You believe you already know all that matters, so would not have been truly interested in my answer. It was not a real question. I only answer real questions." Joseph leaned forward and glared at the man. "Were it not for your own sense of infallibility, you might have paused to wonder why our extraordinary visitor chose to make first contact with a spiritual person like myself. After all, you were available." Some uncomfortable laughter went around the room. "Could it be that there is something about the mind of a person such as myself that is receptive to mystery, to the vast unknownness of existence, and so is ripe for relationship with the genuinely alien? And, inconceivable though it may be to you, might it be that the spiritual impulse is something that the Visitor shares and honors? Perhaps you should give this some thought." Joseph held the man in his glare for a few seconds more before releasing him. The reporter slumped back into his chair, looking both angry and shaken. Joseph felt sorry for him. Even he had been daunted by the authority that had filled his voice.

"Next question please."

Joseph took a sip of water as he looked around the hands that went up in the air. There was one man, of African origin Joseph guessed, who seemed particularly keen and somewhat excited. Joseph pointed at him and waited as a microphone found its way into his hand.

"Is it not obvious, Father Joseph, that you have been chosen because, like me, you believe in Jesus Christ as the one Lord and Savior of Mankind and that our Visitor must also acknowledge this truth? Surely what happened to you, and that it happened at a Christian church, proves that this much superior being has come to Christ."

The question provoked uproar in the room. Real anger was directed at the questioner from all sides. Yet the man looked unperturbed, basking in another kind of righteousness. Joseph knew that this idea had to be stamped on without mercy. Nothing could be more dangerous. He was tempted to answer immediately, but managed to restrain himself, waiting for the stillness to respond. When he was ready, he raised his hand as a signal for order to be restored. Reluctantly and slowly the crowd of journalists complied.

"Nothing in my contact with the Visitor would support such arrogant nonsense." Joseph felt the shock go around the room at the bluntness of his words. "I don't know why I was chosen, but am certain that it could just as easily have been someone from another faith or none. The Visitor's ... vision ... is vast and all of our philosophies and faiths are, at their very best, merely glimpses of something infinitely greater. We must not project onto the Visitor our partial little stories, but must come with humility, ready to have our minds blown open." The man's composure had gone and he was now looking angry, but the stillness had not finished. "I am a follower of Jesus of Nazareth because he sets my heart on fire and leads me into the majestic mystery of life. Yet I know that for others it is the Buddha or Krishna or Allah or the Arwen or the Great Spirit that inspires them in this way. Mine is just one path in a vast land. For me, spirituality is a diving into the Great Mystery, not into false certainty. Mine is a path of unknowing." Joseph looked directly at the questioner. "I'm afraid, Sir, that you and I have nothing in common. In fact, I would suggest that there is little difference between you and the previous questioner in your evangelical fundamentalism. Yours is religious, his is atheistic, but it is a cosmetic difference. Underneath, the mindset is the same and just as dangerous."

Joseph was aware that the vehemence of his attack had stunned the room, but he felt no remorse. People could die because of what the questioner had said. The man had not finished and stood up, clearly furious.

"How dare you call yourself a Christian!" he thundered.

"I never did," Joseph retorted instantly. "I called myself a follower of Jesus. The man who walked two thousand years ago would not recognize much of what now carries the sorely abused label of 'Christian'."

The man was now incandescent with fury.

"Then clearly the intruder must be the devil to have turned your mind so. It really is as prophesized in the Book of Revelation. You, Joseph Williams, are antichrist!"

The tension in the room was near breaking point. Joseph could see security staff moving towards the questioner, about to intervene. He waited for the stillness to lead the way. He found himself starting to laugh. Gradually, many in the room joined in and the man, though still furious, sat down. The security people moved back into the shadows. Joseph noted their presence and wondered how many others were spread, invisibly, around the house and grounds. He hoped that Alex had laid his plans well. The laughter died away and, although the tension was eased, Joseph felt daunted by what the last three questions had revealed. So deep were human divisions, infected with terrifying certainty, that the arrival of the Visitor could easily ignite mayhem. Most human minds would see what was happening through the filter of their beliefs, histories, fears and needs. Few would be able to lay these aside and open to the devastatingly new. That he should be in the middle of all of this, filled him with trepidation. And as the fear grew, so the stillness receded a little. Yet he was fascinated to see that they could coexist. In a determined fashion, he focused his attention on the stillness.

"Are there any more questions?"

Fewer hands went up this time. Joseph pointed to a woman who he guessed might be from the Middle East.

"Father Williams, to whom do you answer? I too have seen that you sit before us alone. Do you make a deliberate statement with this? Do you say that you are subject to no authority but your own? Should not the General Secretary to the United Nations be at your side? Or do you take all power to yourself in this matter?"

The room was very quiet again now. It was a good question and deserved a good answer.

"I sit before you alone because last night I had an incredible experience that I thought should be shared with the people of the world. I was the only one to have the experience and that is my authority. There would have been no point anyone else sitting up here. I also sit here alone, without my clerical collar, because I felt strongly that I wanted to present my story to the world directly, as a simple human being, no different to anyone else. I have no idea what the future might hold, but we should all remember that the Visitor has chosen not to communicate with governments or the United Nations. So it isn't a case of my excluding such august institutions, but that they are being bypassed. I think we should be willing to honor the Visitor's wishes."

The reporter had not finished.

"So this is not just another example of the Western World's obsession with individualism?"

Joseph marveled at yet another way in which cultural bias could distort perceptions of the Visitor's presence.

"That is not my motivation." He paused to bring emphasis to his next words. "But perhaps it is part of the Visitor's agenda. For is not the growth of consciousness concerned with an ever-increasing individual experience of reality, in as many minds as possible? Only time will tell, I think."

The woman looked as though she wanted to continue the conversation, but Joseph sensed that it was time to bring the conference to an end. He was tiring, but he also knew that it was better to leave people wanting more, so that what had been said would stay in their minds for longer. He decided to take one more question and then leave, but not to announce this in advance. He wanted to take the security people by surprise.

"Another question, I think."

Hands were raised and Joseph was drawn to a man right at the back, who was very close to some of the bright spotlights that were arrayed around the room. In the glare, the man's features were invisible, yet there was something about him that attracted Joseph. The feeling intensified as a rich, almost musical voice spoke out of the light, in what Joseph judged to be an Indian accent.

"Father Joseph, what do you need us to do?"

There was something about the question that carried great power. Joseph knew this was because it came from the stillness in which he also bathed. It was the stillness speaking to itself. Ultimately, the stillness was not personal. It belonged to no one and expressed itself in infinite ways.

The stillness answered itself.

"I suppose it's very simple, but perhaps too simple. In the time to come we must all be willing to doubt everything we know - and find a deep joy and adventure in this. We must come together as simple human beings, staring in wonder at the mystery of existence, at the astonishing fact of now. We must be prepared to let everything go, so that something incredible may be born. Thank you."

Before anyone could react, Joseph stood and walked quickly from the room. Within seconds he was out in the corridor, shutting the door behind him as the noisy reaction to his departure began. He almost walked into the bishop, who stood there, her face a picture of concern.

"Go quickly," she said. "Those government people. They're going to take you." Then she grabbed his hands. "And look after him. He's all I've got." Before Joseph could reply, she turned and walked away.

Chapter 16

Joseph got to the kitchen as quickly as he could. He had wanted to run, but knew it would draw attention. His heart was pounding and he could feel the adrenaline rising. This was not something he was used to. He had always preferred a good book and a comfortable chair.

Alex was waiting for him, looking anxious.

"Hurry, put this on," he said holding out a yellow workman's jacket with a luminous stripe running across. "We have little time."

Joseph looked at it doubtfully, before doing as instructed.

"Won't we be rather obvious in this?"

Alex shook his head, while putting on a similar jacket.

"On the contrary, we are going to hide in plain sight. We are going to be so visible that no one will be in the least bit suspicious. But we must disguise your face a little, just in case. Put this on as well."

Alex handed Joseph a dark woolly hat and waited while he pulled it over his head.

"Right, come with me."

He led Joseph to the corner of the kitchen and opened a door into a storage room. Although Alex did not turn the light on, all around Joseph could see the vague outline of shelves containing tins of food. At the far end of the room, Joseph's shin connected with something hard. A small cry of pain escaped.

"Sh, you must be quiet." Alex complained, showing little sympathy. "Now, reach down to the box which you just dented and find the rope handle. Lift the box. I will do the same at my end."

Joseph groped down in the dark and encountered a large rectangular wooden box. He felt his way a bit further and soon located the handle. The rope was thick and rough, and Joseph hoped that they would not be carrying the box too far. He had no wish to get blisters. He lifted his end of the box with some effort. It was heavy. Then he felt Alex do the same and the weight, if anything, seemed to increase.

"What have you got in here? It weighs a ton," he whispered.

"Only a few potatoes, they were all I could find. We need to look as though we are carrying something that is real. I am surprised you find it heavy. Perhaps you need to spend more time in the gym."

In the darkness Joseph could not see whether Alex was smiling.

"Now, Father Joseph, in a few moments I am going to open a door and walk outside. We are at the far end of the courtyard and all we are going to do is make our way to the nearest store room in the old stable block. We are going to make no attempt to hide and will simply look like two workmen carrying a large heavy box. I have deliberately made this journey several times over the last few hours wearing this coat, so any observant eyes should not be surprised by what they see. We will resist the temptation to hurry. Do you understand?"

Joseph took a deep breath. His stomach was clenched and he was sweating heavily.

"Yes. Right," was all that came out.

Barely had the words left Joseph's mouth when in front of him a rectangle of semi-light broke the darkness. Alex had opened the door. A tug on the rope handle told Joseph that they were moving. The box was awkward to carry and Joseph immediately hit his shins again on the hard wood as he tried to shuffle along. Fortunately they were out into the courtyard in a few moments and able to adjust their position so that they could walk side by side, with the box hanging between them. They walked slowly across the open courtyard towards the nearest storeroom. It was no more than about twenty yards away, but in the bright moonlight he felt totally exposed. The temperature had fallen and his breath billowing before him did not help to alleviate this feeling.

Then a different kind of chill went through him as he realized that they were not alone. Out of the corner of his eye he saw, at the far end of the courtyard, a group of figures clustered around the large four-wheel drive vehicles that he had seen arrive earlier in the day. He could not help himself, but had to risk a glance to see what they were doing. He was relieved to see that their attention was elsewhere, as they listened to a figure that stood at the center of the huddle. He got the impression that they were receiving instructions on something. With an involuntary shiver, the thought occurred that it might be to do with him. He quickly turned his gaze back to the storeroom they were heading for and tried to focus on that.

In what seemed like both an eternity and an instant, they were there. In a calm and unhurried fashion, Alex opened the door and they edged their way inside, gently closing it behind them. They put down the heavy box with relief. Moonlight seeped through a window and in its eerie glow Joseph and Alex looked at one another and erupted into stifled, tension relieving laughter. Joseph felt exhilarated. For the first time in his life, he began to understand the attraction of dangerous sports. Alex quickly got control of himself and grabbed something off a large hook on the wall.

"Take off your coat and put this on instead. Now we must merge into the darkness."

Joseph removed the luminous jacket that he had worn for no more than a few minutes and donned a dark colored anorak. Alex did the same, in the process catching his arm in the gloom on some unidentifiable machinery. A hissed swear word followed. His English was even better than Joseph had realized.

"My apologies, Father, if I offend your sensibilities, but that hurt. Now we must pull up the hoods on these coats so that our white faces do not shine out of the darkness. It is fortunate that you priests dress in black, otherwise the rest of your clothing might give us away." Alex leaned forward in the dim silvery light and grasped Joseph's arm. "We must move fast. The presence of those men in the courtyard suggests that you will soon be missed. We are going out through the window at the rear of this room and will then follow the perimeter wall. Keep close to me. The wall will put us into shadow, so we should be invisible to anyone looking in our direction."

Alex turned and made his way to the rear window. It was already open and Joseph guessed that Alex had done this earlier as part of his preparations. Within moments they were both outside in a narrow passage, with the rear wall of the storeroom on their left and the high perimeter wall to the right. Above, a slot of starlit sky looked down on them. It caught Joseph's attention and for a few moments something within him lit up. Without hesitation, Alex set off and in the semi-darkness Joseph struggled to keep him in sight. The ground underneath was uneven and Joseph worried that he might stumble. After they had travelled a little way, he began to hear muffled voices to his left and guessed that they must now be approaching the group of security people on the other side of the old stable block. His mouth went dry and he redoubled his efforts to keep up. Joseph was so relieved when the voices faded into the distance, that he lost concentration and collided with Alex who had suddenly stopped. Joseph thought he heard another whispered swear word and was not sure the bishop would approve of her man's bad language. Joseph could see that they had reached the end of the stable block and before them stretched the moonlit lawns which they had walked across earlier that day with Leola. But he could also see that, immediately next to the perimeter wall that ran away from them, was a dark line of shadow. If they kept to that, it should be almost impossible for them to be seen. No sooner had these thoughts crossed his mind than Alex was off again. Crouching as low as they could, they ran forward along the wall. As he ran, Joseph began to wonder where Alex was taking him. So complete was his trust, and so absorbed had he been by the press conference, that he had just done whatever was asked of him. Now, for the first time, he tried to puzzle out Alex's plan of escape. They were going in the direction of the trees and brambles that hid the hermit cell. Perhaps Alex was intending to scale the wall at that point, hidden from view. Yet when they had emerged from the cell earlier that day, they had heard police on the other side of the wall. Joseph realized that Alex must have something else in mind, but could not figure out what it might be.

His thoughts were suddenly interrupted as he sprawled forward, landing on something large and soft. The blow to his chest and midriff forced the air from his lungs with a loud gasp. He froze, waiting for shouts of alarm and lights to be shone in their direction. But nothing happened. The night remained still, with only the distant sound of traffic to be heard. As he lay there, it dawned on him what had cushioned his fall. The large soft lump on which he lay was Alex.

"I tripped," Alex whispered grumpily. "Now get off me so we can get going again. We must hurry."

They got to their feet and continued along the base of the wall. It did not take long to reach the edge of the trees that hid the hermit cell. Alex stopped and turned his head towards Joseph.

"Now we must crawl a little distance. It is the only way to get through the brambles in this place. We cannot risk going to the opening we used earlier. Pull up your hood as far as it will go and tie the drawstrings. It will give some protection from the thorns. Then follow me."

Joseph did not like the sound of this, but did as he was bid. Alex went down on his stomach and began to wriggle forward. Joseph heard the sound of twigs and thorns scraping on the fiber of Alex's coat and realized the good sense of the advice he had been given. As soon as Alex's feet disappeared from view, Joseph lay down and began to inch forward. He clawed at the hard ground, fingers connecting with twigs and half buried roots. He could see nothing except an unfocussed impression of the ground immediately in front of his nose. Through the anorak, he felt the brambles pulling at the fabric, catching for a few moments before giving way. There was an instant of sharp pain as his knee went down on a hard stone, to be followed by a throbbing ache. He bit his lip to avoid crying out and concentrated on moving forward. Then he felt strong hands grab his coat and pull him clear. He got to his feet with difficulty and felt more pain as he tried to put weight on the still aching knee.

"Are you alright?" Alex whispered in the dark.

"Yeah, just banged my knee a bit. I'm sure it'll wear off," Joseph replied trying to sound confident.

"O.K., let's keep going then," Alex said as he turned and moved away.

There was just enough moonlight filtering through the branches to be able to see. Slowly and carefully they wound their way through the trees, trying to make as little sound as possible on the cold crunchy ground. At first, Joseph had to limp along, but after a short while, to his great relief, the knee began to recover. Then, suddenly, they were in the clearing, with the vague outline of the hermit cell forming a dark shape a little way in front. Alex held up his hand to signal Joseph to stop and put his finger to his lips. They stood very still, listened and, sure enough, heard muted voices from behind the dark line of the wall about fifty feet away. The police were still there. Alex made his way forward very slowly, intent on making no sound. Joseph crept along behind, stepping as gently as he could. It reminded him of a time when he had stalked a rabbit while on a country walk with Clare. They had spotted it munching away on some grass and she had bet that he would not be able to get within ten feet before it ran off. With enormous care he had managed to steal almost up to the rabbit before it bolted. Clare had said that she was very proud of her hunter-gatherer husband and that she now knew they would be fine if civilization came to an end.

Overhead, a cloud went in front of the moon and the light became even dimmer. But Alex did not stop and soon they were at the steps leading down into the hermit cell. Carefully, they found their way down the treacherous stones and, looking over Alex's shoulder, Joseph could just make out that the door to the cell was open. Clearly, this was another example of Alex's preparations. They felt their way inside, Joseph trying to remember the layout of the room to avoid tripping over anything. Then Alex whispered in his ear.

"The torch."

At first, Joseph did not understand what he meant, before remembering the lump in his jacket pocket. He unzipped the anorak and pulled out the small torch that Alex had given him earlier. He put his hand over the bulb before turning it on, so that light did not spill out through the open doorway. He then carefully removed his hand, making sure that the torch was directed towards the far corner of the room. As he did so, Alex gently closed the door. It made no sound and Joseph guessed that Alex must have put a lot of lubricant on the hinges since their earlier visit. Once the door was finally shut, in the limited light of the torch, Joseph saw Alex lean back against it, put his hands on his knees and let out a huge sigh. Then he looked up at Joseph and slowly his face cracked into a huge smile and a slow, rumbling laugh found its way to the surface.

"Now that was exciting. Takes me back to my younger days in Athens. I had forgotten how good the fear feels."

Joseph knew what he meant. He felt intensely alive, but terrified at the same time.

"Perhaps I missed my real vocation, Alex. Maybe I should have been a spy."

"Hah! With all due respect, Father Joseph, you are no James Bond." Alex straightened up and moved towards the rear of the chamber where his cardboard box of wonders still lay against the wall.

"Shine the torch over there please, Father."

Joseph did as he was asked and watched as Alex's hand reached down into the box, moved a few things around and re-emerged holding a large powerful flashlight.

"We will need more than your little torch for where we are going," he commented.

Joseph could contain his curiosity no longer.

"Alex, what do you mean? We're still in the grounds of the house. How are we going to escape from this hole in the ground - nice though it is?"

Alex said nothing, but just switched on his flashlight and moved the beam theatrically along the wall until it illuminated the second mysterious door, which Joseph had spotted that afternoon.

"I recommend that you fasten your coat, Father, for where we are going is rather wet."

Joseph stared at him for a few moments and then decided that further questions were pointless. Alex's love of mystery and theatre were too great. Carefully holding the torch between his teeth, he reached down and re-zipped his coat, watching as Alex moved to the second door and slowly drew back two large bolts. In the illumination provided by Alex's flashlight, Joseph could see that the bolts and hinges were covered in thick grease. Alex saw him notice.

"It took me quite a while and a lot of effort to free this door after I first found the cell. It had not been opened for many years."

Once the bolts were free, Alex loosened the latch and pulled the door open. He had obviously done his work well and no sound came from the decrepit, rusting hinges. The door opened wide to reveal utter blackness beyond. The only indication of what lay ahead was the occasional echoing sound of dripping water and a waft of dank moldy air. Alex shone his flashlight into the doorway and Joseph could see a series of steps going down into the darkness.

"What is it?"

"Our escape tunnel," Alex whispered mischievously. "It will be just like a war film. Follow me and walk carefully. The steps are covered in lichen and very slippery."

Joseph followed Alex into the tunnel and immediately discovered the truth of what he had been told about the steps, as his foot went from underneath him. His hands shot sideways in a reflex action and he managed to steady himself against the walls. He decided to keep his hands there as he cautiously advanced. He noticed that his palms were against stone, not soil, and realized that the tunnel must have been carved through bedrock. As he looked more closely in the wavering torch light he could see chisel marks in the stone. After going down about twenty steps they reached the bottom and Joseph could see the passage running away in front. In the distance, at the limit of Alex's flashlight, it curved away to the right. The walls were now very wet and he could see large pools had gathered in the uneven parts of the floor. Some were so wide that they would have little choice but to walk through them. Joseph hoped that they were not too deep. The damp moldy smell was now very strong. In the distance was another sound, faint but clearly discernable. It was the sound of running water.

"We are lucky that it has been a cold dry winter," Alex said over his shoulder, as if reading Joseph's thoughts. "When there has been much rain, the pools down here can be very deep."

"What is this?"

"Be patient my friend, soon all will become clear."

With this, Alex set off down the tunnel, splashing through the pools, the beam from the flashlight bouncing off the walls. Joseph followed, finding that he had to crouch slightly to avoid scraping his head against the roof. This did not stop drips of water wetting his hair and running down his neck. He swiftly raised the hood of his coat for protection. At first he tried to avoid the pools, but found this was impossible and so tried to accept with equanimity the freezing cold water that filled his shoes. As he walked along he noticed small niches cut into the wall, similar to those in the hermit cell itself. He guessed that candles would at one time have flickered away, casting their uncertain light through the tunnel. Yet why an ornamental hermit would have needed such a tunnel was beyond him.

The explanation began to reveal itself as they turned the corner at the end of the passage. Alex stopped and beckoned Joseph to stand by his side. At first Joseph was bemused as he did not think there would be enough space, but as he moved forward he realized that the tunnel had ended and they were standing on a large platform cut into the rock. He tried to shine his small torch around to get a sense of where they were, but its light would not reach the far wall. He then knew that they must be in some kind of cavern.

"I will show you," Alex said. "We are standing on a rock-cut platform that stands about four feet above the floor of the cave."

As he spoke, Alex shone the much more powerful flashlight along the surface on which they stood. Joseph could see that it was about eight feet wide and ten feet long. Away to his left, some steps led down onto the main floor. The beam then took in the rest of the chamber and Joseph caught his breath as a sea of multicolored reflections sparkled into life as the light touched them. He saw that elegant stalactites and stalagmites decorated much of the space, and were coated in whatever caused the twinkling colors.

"There are small crystals and jewels set into the walls. Two hundred years ago, the chamber would have been illuminated by many candles and the effect would have been bewitching. The stalactites and stalagmites are artificial, created when the cave was carved from the rock, but are no less impressive for that."

The flashlight then found its way across the floor, revealing a narrow, but fast-moving stream that tumbled along an artistically carved channel. It emerged from a hole in the farthest wall of the cavern and exited out of a similar, but slightly larger gap at the other end.

"I think that the stream must have been diverted from elsewhere, but I have not been able to find the source," Alex explained.

"What was this place for?" Joseph asked as his eyes drank in the amazing light show.

"It is the grotto where the hermit would be displayed to the landowner's friends. He would sit on the platform, immobile and apparently at prayer while the nobility gazed on. I think the cell was a more private place."

"It must have been an amazing sight," Joseph remarked, his eyes still mesmerized by the cave.

"Indeed, and I think only visited by myself in a very long time."

Joseph thought back to the route they had followed. He began to understand Alex's plan.

"This tunnel goes under the road. We're in the arboretum!"

"That is correct. The tunnel predates the road by centuries. It is cut deep into the rock and so was not revealed when the road was laid down. The tunnel and cell must have been made to give the hermit some privacy. There are hints in the records that the cell was constructed for William Stokes, years after the grotto was first established. It is maybe a sign of the esteem in which he was held."

"I visited the arboretum with Clare a couple of years ago. I don't remember seeing the grotto and no one's ever mentioned it to me."

"I think that after Stokes's death the entrance was sealed and it eventually faded from memory. The records are not complete and so I am only guessing. But, think harder my friend. You saw the stream did you not?" Alex shone the flashlight along the running water.

"Yes, I remember it well. It runs in a small valley through the arboretum. It never occurred to me to question where it came from."

"No. And so it has been for many years. From the outside, it just appears to emerge from a cleft in the rock. Yet if anyone were to look closer they would see that what appears to be stone is, in fact, a wall which is so old and covered in moss and ivy that it seems natural.

Joseph looked around in wonder, until the urgency of their situation suddenly reasserted itself.

"Alex, this is all very interesting, but how do we get out of here if the cavern is sealed?"

Alex sighed. "I'm afraid, Father, that it means getting very wet."

Joseph did not have time to reply before Alex marched off towards the steps. Joseph hurried after him, the thin light from his torch a poor relation to the Greek's powerful flashlight. They found their way carefully across the damp lichen covered floor to where the stream found its way outside.

"We go through there," Alex said, pointing towards the hole.

Joseph looked down and could not believe what he was seeing. The fast moving water appeared to be at least a couple of feet deep and there could be no more than the same distance between the surface and the height of the opening. He looked at Alex, unable to say a word.

"Do not worry, Father Joseph, I have been along the passage before and it is only a few feet before we reach the outside. We will just get a little wet along the way. The material at the end is very weak with age and I am sure that I can knock it aside without trouble."

Joseph was suspicious.

"And what month of the year did you undertake this journey,

Alex?"

"Oh, August, and I have to admit that the water was much lower."

Joseph made to argue, but in the same instant knew there was no point. It was this or go back. It was time to plunge in again, but literally on this occasion.

"Let's go," was all that came out.

Alex stepped down into the stream, emitting yet another swear word as the cold bit into him. He turned to Joseph, taking a deep breath as he tried to adjust to the freezing water.

"Come on, Father Joseph. The sooner we begin, the sooner it is over."

Joseph gathered himself and then stepped into the flow. The cold stopped him in his tracks. It felt as if his legs had been encased in ice. But Alex gave him no time to think and crawled into the opening, flashlight glinting off the surface of the water. Joseph lowered himself, gasping as the cold slid up his body. Then, to his surprise, it got easier. He suspected his brain had reached some sensation threshold where a trip-switch had flipped to an off position. He held his small torch between his teeth and crawled after Alex, being pushed along by the current. He did not have far to go. The opening was only about six feet deep. In blocking the entrance to the grotto, the nineteenth century workmen had erected two walls and filled the gap between them with rubble, leaving a small protected tunnel for the stream. He had only just got into the constricted space when he had to stop. Ahead was Alex, banging away with the sturdy flashlight at the outer wall. All Joseph could do was watch the freezing water stream between his arms, a few inches from his face. A violent shiver went through him. Even though he had become almost immune to the cold, it was having an effect on his body. He wondered how long it would be before serious damage was done. His morbid thoughts were interrupted by Alex.

"Yes!" his Greek friend exclaimed triumphantly.

Joseph looked up and saw that the light in front had changed. It had become more silvery and pervasive. Before he could ponder why this might be, Alex was gone. It took Joseph a few seconds to realize what had happened, before he plunged forward into the gap that Alex must have created. The surging water now came to his aid and he was almost carried through the outer wall into the night air. The next moment he was being pulled from the water. They waited together on the bank, regaining their breath. Joseph looked around and in the dim moonlight saw the outline of the hole from which they had just emerged. He looked up and noticed the rise in the ground on which he and Clare had once stood. He realized that they must have been almost directly over the grotto.

Alex's hand touched his arm.

"Come, Father, we must hurry. Friends are waiting for us. Turn off your torch, so its light does not give us away."

Joseph took the torch from his mouth and did as he was asked. He had actually forgotten that it was there.

"Friends?" he enquired of Alex.

"Yes, but no time to explain. We could not do this alone. Now we must make for the far wall where there is another entrance to the arboretum. But do not run. We cannot see properly and must not risk falling."

Alex headed off down a path away from the hidden grotto. Joseph followed, marveling that he was not exhausted and frozen to the core. He now understood the power of adrenalin. As they walked, he suddenly felt a need to look upwards. The glimpse of the night sky at the back of the storeroom had worked its magic. The night was not so clear now, but through the branches many stars could still be seen. He wondered what Alex and he would look like from such a distance and how unimportant their dramas. Even now, in the midst of such adventure, he wanted to be out there among the stars, swimming in the blackness. He had wanted this since he could first remember and it had never been as strong. He had no doubt that this was connected with the Visitor. For the first time it occurred to him that this deep desire might be connected with his singling out. It was too overwhelming an insight and he quickly suppressed it.

It took them only a few minutes to reach the far wall. Despite Alex's warning, they had found themselves breaking into a gentle trot.

"Shine your little torch on the wall for me, Father."

Joseph did so and saw in front of them an old wooden door that filled an archway in the high wall. It was identical to the one by which Clare and he had entered on their visit. Alex searched with his hand in the thick ivy on either side and then pulled out a large cast-iron key. Within moments the gate was open and they stepped through onto a dirt road that wound its way across undistinguished, moonlit heathland. To his right, not far away, Joseph could see the lights of the nearby housing estate. After the excitement of the escape and the intensity of their underground journey, the sudden stillness and silence felt slightly strange and he gave himself a few seconds to adjust. As he did so, he heard Alex doing something on his mobile phone, before breathing a sigh of relief and putting it back in his pocket.

"We are lucky it still works, Father. I forgot to take it out of my pocket when we went through the stream. Fortunately it survived the water."

"What would have happened if it hadn't worked?"

Alex did not reply, but in the dim light he looked at Joseph and smiled. Joseph felt a shiver go through him, but he was not sure if it was from cold or fear at what might have been.

"Now we wait, Father. It should not be many minutes."

Joseph did not bother to ask what they were waiting for. He knew Alex well enough by now to know that he would not get a straight answer. He concentrated on burying himself more deeply into his coat as the shivering intensified. His knee was also starting to hurt again and he surmised that the adrenalin rush was now exhausted. Fortunately, he did not have long to wait as within a minute or so headlights appeared at the end of the track where it merged into the lights of the estate. The twin beams approached slowly, treating the potholed track with respect. For a moment, Joseph's heart was in his mouth as through the gloom he recognized a four-wheel drive vehicle with black tinted windows.

"Do not worry, Father Joseph, this is one of ours," Alex interjected, sensing Joseph's alarm.

The vehicle stopped in front of them and the rear door opened.

"In we go. You first, Father," Alex instructed.

Joseph climbed into the back with difficulty. His body was aching all over and had no energy left. Alex leapt in behind him. Joseph found himself sitting behind two men who neither spoke nor acknowledged the presence of Alex and himself. He found this unnerving and looked at Alex. The Greek just shook his head and put his finger to his lips. No sooner was Alex in, than the vehicle moved off through the night. In the darkness, out of habit, Joseph tried to find the seat belt as they bumped along, but gave up as his exhausted body would not function properly. He was now shivering constantly and the pain from his knee had become excruciating. He settled back in the seat and just surrendered to the situation. He was too tired to do anything else. He eyes drifted to the glowing clock at the center of the dashboard, causing him to sit up straight again in disbelief at what he saw. The escape felt as if it had lasted a lifetime. Yet the clock told him that less than twenty minutes had elapsed since he left the press conference.

Joseph fell back into the seat and gave up trying to think.

Chapter 17

Joseph stopped and looked out over the great plain of Thessaly. The steep climb up the narrow rock-cut steps had left him out of breath and his knee had started to ache again. He was grateful for the opportunity to recover.

It was early evening and the sun had already sunk below the mountains to the west, but there was still enough light to see. In the distance the Peneios River wound its way across a vast, spacious patchwork of green and brown fields. Clusters of houses with red roofs and white walls, appearing tiny from his great height, littered the plain. Occasionally they huddled in small settlements. Joining them together, thin ligaments of tarmac grey snaked across the immense area of land that stretched away to yet more mountains in the distance. Here and there, diminutive points of light crawled along the roads as car drivers navigated the twilight. It was cold and there was a slight drizzle, but it was an improvement on the weather he had left behind in England. Only twenty-four hours earlier he had been sitting before the world's media. Now he was hidden away in northern Greece, his whereabouts known only to a handful of people. It was a great relief.

Then, just for a moment, Joseph wobbled slightly as mild vertigo swept over him. Although the sensation did not last for more than a few seconds, it affected his confidence. He had never been particularly afraid of heights, but he was standing on the summit of a narrow pinnacle of rock over a thousand feet tall, which had its roots in the foothills of a range of majestic mountains. His reaction was understandable. He looked around the dark grey sandstone plateau, no more than a few hundred yards wide in any direction, for a suitable boulder or outcrop of rock on which to sit. He walked carefully across the undulating cracked surface, avoiding the dark green scrub that clung onto the rock wherever it could get a foothold. It was with a feeling of thankfulness that he spotted a solid looking outcrop with comfortable contours. He sat down and immediately felt better. A sudden gust of wind blew the drizzle against his face, but he did not raise the hood of his trusty anorak. It felt good and clean. It brought with it a sense of being alive and connected with nature. A thought struck him and he paused to listen carefully. He was surprised to discover that he could not hear any sound apart from the gentle moan of the wind and the almost imperceptible patter of drizzle on his coat. Even the birds were silent. Perhaps they were already roosting, snug against the damp cold.

The pinnacle of rock on which he sat was but one of a range of precipitous steeples that rose from the north-western edge of the Thessalonian plain. Cut by water, wind and temperature from the cracked sandstone of an ancient seabed long ago raised from the ocean floor, they resembled gigantic fissured stalagmites. As Joseph raised his eyes from the plain and looked around at the other rocky pillars, with their wonderful variety of shapes and sizes, he could see on some the attribute that made the Metéora rocks famous. Here and there, on the top of pinnacles or carefully molded into small gorges and ledges in the rock face, were the monasteries of the Greek Orthodox Church that had been present in some form for at least six hundred years. Before that, hermits had climbed virtually sheer rock faces seeking safety, solitude and an inspirational setting for prayer. As the monastic buildings had developed, many had remained accessible only via rope ladders or baskets hauled from far above, requiring strong nerves from both monk and visitor alike. Only in recent times had the surviving communities relented and cut daunting steps into cliff faces or built bridges from adjacent rocks to make access easier. Over the centuries many communities had been established, but the ravages of more recent history had reduced this number to only a few. Joseph knew that many of the buildings he could see would be empty shells. Alex had already told him that a few years earlier the community with whom they were staying had quietly taken over such a deserted monastery.

As Joseph looked around, Clare came to mind, as she had frequently over the last couple of hours. They had been planning to visit Greece when she had died. The eerie coincidence had struck him. Both had always been drawn to this mysterious, mythical country where western civilization had its roots. They had read extensively and worked out a detailed itinerary of all the places they would visit. And Metéora, with its amazing landscape, had been top of the list.

In that moment he missed her greatly.

He took a deep breath and made an effort to get his mind onto other things. Now that the fear and excitement of the last twenty-four hours were over, Joseph suspected that he had gone into a dilute form of shock. The result was that his deep need for Clare, which had faded a little, had returned re-energized. She had always been the one who understood and helped him cope with the challenges of life.

Yet it was not the shock that was the problem. He could cope with that.

What was beginning to really worry him was that his mind was a mess.

It was why he had climbed the steep, damp steps to get to this place. During the climb his thoughts had calmed a little as he had focused on putting one foot in front of the other, but now that he was still again, the frenzied mental chaos was returning in full force.

Since he had awakened a little while before, something had snapped. His mind had been strained beyond its limit over the past two days. It had been filled to overflowing to such an extent that it could absorb no more and had gone into freefall. It seemed to be almost outside his control, as it leapt from one train of ideas to another. As he tried to get a grip on one lot of thoughts, another forced its way in and, before he knew what was happening, had taken over. As a result, everything was becoming an insurmountable problem. Everything was wrong. He was starting to feel angry and depressed. He had no doubt that the future held even more extraordinary experiences, but he could not imagine being able to cope. A quiet panic was beginning to take over.

With a huge effort, he turned his thoughts to his escape from the bishop's house and the subsequent extraordinary journey to Greece. He hoped that following the story methodically in his mind would help bring some calm.

Whoever Alex's shadowy friends were, they had known what they were doing. After being collected by the silent men in the four-wheel drive vehicle, the road journey had been short. Within hardly any time they had pulled into the entrance of a small private airfield where a light aircraft had been waiting with its propeller whirling. As he had climbed into the plane, through the back draft, a whiff of exhaust fumes had imprinted itself onto his memory. Even now, gazing out over the Thessalonian plain from his rocky crow's nest, he could recall the pungent smell. A cramped bumpy journey of about half an hour had brought them to a major airport, which in the darkness Joseph had been unable to identify. It had just been a mass of lights, subdivided by large patches of darkness. After landing, the plane had gone under its own power straight into a large hanger at the edge of the complex. The building had been brilliantly lit inside and the sudden illumination had been magnified through the rivulets of water running down the windows of the small aircraft, causing his eyes to hurt. As the discomfort had died away, Joseph had been able to watch as they carefully maneuvered alongside a small executive jet. Within moments of pulling up alongside the sleek airplane, he and Alex had been bundled unceremoniously from one machine to the other. Waiting inside was a steward who had directed them to their seats and made sure their safety belts were properly fastened. Even while this was happening, Joseph had been able to feel and hear the engines of the aircraft come alive and within moments they had been outside the hanger taxiing for take-off. He had gazed around the small plane as much as he could given the constraints of the seat belt and had been pretty sure that, apart from the crew, he and Alex had been the only passengers. It was only as they were soaring into the air that Joseph had realized anxiously that he did not have his passport with him. He had mentioned it to Alex, who had laughed and assured him that it would not be a problem. As Joseph thought about it, he could see Alex's point. He was pretty sure that they had just left Britain illegally, so it had seemed a good bet that Alex's powerful friends had the next bit worked out too.

After that he had dozed fitfully between cups of coffee provided by the steward. He had managed to force down a couple of sandwiches, but his stomach had not really wanted to know about food. Time had passed slowly, with only intermittent conversation with Alex. Joseph had wanted to know more about where they were going, but had received only evasive replies. He had also asked about the people who had arranged his escape, but with the same result. Joseph had not been able to work out whether Alex was simply being his usual enigmatic self, or was disinclined to talk. Joseph suspected that at least some of the reticence was rooted in the latter and it occurred to him that leaving Jennifer behind to face the music on her own was not resting easily with Alex. After a couple of hours Joseph had sensed a change in the feel of the plane and, looking out, had seen that they were now descending through the darkness. Craning his neck to see forward, at first he had been unable to see anything through the vague billowing mass of cloud. Then they had broken through and he had seen a vast spread of light below that could only be a major city. Ten minutes later they had landed and the plane was maneuvered over to a corner of the airfield. In the darkness, Joseph had initially been able to see the vague outlines of commercial aircraft, but after a while this had been replaced by what he was sure were military silhouettes. A car had been waiting and they had been whisked off into the night, emerging from the airport onto brightly lit, but mainly deserted city streets. Joseph had guessed that wherever he was, it must be late. It was as they had stopped at traffic lights that he had realized where they were, at least in general terms, as he saw road signs with Greek lettering. It had not been a great surprise. Greece was where Alex's contacts were based and it was an obvious place to hide him out of sight.

Even then, the bitter-sweet memory of the visit he and Clare had planned had come to mind.

The lights had then changed and they had zoomed off through the streets, eventually leaving the city and heading out into more rural areas. The rest of the journey had been a blur of shadowy images. There had been no moonlight. The cloud through which they had flown had been too thick. The indistinct outlines of innumerable olive trees and immense mountains had been broken only by the empty streets of small, unnamed towns as they sped through. Eventually, the car had wound its way up narrow switchback roads carved into the side of a range of mountains that loomed over them in the darkness. Looking from his position in the back of the car, Joseph had caught glimpses of precipitous drops and sheer rock faces as the headlights had swept along. Although invisible in the darkness, he had realized that in daylight the drive would have been spectacular.

The end of the journey had taken him by surprise. One moment they had been driving along, zigzagging their way around hairpin bends and the next they were pulling to a halt in a small grassy space by the side of the road.

"We get out here." Alex had instructed.

The car had driven away as soon as they were out and they had listened as the sound of its engine had quickly faded into the distance. Then they had just waited in the dark chilly silence, somehow aware of the towering mountains all around even though they were virtually invisible. They had not spoken. Joseph had run out of things to say and Alex seemed to have gone deep into himself. It was Joseph who had first seen the light. It had seemed to be floating unsteadily in the air, while it slowly descended The effect had confused Joseph who had wondered if he was seeing a distant aircraft through turbulent atmosphere, until he realized it was set against the dim outline of a mass of rock. He had broken the silence and drawn Alex's attention to it.

"Ah, they are coming down for us," he had replied, starting to get a little more cheerful. "Soon, Father Joseph, we will be in a warm bed."

Joseph had not asked more questions. He was learning. Instead he had just watched as the light became stronger and eventually ceased its descent. A few moments later a female voice had called out to them in Greek from the darkness, to which Alex had responded.

"Come, Father, we must go," he had said, touching Joseph's arm before moving off towards the light.

Joseph had followed, stumbling in the darkness over uneven ground. Then a brainwave had struck and he had taken from his pocket the small torch that he had brought all the way from England. Its light, though dim, had been useful and reassuring. They had soon come to the source of the light and Joseph had immediately recognized a nun of the Orthodox Church, carrying a large electric lantern. Her young white face, eerily framed by a black veil, had almost appeared to be floating in the air as her even blacker robe melted into the background. She had greeted Alex quietly, but it had been clear to Joseph that they knew each other well. Then she had turned and walked towards the almost invisible rock face that reared over them. Alex had signaled Joseph to follow and had then brought up the rear. After a few yards they had come to an area of sloping rock and Joseph had struggled to make his way up the steep, smooth incline. The grunting from behind had told him that Alex was also struggling. The young nun leading them had gone up easily, giving the impression of barely touching the ground, and had waited for them where the sloping surface met the cliff face. She had then led them along the top of the slope until they had come to a deep vertical fissure in the rock face. She had turned into the cleft and, in the light provided by the lantern, Joseph had seen narrow steps cut into the rock a few yards ahead disappearing upwards into the darkness. It had been a long climb as, like the road they had been on, the steps had wound their way backwards and forwards up the side of the mighty crack in the rock. Joseph had been glad that in the darkness he could not see the mind-numbing drop that must be waiting for him should he slip. He had lost track of how many turns they had made, let alone the number of steps they had climbed. All he had known after a while was that his legs, and especially his knee, could take no more. He had been summoning up the nerve to ask for a rest when suddenly they had burst out onto a perfectly flat surface. Joseph had directed his little torch downwards and seen beautifully laid flagstones. He had then shone the torch a little further and in the barely adequate light had gained the impression of a large courtyard. The nun had led them across the flagstones and a large building had loomed out of the darkness. A door had then opened, flooding the immediate area around the entrance with dim yellowy light.

Joseph and Alex had followed the nun inside and found themselves in a wide candle-lit passageway. In the distance they had been able to hear the unmistakable sound of Orthodox chant, with the deep visceral drone of the bases harmoniously overlaid by the more delicate sound of higher pitched voices. An early morning office had been in progress. It was a sound with which Joseph was familiar, but something had nagged at him, taking a few moments to pin down. Then he had realized what it was. He could hear quite clearly both male and female voices. This had been a complete surprise. It seemed that the monastery housed both nuns and monks. He had never heard of such a practice before.

The walls of the passageway were unplastered and made of large, smooth stone blocks. Beautiful gold candle-holders were spaced regularly down the length of each wall, the light from the flickering flames shimmering in the gleaming metal. But it had been the ceiling that had caught Joseph's attention. It was covered in a magnificent fresco of the Last Supper, with Jesus at the center, hands holding out the broken bread of the Mass towards the viewer. It was so well painted that it looked almost three-dimensional and Joseph had felt himself being pulled into the image. Suddenly the vision he had experienced at the Mass on the day the Visitor arrived had come to mind, almost causing him to gasp out loud. He knew in that moment that the vision and the fresco were linked; that one presaged the other. Then he remembered his even earlier dream when he had met his brothers. Once more he knew that he had glimpsed the deeply connected story of which he was a part.

Alex and the nun had noticed his reaction.

"Are you alright, Father?" Alex had enquired.

"I'm more than alright, Alex. This fresco is magnificent and I feel as though I've seen it before … in a vision. How old is it? Who's the artist?"

Alex had looked both pleased and embarrassed at the same time.

"Er… well … actually it is modern, only painted a few years ago when this monastery was revived. Your reaction to it is most … gratifying."

Joseph had been going to ask again about the artist when the truth had dawned on him. Alex was the artist. Joseph had stared at him, awed by his skill. This was no ordinary painting, but an icon in the true sense of the word. It was not just a picture, but a doorway through which the mind was drawn into profound relationship with what lay behind the image. It could only have been painted from the depths of illumined consciousness. And that he should have seen it in advance, in a vision, both inspired and shook Joseph. He had managed with difficulty to drag his eyes from the fresco and once more engage with Alex and the nun. He had immediately noticed that she was looking at him and realized that it was the first time she had done this. Her gaze was direct and welcoming. He suspected that his reaction to the fresco had made her see him in a new and approving way. She had smiled at him before turning to Alex. A brief conversation in Greek had followed and she had then walked away in the direction of the chanting. As she had gone through a door at the end of the corridor the chanting had briefly grown louder, before returning to its previous level. A whiff of incense had drifted from the direction of the door as it had closed after her.

"We must look after ourselves for a while as the sisters and brothers will be at prayer for some time," Alex had informed him in a quiet voice. "I know my way around, so it shouldn't be a problem."

He had then led the way to a side door, which he had opened and beckoned Joseph to go through. Before doing so, however, Joseph had been unable to resist a final glance at the fresco on the ceiling.

"Alex, it's wonderful."

"Father, you are too kind. To God be the glory," Alex had bumbled in reply. Then he had sighed and looked sad. "Perhaps one day Jennifer will come here and see my work."

Joseph's heart had gone out to his friend.

"When I get back, I will tell her all about it."

Alex had looked pleased at these words, before ushering him through the door and up the spiral staircase that lay beyond. They had breakfasted in an empty refectory on bread, feta cheese, olives and tomatoes. Alex had then shown Joseph to a small room, simply furnished with a bed and a few other items. On the bed had been a pair of old-fashioned looking pajamas.

"Leave your clothes neatly folded outside the door and they will be cleaned and repaired while you sleep," Alex had instructed before leaving. Out of shyness, Joseph had not intended to comply. But then he had noticed the battered state of what he was wearing. He had stripped off completely, washed in a sink in the corner of the room, put on the pajamas and then placed his clothes where he had been instructed. He had collapsed into bed and his last coherent memory was of dawn light beginning to filter through a small window.

Joseph had slept for most of the day, waking up disorientated and leaden. When he had worked out where he was, he had splashed his face with water and searched for his clothes before remembering what he had done with them. Sheepishly, he had put his head outside the door and discovered them waiting for him in almost mint condition. He had no idea how this had been achieved so quickly. He had dressed, hesitating as his hand encountered the white strip of plastic in his jacket pocket. After a few moments thought, he had left it where it was. With some trepidation he had then made his way to the refectory. He was always nervous with new people, in new surroundings. It was part of his shyness. He had been relieved when the only person he encountered was Alex, sitting at one of the long tables with a mug of coffee. He had been greeted like a long lost brother and had suspected that his Greek friend had been waiting for him to emerge. After Joseph had helped himself to some coffee and milopita, a traditional Greek apple cake, they had talked for a while about nothing in particular. Joseph had realized that neither of them wanted to wrestle with anything weighty. There had been so much to say, but it was not the time. The elephant in the room would have to wait.

Yet after a while, even this began to feel too much for Joseph. It was when he had begun to realize that something was wrong with his mind. Suddenly he had felt that he could not take in one more idea or word. The desultory conversation had rambled on a bit longer, but Joseph had known that he had to do something. Interrupting, he had asked Alex whether there was anywhere he could go to be alone. He had felt so bad that he had not cared if Alex thought him rude and took offence. His Greek friend had looked at him thoughtfully for a few moments in silence.

"Of course, Father," he had replied. He had then leaned over the table and gently gripped Joseph's hand. "Do not worry. I will help you in any way I can."

It had brought a lump to Joseph's throat.

After collecting his coat, Alex had led him out onto the paved forecourt to the monastery where they had arrived the previous night. On the way they had passed some monks and nuns who had not acknowledged them. Alex had whispered that they spent much of their time in silence, which must be respected. Joseph had no problem with this. Years before, prior to meeting Clare, he had been drawn to the monastic life and had seriously considered joining one of the contemplative silent orders. In the end, however, he had not quite been able to do it. It stirred something deep within his soul, but also, for reasons he could not understand, it had felt like a backward step. He had an intuitive feeling that it was something that had been done and must now be left behind; that much of its attraction for him had its roots in feelings of familiarity and security. At the time he had not been able to understand such feelings. Now he had strong suspicions as to what lay behind them.

As Alex had led the way across the large forecourt Joseph had been able to see what he had missed in the darkness the night before. At the front edge, at the opposite side to the monastery, was a curved stone balustrade that marked the top edge of a sheer cliff face, several hundred feet high. Joseph had broken away from Alex and gingerly peered over the edge. He had been able to pick out the rocky stairway which they had ascended in the darkness and, beyond it, the slim ribbon of road they must have driven along. He had then turned away from the balustrade and examined the monastery itself. The forecourt was roughly semi-circular, about forty feet wide at its maximum depth, with its straight side against the building. Tastefully positioned around it were large tubs and troughs that Joseph guessed would start to come alive with flowers once the better weather arrived. The building itself was tucked beneath a massive outcrop of rock below the summit of the pinnacle and had been constructed from the same dark grey stone. Joseph had wondered if the cavity in which the building rested had been carved out of the cliff face and the stone used in its construction. Regardless, the result was that it blended into the background almost perfectly. From even a short distance, it would be wonderfully camouflaged. It was hidden in plain sight, just as Alex and he had been the night before as they crossed another courtyard. Joseph had then wondered for a few moments whether this was more than just coincidence. Perhaps this was a theme that manifested in myriad ways within Alex's group.

"What an amazing place," he had said to Alex.

"Indeed. Perhaps later there will be time to tell you a little more about it." Alex had then pointed to a set of steps in the far corner of the courtyard that ascended a short way before disappearing around a rocky outcrop. "Follow the path to the top and you will find the place you need. But do not be gone longer than an hour or so, for tonight we are honored. We will dine privately with the Hegumeni and Hegumen; the Abbess and the Abbot. There is much to discuss." Then, to Joseph's great surprise, Alex had given him a hug before walking back towards the monastery.

So now Joseph sat with his eyes fixed on an impossibly distant horizon, attempting to bring some order to his mind. Yet the more he tried, the more confused and hyperactive his thinking became. His thoughts went around in circles of infinite regression. The illumined consciousness and the deep sense of inner guidance that had been so strong seemed but a dream in his present condition. He could not imagine ever experiencing them again.

Then he remembered what he had encouraged parishioners to do when their minds were full of worries and confusion. It was strange how difficult it could be to take one's own advice.

He remembered to pray.

He began to talk to God.

He talked to him as a listening friend, not caring what was said, except that it be the truth of how he was feeling.

At first he was self-conscious and his words were wooden, but then he recalled how he had talked to Clare only a couple of mornings before. This helped. Gradually he lost himself in the experience and before long he could not stop talking. It poured out. He described everything that had happened, shared all his hopes and fears, and slowly the pressure in his mind began to ease. Speaking these things out loud to someone who truly listened, enabled a stillness to descend. The frantic demons of his mind were gently exorcised.

And he knew that someone was listening.

He knew this in the same way he had known when he encountered a different kind of "someone" in the blue beam of light outside his church.

It was a primal knowing.

After a while, the talking naturally faded away, spent and drained of energy. His mind became very quiet and, without effort, he started to become extraordinarily aware of the moment and place that he occupied in the universe. His mind, that had been spread wafer thin across the past and future, began to concentrate naturally in the eternal now. Mental time dissolved, deprived of the energy on which it depended. Everything that he could feel, see and hear became incredibly intense and alive. There was a deep sense of oneness with all that existed. The illumined consciousness, that had seemed so impossibly distant only a short while before, was back.

The sound of a distant bell restored him to the normal world. It was not an awakening, for what he had tasted was an extraordinary experience of acute wakefulness, but a return to a more thought-based expression of consciousness. He guessed that the sound was coming from the monastery that lay beneath the rock on which he sat. And he knew that bells in monastic communities meant that something was about to happen. He remembered what Alex had said about dining with the Hegumeni and Hegumen. It was likely the bell meant that it was dinner time. He also recalled Alex saying that there was much to discuss. At the time, Joseph's mind had recoiled from the prospect. Now he welcomed it.

He stood up, taking a long final look at the Thessalonian plain that stretched away into the distance. Then he turned and made his way back to the steps.

Chapter 18

It was almost dark as Joseph descended the steps that led back to the monastery forecourt. He kept his hand against the rock face as an anchor and gradually found himself marveling that the grainy surface that pressed against his palm had once been desert, then the bottom of some exotic ocean, before mighty seismic upheaval had raised it to the heavens as a glorious range of mountains. As the thought sank in, it literally stopped him in his tracks. He stood in the dark, running fingertips over the rock, becoming aware of every nuance of texture and shape. He began to sense the age of the rock, not as an abstract number, but as an atmosphere, an ancient presence with which he joined. It brought with it a profound appreciation of his own firefly existence and the passing nature of the challenges that lay ahead, extraordinary though they were. In that dark, damp rocky place, life felt a little less personal.

After a few minutes, the intense connection with the rock began to fade and he resumed the descent. By the time he reached the paved forecourt, night had fallen and he struggled to see. At first it surprised him that there was no lighting, until he remembered the community's obvious preference for privacy. They wanted no lights shining out that could be seen for miles. They sought to be invisible in plain sight. Joseph was wary of walking across the open space in the dark and took from his pocket the small torch that Alex had given him the previous day. The batteries were now failing, but the faint light it still gave out was just about sufficient. He picked his way towards the monastery, keeping within the small arc of light that splayed out across the stone slabs. The drizzle had turned to rain and the torchlight was reflected back in myriad ways as it caught the film of water that clung to the surface. Joseph suddenly became aware of how wet he was and went to pull up the hood of his coat, but as soon as his hand touched his hair, which was by now plastered to his head in a damp mass, he realized the futility. He hoped that there would be time to tidy up before dining with the Hegumeni and Hegumen. He reached the monastery building and was impressed to see that, even at such close quarters, not a glimmer of light could be seen. He found his way along the wall to the large door and let himself in. Everything was transformed as he once more entered a world of light. He was in the candlelit passage where he had arrived the previous night. It was empty and in the distance he could again hear the sound of prayerful chant. He realized that the bell he had heard must have been summoning the monks and nuns to their evening office. He was relieved that there was still a while to go until dinner and that he would have time to make himself presentable, but also felt slightly guilty that he, a priest, seemed to be missing all the services.

His guilt vanished in an instant, however, as his eyes once more caught sight of the majestic fresco that hung overhead. He moved to stand directly beneath the figure of Jesus as he held out the bread of the Mass, which had been painted with astonishing realism. Joseph almost felt that he could reach up and take the sacrament that was offered. The gentle background of sacred chant lulled his mind. He found himself starting to encounter a similar quality of connection with the image as he had with the ancient rock a few minutes earlier. Yet at the same time, paradoxically, there was something completely different about the experience. The icon of Jesus connected him with another rhythm of existence to that of the rock, a multifaceted level of awareness and individualized being. In the image, in the invocation of that name and presence, he was meeting himself and everyone else at a depth where the fleeting mirage of worldly identity had no substance. And he was also touching what lay beyond even this. After a few minutes, as with his experience with the rock face, the intense connection naturally faded and he found himself drawing away, both physically and in consciousness. He took a deep breath to bring himself fully back, whispered a prayer of thanks and returned, after several unintended detours, to the small bedroom.

Joseph re-emerged ten minutes later, having done his best to make himself respectable. His trusty metal comb had proved its worth once again and he had been relieved to find that no mud had found its way onto his clothes, despite the wet conditions. He looked along the narrow corridor to get his bearings and then found his way to the refectory where he presumed the meal would be served. It was deserted and he surmised that the nuns and monks must still be at prayer. Behind two large double doors on one side of the long room he could hear the distant clashing of pots, plates and pans that betrayed the location of the kitchen. Yet there were no voices. Even the cooking, it seemed, was performed in silence. He looked around and wondered where to wait. Two long wooden tables had been placed length ways, about ten feet apart, and a third, shorter table had been placed across the top joining them together. He guessed that the Abbess and Abbot would sit at the top table and so it would make sense to position himself there. But he wondered if this might appear presumptuous and wavered in indecision. He finally hit upon a compromise and sat down at the edge of the top table, ready to leap up nonchalantly should he detect any sign that he had breached etiquette.

Joseph sat in a silence broken only by the faint kitchen sounds that drifted through the closed doors and began to examine the room with more care. Even though he had been in there several times during his brief stay at the monastery, he had never really noticed it. His mind had been on other matters. Yet now, as he gave it proper attention, it slowly dawned on him that it was no ordinary room. There was something about it, very difficult to define, that affected consciousness. His mind felt as though it was soaking in a warm bath, as if it was being gently massaged, with each knot and wrinkle being softly smoothed away. It was a beautifully restful place. He looked around, trying to work out what was creating such an atmosphere.

The refectory was rectangular in shape, with the top table across the shorter axis of the room and the main tables running lengthways. He looked over his shoulder and saw that in each corner was a small wooden door within a sharply curved arch. Turning back, to his right, were the closed doors that obviously led to the kitchen. As he looked down the long axis of the room, he could see a pair of double doors at the far end that he knew led to the rest of the building. On the left-hand wall were three large arched windows. Now that night had descended, no light entered through them, but Joseph could remember how bright the refectory had been earlier in the day. Thinking back, he also recalled that they were made of clear opaque glass that seemed to produce a subtle crystalline quality to the light. He wished he had been more present in his mind at the time to have noticed properly. The walls were of the same simple stone as the rest of the monastery, except that they had been laid with great precision. Every joint was perfectly aligned, with the flowing grain of each block of sandstone having been painstakingly matched with its neighbors. Joseph walked over to the nearest wall and at close range the extraordinary accuracy was even more apparent. As he examined the wall, he realized that this sense of the profound, almost loving care with which the stone had been laid was a powerful element in the overall effect of the room. As he looked around he saw that everything in the room reflected this approach. From the construction of the impressive wood-beamed roof and the stone-paved floor to the positioning of the tables and chairs, everything had been done with the utmost mindfulness. Even the simple cutlery, drinking vessels and other tableware had been positioned with great care. Nothing in the room suggested absent-mindedness. This was not the result of some sort of pathological obsession, but was the inevitable consequence of minds that were very present in each moment as they interacted with the material world.

It was deep art.

Joseph walked away from the wall to the center of the refectory knowing that he had seen part of the room's secret. But there was something else at work that he had not yet pinned down. He stood there, allowing his thoughts to still, while holding the question gently in the flow of consciousness. After a minute or so, the answer eased its way to the surface.

He saw that the room had an extraordinary simplicity.

It contained nothing that was unnecessary to its purpose. There were no paintings on the walls, ornate stained-glass windows or sumptuous rugs. There was nothing in the room that would stimulate the mind beyond what was strictly necessary for its function. So the mind could rest in a place that sought to add as little as possible to the usual frenzy of thought. Yet despite this insight, something still puzzled Joseph. He had been in many places that were merely functional and they had not felt like this. He wondered what it was that saved the refectory from a sense of lifelessness. Then he saw that it was the deep art with which it had been constructed and was maintained. The deep art and the pure simplicity together flowered into something that was greater than both, a presence, an atmosphere that had no name but which tasted far better than the most expensive wine. The moment that Joseph saw this, he connected with it even more strongly. He stood at the center of the room basking in its subtle glow. As he did so, he understood with a new clarity the nature of sacred space. He also sensed how minds so affected would, in turn, imprint their pattern on the fabric of reality in such a place. And he knew, from somewhere deep within, that this inter-relationship opened doorways to the inner planes of existence; to God and all that lay between.

He recalled Clare's gift for evoking the same effect with a room and also the garden at the rear of the rectory with its ability to shape and focus the mind. He realized that the gift of sacred space could manifest in many different ways.

Then Joseph remembered something he had read years before in a nineteenth century novel about magic. The main character had created a house where every room was designed to affect the mind in some way and thereby open it to what lay behind the frothy surface of life. Some rooms were like this one, in that they would bring stillness to thought and open awareness to the eternal now. Others stimulated the senses in order to open the imagination, to focus energetic thought, so that it might connect symbolically with deeper layers of reality. It occurred to him that what he had so far seen of the monastery seemed to follow this model. The extraordinary fresco painted by Alex, the simplicity of his bedroom and the precision of the refectory suggested that everything in the building had been designed with clear intent. It was a house of prayer in the deepest and widest meaning of that phrase. He wondered what the remainder of the monastery was like.

Joseph's meditation was suddenly interrupted. As well as the clatter of culinary preparation from the closed kitchen, he began to hear the sound of approaching people, still distant, but getting closer. The nuns and monks had concluded their office and must be heading to the refectory. His old insecurities immediately reasserted themselves alongside the deep sense of inspiration he was feeling. He quickly headed back to his perch at the end of the top table and began to feel nervous. He was still surprised at how he could experience such profound awareness alongside his normal human frailties. In the past he would have presumed that the former would have eliminated the latter, but he was now beginning to see that opening to transcendent consciousness was an expansion, not a moving on and leaving behind.

The first of the monastics entered and Joseph felt very exposed sitting on his own at the top table. Until now, apart from the nun who had met them by the road, his few encounters with members of the community had been limited to passing in corridors. This was the first time he had met the whole community. He watched as the monks aligned themselves along the right-hand table and the nuns, facing them, along the other. Joseph noticed that there seemed to be equal numbers. Dressed in black from head to toe, both wore robes of similar cut and design. The only differences in their attire were the beards and rigid conical hats of the men compared with the head covering veils of the women. There were about thirty of them and he was surprised to see the wide range of ages that were represented, from the venerable elderly to those who would be still in their twenties. They remained in silence, but in an easy and relaxed way. It was not a self-important, overtly pious silence that Joseph had sometimes encountered with such communities. Everybody was taking the practice of silence seriously, but not too seriously. Indeed, Joseph noticed that one of the younger monks was trying to catch the eye of a couple of the nuns, who were studiously not looking in his direction while trying to suppress smiles. They were clearly sharing some kind of joke. An older nun glanced towards them, before looking at Joseph and raising her eyebrows in mock resig-nation. Joseph smiled back and for a few moments relaxed a little. He wondered if she was the Hegumeni and one of the older monks was the Hegumen, but the thought brought with it the realization that they were on the main tables and he was on his own at the top. Also, he was sitting while everyone else was standing, obviously waiting for something. His self-consciousness returned with even greater force. He wanted to stand, but in that irrational way that so often takes over in such situations, feared that it would draw attention to the fact that he had not been standing in the first place.

The arrival of Alex felt like a blessing from heaven. He walked through the doors at the far end of the room and marched confi-dently behind the line of silent monks to where Joseph sat alone. He took a long look at Joseph's face and tried to suppress a smile.

"I have been looking for you, Father. I wondered where you were hiding." He made no attempt to keep his voice down and seemed to be enjoying the situation. "We are not dining in here, but in a private room as there is much we need to discuss." Alex then turned to the older nun who had smiled at Joseph. "Mother Adriadna, it is requested that you preside at tonight's meal in the absence of the Hegumeni and Hegumen."

The nun bowed her head slightly in acknowledgement, before looking at Joseph and speaking slowly in heavily accented English.

"And may I welcome Father Joseph to our community. We know that you have much before you and be assured that you are in our prayers." She paused and looked at him deeply for a few moments. "Yet from what I can see, you are chosen for what awaits and have within all you will need."

Joseph was taken aback by her words. There was something about Mother Adriadna that was very direct. She only ever said exactly what she meant.

"Thank you," was all he said. But it was not politeness. It was his turn to mean exactly what he said.

Chapter 19

Joseph followed Alex over to one of the small doors behind the top table, the one nearest to the wall with the arched windows. Alex knocked respectfully and then entered. Joseph followed and found himself in a circular room about twenty feet across with a round table at the center, about which were four evenly spaced chairs. On the opposite side of the room from where he stood was another door, which he surmised was the point of entry for the two people that were busy preparing the table. They had certainly not passed him in the refectory. He would undoubtedly have noticed two such memorable figures. The Hegumeni and Hegumen were a striking visual contrast. She was short, no more than five feet tall, with a slender delicate frame. The Hegumen, on the other hand, was a huge bear of a man, of Greek features, with one of the most imposing beards Joseph had ever seen. His age was difficult to judge, but Joseph would have guessed that he was middle-aged. Both were dressed in the same black robes and head coverings as the other monastics and, surprisingly, wore no obvious symbols of their status. As they turned to greet their guests, Joseph could see that the Hegumeni's copper brown face, framed by her black veil, was almost childlike. Its bone structure suggested an Egyptian heritage. To Joseph, she seemed quite young to hold such high office, the equivalent of an Abbess in a western convent.

Alex made a polite cough.

"Mother Anastasia and Father Anastasios, may I present Father Joseph Williams."

Joseph found himself being regarded by kindly eyes, although the Hegumen's face carried a hint of shyness. Joseph nodded to them and tried to smile as best he could. Anastasia confidently returned the smile, walked forward and took both of his hands.

"Father Joseph, we are most honored by your presence. We give thanks to God that we are able to be of assistance to you at this most holy of times." Her English was perfect, although enunciated in a distinct North African accent.

Joseph found himself looking down into large dark brown eyes that examined his so directly that he began to feel uncomfortable. Held in that gaze, his earlier thoughts concerning her youth quickly evaporated. What shone from the depths of her cavernous pupils was anything but young. With great effort he managed to put some words together.

"The embrace of your community at this time is wonderful, Mother Anastasia."

But in the light of that searching gaze his words felt formal and empty. He knew that he had to say more; that his heart must speak instead of his brain.

"I feel very alone, Mother. Something incredibly strange is happening to me. If I think about it too much, it is very frightening. So to have such friends as your community and Alex is beyond price."

Anastasia looked pleased and after a few moments dropped her hands.

"There is much that we must talk about, Father, for time is short. We ... sense ... that the next chapter of your journey is imminent and we must help you to prepare. We have some ... understanding ... of the Visitor, as you call him, that may guide you in the time to come." She stepped away from Joseph. "But that is for later. First, Anastasios and I must serve you food as is our custom with guests. Please sit at our humble table."

Joseph was stunned for a few moments by Anastasia's claim to have some understanding of the Visitor. It took a few seconds to sink in. When it did, it was all that he wanted to talk about. Someone was offering to explain, at least to some extent, the event that had turned his life on its head. The idea of first eating seemed unthinkable - like having to wait until Christmas day as a child to open presents. But he managed to get a grip on himself and moved over to the nearest seat. Alex, watching his face carefully, sat down opposite.

To calm his mind, Joseph concentrated on observing the Hegumeni and Hegumen as they carried over steaming pots and began ladling food onto plates. He immediately noticed how graceful they were, even when performing such a simple task. As they moved they carried an air of stillness. It reminded him of a gifted ice dancer, a living symbol of repose with motion. They also had an aura of gravity. There was a sense that they became the center of wherever they were and whatever they were doing. He realized that, once more, he was observing precision and simplicity in complete harmony, an outward manifestation of the quality of their minds. The plates were handed around and the Hegumeni and Hegumen took their seats on opposite sides of the circular table. Joseph had a sense that this positioning mattered, that it was an expression of their relationship. He could not have imagined any other seating arrangement. Anastasia, on Joseph's left, addressed Anastasios

"My Father and Brother, will you give thanks for the gift that lies before us?"

Joseph was fascinated by the form of address that Anastasia had used. At one level, it could appear as a natural way to address a priest and fellow monastic, but Joseph suspected something deeper. Fragments of past reading struggled to come together in his mind to do with ancient Egypt and the Western magical tradition. His thoughts were interrupted by a faint, but astonishing sound that began to fill the room. Its source was Anastasios. Joseph glanced at the massive bearded figure and saw that his hands were held in front of his chest, palms together, while his eyes were firmly closed. The sound was a deep rumbling drone emanating from somewhere within the big man's chest, through a mouth that was barely open. Joseph found his eyes closing as the vibration penetrated the fibers of his being. He was suddenly aware, without knowing how, that the sound was bringing the four of them into a strange connection and he allowed himself to sink into the experience. Then the chant started. Somehow, Anastasios seemed able to maintain the drone and at the same time enunciate words at a slightly higher pitch. It was an extraordinary performance. The words touched Joseph deeply, even though he could not understand them. He guessed that the language was liturgical Greek, but some of the words had a markedly different texture and he suspected that they were from another source. It was not necessary for him to understand the literal meaning of what was being said. You do not need to speak Swahili to feel the love of a mother speaking to her child in that language. Words used in a certain way become containers for something far greater. This is how it was with Anastasios' chant. It was filled with gratitude and humility.

It lasted no more than a couple of minutes, but was followed by a silence that went on just as long. As Joseph eventually found his eyes opening, he looked across the table at Alex. He knew that he had now seen a little further into what drove his friend.

"And now we eat, thank goodness," Anastasios rumbled in one of the deepest voices that Joseph had ever heard. His humor lightened the atmosphere and the four of them began to tuck into the collection of vegetables that filled their plates. Joseph had no idea what they were, but the aroma was wonderful. He suspected that some spices were involved, but had always relied on Clare to identify such things for him. One thing that he did notice, however, was that his relationship with the food had changed. Before Anastasios' prayer, the food had just been food. Now it felt like something special, like an amazing gift. His enjoyment of the meal was interrupted as Anastasia leaned over and placed her hand lightly on his wrist. Joseph was beginning to notice how tactile she was, which he found surprising in a nun.

"Father, may I ask a great favor? Will you tell us about your encounter with the … Visitor? I know that you may be weary of this, but although we have seen the television pictures and heard what you said at the news conference, we need to hear it from you directly."

Joseph was surprised again. He had assumed that the monastery would be cut off from such an example of modernity as a television set.

"Mother Anastasia, it's something that I'd very much like to do. I desperately need to make sense of what has happened over the last few days and I'm sure that you'll be able to help."

Anastasia looked pleased.

"You are very kind, Father Joseph. I think it is very possible that we will have some … insights. Please continue. But do not let your food get cold while you talk."

So, between mouthfuls of food, Joseph told them about the church service and his experience in the blue light. He also told them about Leola and the bishop. Then, after a glance at Alex, who nodded reassuringly, he recounted his puzzling vision from the hermit cell. When he finished, there was silence in the room and Anastasia held him in her most penetrating gaze. To break the contact, Joseph looked to his right at Anastasios, hoping to discover a response that was less intimidating. He was disappointed to find that, if anything, he was being regarded with even more intensity by the Hegumen. Both held him in the center of their awareness, but he sensed that the focal point of their concentration was beyond the surface. In desperation he glanced up at Alex on the opposite side of the table and was rewarded by another slight nod of the head and a reassuring smile.

It was Anastasios who broke the spell.

"I need more food," the cavernous voice announced.

Joseph was relieved that he was no longer the center of attention, but was a bit puzzled to see that despite his proclamation, Anastasios' plate was still nearly full. He had clearly not taken the advice of his opposite number. It was a temporary situation, however, as he swiftly demolished the contents and reached for the large bowls that steamed invitingly at the center of the table.

"Father Joseph, can we offer you some more," Anastasia asked politely, while glancing over at Anastasios with a look of mild reprimand.

"Ah, yes, of course," the Hegumen exclaimed, diverting the bowl in Joseph's direction, while trying to make it look as though this had always been his intention.

"Thank you. That would be good," Joseph replied, attempting to keep a straight face. After spooning some more food onto his plate he looked over at Alex.

"And you Alex?" he enquired innocently.

Alex quickly caught onto the joke and nodded his head enthusiastically.

"Why yes. I am most hungry tonight."

Joseph passed the bowl over and Alex filled his plate to overflowing, before looking at Anastasia.

"And you, Mother Anastasia? I think that there is a bit left."

The bearded Hegumen shifted in his seat at these unwelcome words.

Anastasia looked down at her plate on which very little had been touched.

"No, thank you, Brother Alex." She looked over at Anastasios with a twinkle in her eye. "I fear there may be others in greater need."

The bowl eventually found its way to Anastasios who, after inspecting the contents, looked at Alex, snorted slightly and then ladled a mountain of food onto his plate. He looked at Joseph.

"I think you have not finished, Father Joseph."

At first Joseph was confused, thinking that he was referring to the food, but the look on the Hegumen's face told him that it was not so simple. Before he could respond, Anastasios spoke again.

"There is more to your story than you have shared," he

rumbled. "I can see it in you."

Joseph felt disturbed. Only Clare and Leola, he had recently discovered, knew about the Teacher and his dreams. He had told no one about the experiences of expanded consciousness that had been growing in intensity and power since the arrival of the Visitor. Anastasios was treading on sensitive ground. Joseph was a profoundly private person, but it was also more than that. He had a strongly rooted sense that such matters were not for general conversation. Secrecy would have been the wrong word to describe this conviction. It was more a feeling that great discretion was needed. He did not know where this impression came from, but it arose from somewhere deep within. Anastasia saw his discomfort.

"Perhaps, Anastasios, we are being too forward and should be satisfied with what Father Joseph has felt able to share."

The Hegumen grunted, clearly not in sympathy with Anastasia's sentiment. Joseph was grateful for his honesty. It helped him to see what he must do. If these people were to help him, he must not hold back. He looked at Anastasia and smiled.

"I fear that Father Anastasios is correct in all ways. There are things that I haven't shared which I should. But you'll have to be patient. I don't find it easy to talk about such matters."

Very self-consciously, Joseph then told them about the Teacher, the voyage of exploration that had resulted and the dreams. He told them how the Teacher had left on the same day that the Visitor had arrived. The Hegumen and Hegumeni had glanced at each other as he had said this. He then described the increasing experiences of illumined consciousness that he had since experienced. He also spoke about his sense of connection with the Visitor from the moment he had seen the light vessel above Niagara Falls on the television. Then there was a pause and he found himself talking about Clare and her death. He had not meant to. It just came out. There was silence when he finished and Joseph pretended to concentrate on his plate of food to hide his embarrassment. He felt that he had shared very private matters with virtual strangers. But then something happened that astonished him. Anastasios reached over and took his hand. When Joseph looked up, there were tears in the big man's eyes.

"Such a wonderful love you have described, Father Joseph. Compared with that, everything else is but passing clouds." Anastasios gripped his hand even more tightly. "We believe that such a love between a man and a woman is an outward sign of the coming together of immense creative forces on the inner planes. This expression of ... polarity ... is at the heart of our prayer. It ... ." Anastasios stopped in mid-flow and suddenly looked worried. "But perhaps I say too much."

"No, my Father and my Brother, you are right to speak of these things," Anastasia interjected. "Father Joseph has revealed much to us, so in turn we must be open with him. This is a special time when what has been hidden must be revealed if we are to ... respond ... as we should to the Messenger."

So much of importance had been said in a few sentences that Joseph was left struggling to keep up. The passion of Anastasios, as powerful as it was unexpected, had moved him greatly. And the hint as to the inner meaning of the love between a man and a woman, and how this was at the center of the community's prayer, fascinated him. He began to think back and odd things he had noticed in passing began to assume significance; the unexpected presence of monks and nuns under the same roof, and the equal number of both that he had noticed in the refectory. Yet what had left the greatest impression was Anastasia referring to the Visitor as "the Messenger". He had not heard this term used before and it carried all kinds of implications. He was left with many questions but, before he could ask, Anastasia spoke again.

"Now it is our turn to reveal ourselves, Father Joseph, but first I would say that what you have shared does not surprise us. The details we could not have known, but nothing happens without a cause. Your choosing by the Messenger told us immediately that deep forces were at work in your life, the signs of which would be apparent in some way. All of this will make more sense if I first explain the nature of this community."

Anastasia paused for a few moments, staring down absent-mindedly at her plate, obviously searching for the best way to begin. Then she looked up again.

"At first glance an outsider will see a rather unconventional, but still traditional community of Orthodox monastics. Yet I should tell you at the outset that we have no formal connection with the Orthodox Church, which apart from a few individuals is largely ignorant of our existence. Our community is one expression of a wider fellowship that embraces people from many different walks of life. All are required to observe silence in the outside world concerning their membership, unless certain very specific conditions are met. We are Christian in the sense that the Christ is our inspiration and guide. It is He who is our icon, our gateway to the unknowable God who may be known. But we follow a hidden stream of the tradition that is very different to that which the world knows. It has always been the way of the few and has for most of its existence lived in the shadows. We have found it safer that way. You may ask why, here, we still observe the discipline and form of the Orthodox when we are, beneath the surface, so different. I would reply that our expression of the Orthodox way is just as ancient as the exoteric form and has its own authority. I would also say that most of us are creatures of our heritage and it is natural to express ourselves from within our culture, although there are always exceptions such as myself. Do not be fooled by outward appearance, for all you meet here are educated, modern, twenty-first century people. It would probably astonish you to learn that Father Anastasios is an eminent, internationally known mathematician." She leaned forward with a twinkle in her eye. "You must agree that he hides his light under his bushel with great skill."

Joseph glanced over at the Hegumen, who arched an eyebrow

She paused, her eyes searching his for some kind of reaction. Joseph realized that she was unsure as to what his response would be to her words. He reminded himself that few priests were as open as he and many would be shocked by what they were hearing. He moved quickly to put her at ease.

"Alex has already hinted at something like this in a conversation we had a couple of days ago. I am very ... unconventional ... myself and am sure that the great mystery expresses itself in many ways."

Joseph noticed Anastasia and Anastasios look pointedly at Alex, who appeared very uncomfortable. He was suddenly worried that he had got Alex into trouble. There was silence for a few moments, then the Hegumen spoke.

"We trust your judgment Brother Alexander."

As Alex relaxed, Anastasia looked back at Joseph.

"Perhaps the easiest way for me to explain our ... understanding ... is with a simple picture. Father Anastasios, do you have pen and paper?"

Anastasios looked slightly irritated that his eating had been interrupted and rummaged in his voluminous robe. From some hidden pocket he produced a stubby pencil and a small pad of paper, and then pushed them across the table towards Anastasia.

"I knew we could rely on the Hegumen to have writing materials about his person. He likes to note down immediately any ideas that come to him about his latest math problem. He usually manages to resist the temptation to do this during the liturgy, but does occasionally stray."

Anastasios looked across the table at the Hegumeni, trying to appear fierce, before his face broke into a smile.

"Hah! Succumbing to temptation merely proves that I am still human. You should be impressed."

Joseph watched the exchange with interest. He realized that it was like being with a married couple. There was an ease to their relationship that spoke of deep intimacy, yet they were monk and nun. He wondered just how unconventional the monastery really was. His thoughts were interrupted as Anastasia took the pencil and drew something on the paper. She then turned the pad so that Joseph could see what she had drawn. The image was very simple and, for some reason that he could not immediately identify, rang a bell in his mind. Anastasia had drawn a circle with a single line, a radius, stretching from the center to a point on the circumference.

"This is an ancient symbol," she explained. "Its origins are lost in the mists of time. Our tradition borrows it, for it helps us to explore our understanding of reality. Also it may have ... relevance ... with regard to the Messenger."

Joseph was dubious that something so simple could explain so much, but kept his doubts to himself. The use of the term "Messenger" again and its possible link with the diagram fascinated him. Anastasia reached over and carefully traced the circle with her finger. Joseph noticed how delicate it was.

"The outer circle represents the manifest world. It is where our bodies live and we act out our dramas." She then pointed with the tip of the pencil to the exact spot where the radius met the circumference. "And this unique coordinate is you, reality experiencing itself in an exclusive, inimitable, never to be repeated way." She moved the pencil a millimeter along and drew another radius. "And this point might be me, and this, and this, every other living being in the universe." She continued to move the pencil point around the outside of the circle drawing more lines to the center. "Each experiencing life in its own individual way. And notice that at this level, on the outer edge of existence, all appears separate."

She paused and looked at Joseph for a sign that he was following her explanation. She need not have worried, for the simple picture was coming alive for him. Already he could see where it was leading. He began to get excited as something he knew at a subliminal level began to take more concrete form. It was a wonderfully satisfying experience. Such is the power of a symbol. He smiled at Anastasia and nodded his head for her to continue. She placed the tip of the pencil back onto the point where the original radius met the circumference.

"So, let us say that this is you, apparently separate and cut off from everyone else. Yet if we follow the line back to the center, we find a common source for each of us." She illustrated this explanation by tracing each of the radii back to the center of the circle. She then leaned forward slightly to emphasize her next words. "So we are both one and many in the same moment. We are the one, being many." She paused again to see the effect of her words on Joseph, seeming satisfied with what she saw.

"In our tradition we call this common source 'God' and sense an unknowable meaning and purpose in its creative expression." She traced some of the radii from the center to the circumference. "But even though this meaning and purpose is beyond our ability to understand, we believe that when our minds fall into harmony with this flow our inner-being is illumined and inexpressible fulfillment is experienced - even in the midst of difficult times. In this connection we sense also a personal presence. God is always utterly mysterious, but within that ineffability we sense 'someone' with whom we are in relationship." She paused as a thought struck her. "Actually, that reminds me of the feeling you spoke about at the press conference when you described being in the blue light." She was obviously intrigued by the comparison and seemed to lose herself in thought for a few seconds before refocusing. "For us, as for you, that sense of personal relationship comes to fulfillment in the figure of Jesus. He is our vehicle that joins us with God. And there is something else that you said at the press conference with which we would agree. We do not doubt that the great source, the mystery at the heart of existence, is experienced in many different ways, so we bow our heads with respect to all other genuine spiritual pathways. We make no exclusive claims."

Joseph had listened to Anastasia intently, basking in the joy of hearing his own inner intuitions expressed with such clarity. He looked down at the picture she had drawn and wanted to ask a question, even though he was sure that he knew the answer. He placed his finger in the broad area that lay between the center and the circumference.

"But what about this?" he enquired. "You've spoken about the individual and its direct relationship with the Source of All, yet not about what lies between." He ran the forefinger of each hand along two of the radii towards the center. "For example, I notice that as these lines move inwards they get ever closer. Does this mean that as I ... sink ... into the depths of my being, I become less ... separate ... from other human beings?"

Anastasia looked at him with interest.

"Absolutely, Father Joseph. It suggests that at deeper levels the boundary between each of us blurs and new ways of ... relationship and communication ... become possible. It suggests that as awareness moves towards the center, our minds may touch in more direct and intimate ways. The clumsy expressions of relationship and communication that exist at the surface are but poor reflections of true connection. Much of the frustration of life is that, in our ignorance, we try to achieve with our bodies a joining that can only really be accomplished on the inner planes."

Joseph sat back in his chair and, oblivious to the others, stared at the ceiling while he pondered what he had just heard. It was a beautiful way of picturing what he had often experienced in life. He recalled how he and Clare had often laughed at a telepathy they seemed to share. He would think of something and, often within seconds, she would start talking about the same thing. He had also seen this with other people who were very close. But also, very importantly, it offered an explanation for his link with the Teacher and the Visitor. What for most of humanity was a sporadic, uncontrolled experience, must be for them a refined skill with awesome potential. He saw also that in this model, all must be mind; that material existence was merely a temporary aspect of solidified consciousness - the opposite of the commonly held view that consciousness emerged from matter.

He understood the frustration to which Anastasia referred. The need to join with another was so powerful, yet no matter how close the relationship it never seemed to completely fulfill except for very occasional, brief moments. It was a primal hunger that expressed itself physically through sex and emotionally through romantic love and deep friendship. Yet as beautiful as these could be, the hunger always remained underneath. The image of the circle helped him to understand more clearly why this was. True communion was an inner experience. It required a turning within and a seeking of the depths of being. It was about the authentic nature of love. Then a thought struck him. Try as he might, he could not keep it to himself. He leaned forward in his chair and looked in turn at Anastasia and Anastasios.

"This is part of what you explore in this community, isn't it? It's why you have monks and nuns living together in equal numbers." Joseph tried to choose his next words with care - and failed. "It's why I feel as if I'm in the presence of two ... lovers."

As soon as the words were out of his mouth, Joseph was horrified at what he had said. He was sure that he must have caused great offence. His eyes flitted between the Hegumen and Hegumeni in quiet panic. But he need not have worried. They did not share his English reserve about such matters.

"You are very perceptive, Father Joseph," Anastasios rumbled in a matter of fact manner. He stared at Joseph for a few moments. "Actually, I think it is more that you are remembering what you have known since times past." He looked over with shining eyes at the Hegumeni. "I am fortunate beyond words that

Anastasia is my lover. I feel closer to her than any other human being." Joseph glanced at Anastasia for a few moments and, despite her coppery skin, thought he could detect a blush. "Yet at the level of the physical world we are celibate religious. We do not dissipate the energy of our love through the sexual embrace, but seek to redirect it inwards where our joining may be more profound. It is ... a mystical marriage." Anastasios glanced at his lover. "But you must understand that this is a long and demanding practice, and not easy when your partner is so beautiful."

Joseph did not need to look at Anastasia to know that her embarrassment had just increased ten-fold. He glanced up at Alex, who was trying not to smile. Anastasios had not finished.

"Such a calling is not for everyone. It is very hard and only for those who are guided to this path by the inner currents. It is not about avoiding the normal pleasures of life, but of exploring something greater on behalf of all. So in this community are those who have traveled some way along the road, such as the Hegumeni and myself, and also those who are trying to discern whether this is their vocation. The more experienced act as guides to the others. There are always an equal number of men and women here, but over time the individuals will change as some leave and others join."

"So you don't take life vows then?"

"No, absolutely not. Who can say where the inner currents may be calling someone in years to come. Even the most senior of us may feel that the moment has arrived to return to more ... usual ... forms of relationship."

Anastasios looked across at his partner as he said this and Joseph got the impression that this was more than an abstract question for the two of them. Then the Hegumen looked at Joseph, as though assessing whether to say more. After a few moments he seemed to reach a decision.

"I must talk further about this practice, for otherwise you may think we are merely living out come kind of esoteric romantic novel." The Hegumen paused while he considered how to proceed. "The joining between a man and a woman is only one manifestation of a fundamental principle that lies at the heart of manifest existence. We might call it polarity. This is the state where opposites cannot be present without one another. 'In' has no meaning unless 'out' also exists. There cannot be a coin that does not have two sides. In polarity 'one' and 'two' coexist in the same moment. This principle must also apply at the very root of what we are. In the moment when this becomes a conscious realization, the One knows itself through having become Two. Perhaps we might say that it is the moment when God becomes self-aware." Anastasios leaned over and placed his finger at the center of the circle. "In this moment you are an expression of the oneness that lies at the center of all and also," he continued, as he moved his finger out towards the circumference, "a separate unique being. You are both one and two, fully in the same moment. This state has been called non-duality, for only negative language can refer to it. There is nothing within our normal experience, and therefore within our conceptual framework, that can relate to this. It is paradoxical for minds shaped and formed by a linear world. So here we seek to expand awareness to the roots of the male/female polarity that lies deep within each of us, for it is a royal road to joining with God." Anastasios banged his finger at the center of the circle to emphasize his last point, before leaning back in his chair. "Oh yes, one other thing I must add - it is good fun. Even better than eating." With this, he picked up his fork and set about the contents of his plate.

Joseph's mind was racing with questions.

"This ... redirection of energy ... that you talk about. How is it achieved?"

"A good question, Father Joseph, but perhaps Anastasia would like to talk about that. My food is getting cold again."

Anastasia was taken by surprise. Joseph got the impression

that her thoughts had been elsewhere. She looked slightly flustered.

"Yes ... of course." She gathered herself. "It is too large a subject to talk about in detail for we must soon move on to more pressing matters, but at the heart of the practice is a redirecting of desire. The energy of mind, and therefore also of the body, flows in channels laid down by our desires. For most this is an unconscious process over which there is little control. We seek to focus our desire on something greater and deeper, not because the ways of the world are wrong, but because we wish to explore and express a ... heart-felt calling."

"And what is it you desire?"

"We nurture two desires as the primary focus of our lives."

Anastasia thought for a moment and then brought Joseph's attention back to the drawing. She placed her finger firmly at the center of the circle.

"First, we learn to focus our desire with ever-increasing intensity on the Source of All, for which we use the ancient word 'God'. Without this, there can be nothing else. All is grace. All is gift. We are aware that we do not possess our own lives. We did not create ourselves. We desire with all that we are to know God as a living presence. We seek to know God not as a belief or idea, but as an experience. We seek to join with God. Our way to do this is through the icon of Christ, whose energy lives in the hearts of all who are called to tread his particular way. We do this through prayer in all its forms, with a special emphasis on those forms that still the mind and nurture deep awareness. Above all, we do this through the Divine Liturgy of Bread and Wine in what you call the Mass."

The image of the fresco of the Last Supper that hung above the entrance hall came unbidden to Joseph's mind.

"Our second desire is to serve creation through cooperation with all sentient beings. Only when we have progressed with our first yearning can we begin to explore the second." Anastasia moved her finger away from the center of the circle towards the circumference. "We travel to the center, before moving back to the world through all that lies between. Otherwise there is great danger that, despite the best of intentions, whatever we do will be motivated by unworthy, ego-based desires and we may do great damage. We work with powerful tides and currents that are just as capable of doing harm as good. Great caution is needed for our minds are past masters of self-deception. We must be prepared to allow God to show us ourselves with devastating honesty so that we may see the deep roots of our thoughts. This is not an easy experience, but it is always liberating."

"What do you mean by tides and currents?"

She paused and looked at him. Once again, Joseph knew that he was being assessed before more of the community's knowledge was revealed. She made her decision.

"You must understand that this world is an effect, not a cause. It is the end result of incomprehensible forces that move within the deeper levels of reality." She moved her finger in the area between the center of the circle and the circumference. "We live in a sea of infinite potential. Since the beginning of time, powerful creative impulses have erupted from the great mysterious source into this ocean. These waves have surged, intermingled and evolved, and continue to do so to this day. The ever-changing manifestation of which we are a part, is the direct result. Yet, extraordinarily, sentient beings share this gift for creation. We can surprise God. We are all latent artists and our waves of newness interface with the great primal surges. Thus we can be co-creators, although for most of us this is an occasional, largely unconscious and therefore erratic experience. Some of us, however, understand what is happening and aspire to swim consciously in this water of existence that it may be influenced. But our minds are tiny in comparison with the Source of All and so our energetic impulses can too easily be swallowed up by the great maelstroms of divine movement. Those of us who work consciously in this way watch for moments when particular tidal flows and currents are at a point of balance, a tipping point, where our otherwise insignificant contribution may determine the way in which matters fall. Thus we can sometimes change the world for the better, as eventually these new waves of creation manifest into worldly form."

"How do you do this?"

"Having connected as best we can with God, with the divine center, the Source of All, we use the great mechanism of creative power that we have been given. We use the energy of deep imagination to create new waves and rhythms in the sea of existence. The methods are ancient, passed down from times long forgotten. It is time, also, that has proved their efficacy."

None of this was new to Joseph. This was the Western magical tradition that he had researched in the past. But both the reading he had done and what he had just heard had left a great question in his mind, a challenge to the wisdom of such practice. He tried to soften his voice so as not to sound confrontational.

"But Mother Anastasios, how can you know how to bring goodness into the world? How can the limited human mind work in the complexity of the inner planes? Aren't you just as likely to bring disaster?"

His question brought a snort from Anastasios, who was helping himself to more food. Anastasia looked at Joseph patiently.

"That is a question of much wisdom, Father Joseph. Would that others who dabble in these realms ask it of themselves." She paused for a moment before continuing. "First, is not the point you make, if accepted, an argument against action in the material world also. Can we claim to understand all of this?" she said opening her arms wide. "Second, we are working within an ancient tradition and draw on its insight and understanding. Yet I accept that there can be no certainty as to outcome, as also there cannot be in the world. Most importantly, you must remember that before entering into these waters we seek to be guided by God. We do not rely on our judgment alone. We believe it to be God's will that we do this creative work, that it is a natural expression of what we are made to be." She paused and looked over at Anastasios for a moment and he held her gaze. "Yet your question is of the utmost importance and do not doubt that we challenge ourselves with it from time to time."

She stopped, but Joseph had a feeling that she had not finished speaking.

"I must also correct something in your question. I never said that we work to bring goodness into the world. I said that we seek to change the world for the better."

Joseph was puzzled as to the distinction. Anastasia saw it on his face.

"Father Joseph, I do not know what goodness is. Everything is too complex at the level of the world. I may be certain that my motives in a situation are 'good', yet because of the complexities of the mind be unaware of hidden baser motives. On the surface it may appear that my actions bring healing to a situation, yet it may be that in the longer term I have prevented real progress. How often have we seen the beautiful arise out of what we call bad and evil result from the best of intentions? So you must forgive me if 'goodness' is a word that I am reluctant to use." She paused before continuing. "Our ... conviction ... is that what ultimately matters is the continued evolution of creation; its ongoing unfoldment into what it is meant to become. This is what we work for. Only then will a true end to the suffering of the universe be found. Only then, perhaps, will the true meaning of goodness become clear."

Anastasia's words shocked Joseph, yet at the same time he had an intuitive sympathy with what she was saying. He had often pondered these things himself. He had thought of all the wars that had been fought to defeat evil, only to bring even more into the world. He had remembered the many occasions when he had blundered into a situation, sure he knew what was right, only to be left confused and disillusioned by the result. The times when in trying to be the solution, he had become part of the problem. But his mind still wanted to argue.

"Surely it must be right to seek to bring peace to the world, to feed the hungry and to protect vulnerable children?"

"Of course. Our hearts tell us that there are many things that we simply have to do, but we must never presume to know what the consequences will be. Our most well-intentioned efforts may actually prevent healing and growth. Yet such work is beautiful and the best of what it is to be human. It must be done as an act of faith. It must be done with caution. All of us in this community have done such work in our lives. But it is treating the … symptoms … of a disease, not the cause. Did you not make this same point in your press conference about the intentions of the Messenger? At this time, in this place, it is our role to work at the root. It is the calling of others to feed, water and love the tree while we do what we must. Over time, it may well be that the roles will change."

Joseph was taken aback as he remembered the press conference, and how the same explanation had flowed from his own mouth when asked about the intentions of the Visitor/Messenger. It was strange that he had needed to be reminded of it. He had spoken the words, yet that they not taken root in his mind. The wider implications had not registered. He realized that this was an important lesson about the experience of illumined consciousness. This triggered another memory, something else that he had said. Perhaps this too needed to be grounded in the thoughts of someone else. He looked at Anastasia for a few moments while the question formed in his mind.

"But what is it to evolve in your terms? I'm sure that you're not talking about a further physical evolution of the body."

She smiled at him.

"I think that you answered this question yourself at the press conference. I have talked about the outward surge of the creative impulse from the center, which eventually manifests into physical worlds such as ours. There it continues to evolve in response to outer stimuli and further deep movements within creation. But that is not what we are concerned with, for this is an unconscious evolution. We involve ourselves with what happens when a sentient being that is present at the material level, who has until that moment been transfixed by the outer, turns the gaze of awareness inwards and begins to contemplate for the first time the path of manifestation along which its essence has traveled. It is at this moment that evolution becomes aware of itself and its journey takes on a different flavor, a new direction. It is here that our work starts."

Anastasia ran her finger along one of the radii toward the circumference of the circle.

"It has journeyed to the outer edge and now turns." Her finger sharply reversed its position to point at the center. "It is the moment when that soul suddenly becomes aware of being aware, realizes that it has no idea what it is or, indeed, what anything is. This is a natural, instinctive metanoia that rests in us all, awaiting its moment. It is the impulse of the created to know its creator, although it will be seen through many guises before being so recognized. At first this will be a turning only, not a journey. It will be occasional and brief as the world's seductions pull awareness back to the outer. But over time, the turnings will become increasingly sustained as our deepest impulse asserts its power. Eventually it will become a journey into the mind, into thought and what lies beyond. It will be a discovery that we have no idea who we are, which at first will frighten and then liberate."

Anastasia paused for a few moments to gather her thoughts.

"The nature of that journey will be individual, for our uniqueness is what we have to offer. Some will seek to journey directly to the source; to join with God as our tradition would say." She ran her finger straight to the center. "This has been called the way of the mystic. Others will be drawn to travel toward the center through the vast hinterland of the inner worlds, which has been called the way of magic. It may also be called the way of creation." She spread her fingers within the area between the center and the circumference. "Both paths are beautiful and valid. Some are called to one, some to the other. Over time the emphasis in an individual's life may shift. A few, such as those gathered in this place, practice both. But all must also pursue self-knowledge. All must learn to see with complete clarity the hidden thought dynamics that govern their actions and surface thoughts, for there are many pitfalls and deceptions that await those who neglect this practice. All is ultimately consciousness, so both ways must involve a journey into the depths of mind."

Anastasia paused and looked hard at Joseph, as if to emphasize what she was about to say.

"To evolve in our terms is to grow in the depth of this inner journey. We believe that is what we are for. Through us, the creator comes to know creation and itself. As this flowers we believe that all creation will be transformed and healed."

She paused again before finishing.

"I must be clear, however, that this focus on the inner journey does not mean that we reject the manifest world. On the contrary, it is awesome and wonderful, as is the universe of which it is a tiny part. What we do here," she said, banging the table with her hand, "really matters. We must journey in two directions, rather than one, with both impulses in harmony, informing and guiding the other. Perhaps I should use the word 'expansion' rather than 'journey'."

Joseph was left in silence for a while, entranced by what he had heard. Anastasia was patient and waited for him to gather his thoughts.

"How do you know which ... actions ... on the inner planes will nurture the evolution of creation. Surely this is just as unknowable?"

"Strangely, this is not necessarily so. As one works with fundamental principles, clarity arises. But also we do not work alone. Everything we do is the consequence of deep prayer and collegial discussion. Also we work with others whose ... perspective ... is very different and our interaction helps all to see more clearly."

Joseph looked at her. Something about the tone of her voice had alerted him to the imminence of another revelation about the community. He had a good idea what it might be. His reading had prepared him well, as perhaps had other experiences.

"Others?"

"As I said, we seek to work with other sentient beings." She paused and moved her finger slowly into the space between the center and the circumference, the area that Joseph had highlighted only a few minutes before. "As awareness moves into this realm, between us and God, there are countless other levels of existence to be discovered - and in them a most wonderful proliferation of other living, aware beings. The difference between us and the vast majority of other followers of the Christ is that we work at this level. They serve in the outer world, we in the hidden."

She stopped, again searching Joseph's face for a reaction. He knew that he was now on heady ground and firmly over the border as to what would be acceptable to his fellow priests. A disturbing vision of Bishop Jennifer came briefly to mind. But he did not care, for what he was hearing resonated with his deepest intuitions and explained much that he had experienced. Anastasia seemed to sense his approval.

"In the depths of imaginative meditation and through outward ritual, embracing the energies released by our explo-ration of polarity, we enter into relationship with those beings we encounter who are of goodwill. We do this for the benefit of all, for our worlds are intimately linked. Our evolution unfolds together. As one progresses, the echoes stream out through creation influencing wherever they touch. Everything is like a spider's web. The slightest movement is transmitted and affects the whole structure. Our two-dimensional piece of paper does not do justice to the interweaving of innumerable strands of reality. Also, in order to understand, you must realize that for each of them we are within the circle and they are on the circumference. They are an inner experience to us and we are an inner experience to them. Again, our linear minds cannot really grasp this. There comes a point where these insights become paradoxical. But the center is the same everywhere." Anastasia paused as a thought struck her. "Perhaps you have a symbol within your own culture that may help. You will know, I am sure, the Celtic Knot, that symbol which resembles a loose ball of interwoven wool that has no beginning and no end, each point of the strand never too far from all the others. Maybe this picture is helpful to lay alongside the circle."

"Just don't ask me to draw it," Anastasios mumbled through a mouthful of food.

Joseph's mind was too busy to be sidetracked by Anastasios. He was on fire inside. The words were helping him to connect with a deep part of himself that had been dormant for a long time. The conversation was triggering a reawakening or, as Anastasios had put it a few moments before, a remembering. But he needed to ask another question. It was the question for which Bishop Jennifer would have demanded an answer. He suspected that it lay firmly in the sensitive ground that lay between Alex and her. Before speaking, he glanced over at Alex who looked straight back, seemingly aware of the importance of what he was about to ask.

"Mother Anastasia, you spoke about 'beings of goodwill'? Does that mean you also encounter the malicious?"

Anastasia had obviously spotted Joseph's silent exchange with Alex. She seemed to understand its personal importance.

"Only rarely have we met with that which might be called truly evil. By this I mean a self-absorption so complete that everything else is seen as only existing for its use. Such a view of creation can produce terrible actions. Of course, such individuals may just as easily be met in the outer world. Most beings, however, ourselves included, are naturally a great jumble of the marvelous and the ugly, and everything between. What marks out the beings with whom we work is an acknowledgement of, and a bowing down before the Source of All, however it might be conceptualized, whatever it might be called. Where this is a true part of the soul it produces a humility that allows the mystery of the great source to shine, no matter how imperfect the vessel. We work with those who seek first to know God with all their heart, mind, soul and strength and then to serve. It is not something that can be faked for long. And always, in all things, we seek the guidance of God as we enter into each relationship and act as a community so that no individual may deceive themselves."

Anastasia's answer satisfied Joseph. It reflected much of his own thinking.

"What are these beings like?"

Anastasia thought carefully before answering.

"That is not an easy question to answer, for we meet in the realms of deep mind which is fluid and malleable. Also there are different … lineages … of being that may be encountered. For example, we may meet with beings who have never before had connection with our plane of existence. Or with those who, though from very different spheres, have traveled to this level before."

Anastasia paused, as though wanting to emphasize what she was about to say next.

"Occasionally we are privileged and encounter great beings who have journeyed far into the inner realms, close to the center of our circle, who bring wisdom and guidance. We call them messengers." Her words transfixed Joseph. He needed no further explanation of her use of this term. It was clear what her understanding of the nature of the Visitor was. It filled him with delight. He remembered that the ancient Greek word for a divine messenger was "angel".

Anastasia studied him carefully before continuing, making sure that the import of her words had registered.

"But their message takes a particular form. They do not bring answers, but better questions. They do not lead, but point. They work in symbol and metaphor. They bring experiences more than ideas. They are educators in the original meaning of that term. They seek to draw out of us a potential that is already present, not to impose anything. They know that the unique vision of all must be nurtured if creation is to evolve to its ultimate."

She paused once more, assessing the extent to which Joseph had absorbed what she had said. Seemingly satisfied, she moved on.

"We also encounter the incarnate that travel the inner worlds in their sleep." She glanced meaningfully at Joseph as she said this. "Or we may meet the essences of fellow human beings who have died to the physical form." A knife went through Joseph's heart as Anastasia said these words. His longing for Clare was instantly back in full force. He wondered why she had never returned to see him, to bring reassurance that their love was still alive. He wanted to ask Anastasia about this, but she was still talking. "Some of these souls are fully aware of their condition while others may be wandering, lost in ever-repeating dreams of embodied life. These are but a few examples for the list is limited only by my knowledge. The inner realms are utterly fluid and therefore all possibilities exist, and may be brought into being through the action of creative thought."

Joseph pushed thoughts of Clare to one side and managed to

get his mind back on track.

"Do you see these beings clearly? What do they look like?"

"I would rather say that we perceive them in the mind. This may take the form of seeing, hearing, intuitive impressions or other ways. When we receive an image in our mind's eye, we can never be sure that we are not seeing a shape that we are projecting onto the protean life energy that presents itself, or an image that it puts forth. Perhaps sometimes it is a harmony of both." She paused for a few moments looking thoughtfully at the far wall. "Of course, there are some manifestations of being with which humanity has long had contact and particular images have become firmly established within the collective consciousness. Inevitably, when such encounters occur these archetypal forms are invoked. But what lies behind that representation is impossible to say. We can only 'see' that for which we have a pre-existing concept."

Joseph thought about what he had heard. Once again Anastasia had articulated his own half-formed thoughts and intuitions. But then a question occurred to him. It was a question that cut to the heart of what he was.

"What is Jesus? What is the Christ? Is he just one of these great beings that you spoke about earlier?"

Before Anastasia could reply, the Hegumen broke off from his eating and looked straight at Joseph.

"Oh no, my friend. The Christ that we know in the form of Jesus comes outward from the center. To encounter that ... presence ... is something which words cannot embrace. All our friends with whom we work on the inner planes know this presence in some guise, many of which we can barely recognize. In turn, the name 'Jesus' means nothing to them or the description 'Christ'. But the ... quality ... the particular experience of relationship ... is unmistakable. He ... it ... shines from an unknowable source and light is shaped and colored by what it strikes - but it is still the light."

With that the big man went back to the important task of eating, oblivious to the fact that he had just silenced the room with his majestic words. Then Anastasia took a deep breath and looked at Joseph and Alex.

"It is time that we spoke about the Messenger."

Chapter 20

"We knew something was about to happen. Something of tremendous significance, with deep roots in time."

Anastasia paused and looked down at her hands. Joseph could tell that she was searching for the right words. Anastasios had stopped eating and was watching her with great intensity. The atmosphere in the room had, in a few moments, become electric. Fascinating though the conversation up to this point had been, the climax had now been reached. Joseph's inner senses were suddenly aroused and he felt the presence of intangible others who had joined them for this moment. For a few seconds he had a strong sense of his brothers and had no doubt they were near. He glanced around the room to see if anyone else had noticed and saw Anastasios turn his head to stare at him. He looked as though he was about to say something, but then Anastasia started speaking again.

"We did not know the form the event would take, only that something was approaching. It was as though we could feel the bow wave, the displacement of the inner tides and currents as it advanced. Those we work with sensed it also and were excited by what they perceived. They asked us what was happening, but there was little we could say. The origin of the disturbance was concealed from our vision. All that we could discern was that a temporal cycle was being completed; that something that had manifested before was returning in a new and more profound way. We knew that we would have to wait for the energy of the movement to erupt into the outer world before we would be able to see more clearly. The older and wiser among our friends on the inner planes, although they also could not make out the cause of the approaching surge, told us that they had occasionally seen such things before. They said we were privileged and that great opportunity was drawing near, but also that humanity would require humility and courage to accept the gift that would be offered. They told us that such openings came to all worlds, but only rarely. They were tipping points and could be the precursor to a great evolutionary leap or the harbinger of a fall backwards. These words left us both excited and uneasy."

Anastasia stopped speaking and Joseph could see tension etched on her face. She looked over at Anastasios who nodded in silent agreement and took up the story. His demeanor had now lost any sense of play. He spoke in a tone of deadly seriousness.

"You must understand, Father Joseph, that never before have we experienced something of this nature. Also, there is nothing in the records of our fellowship that can help. The ... taste ... of what we encountered and the words of our friends left us disturbed as we waited to see what would happen. It was clear that humanity was to be presented with a fork in the road. The choice made would determine its future for many ages - or even if it had a future."

Anastasios leaned forward until his face was only a short distance from Joseph's.

"You see, our inner journeying over millennia has left our fellowship in no doubt as to the insignificance of humanity in the unthinkable vastness of creation. We are but one expression of the mighty Source of All that is. It wants us to evolve and grow, but it will also let us wither and die if we refuse to express the potential it has placed in our depths. We are not life. We are merely a single manifestation among a countless multitude that express the life force. That force will continue to create and flower only where it is permitted to flow." Anastasios leaned back a little way. "So you will understand how we have been both troubled and electrified by what we knew was about to transpire. The waiting has been a strain, for we know that much hangs on this time."

Anastasios sat back and nodded at the Hegumeni to take up the story again.

"So you will see, Father Joseph, that when the Messenger ... the Visitor ... appeared over Niagara a few days ago we immediately understood its import. The world saw only that something ... someone ... had journeyed to the Earth across space. We saw also an eruption from the hidden depths of reality." Anastasia paused before continuing. "And immediately the Messenger spoke to the world and left us in no doubt as to its provenance."

Joseph was perplexed.

"I don't remember any words being reported?"

Alex came to life at this point.

"But think, Father, is all communication only verbal? Are there not other ways to speak that say far more than words?"

Joseph thought back to sitting in front of the television in the rectory watching the pictures from Niagara. It felt like a lifetime ago, yet was only a few days. He remembered listening to the story of the Visitor's arrival being endlessly repeated, as the producers desperately tried to fill the void left by its inactivity. Then something clicked in his mind. He recalled listening to an astronomer relating how she had first noticed a point of light set against the moon during the lunar eclipse. A tingle of excitement went through him as her words came to mind. She had described watching the point of light perform a slow dance as it had repeatedly traced a simple pattern against the strangely-colored background.

He now knew why Anastasia's drawing of a circle with a radius had felt familiar.

It was the same design that the Visitor had drawn.

It had spoken wordless words through the power of a symbol and thereby said so much. It had greeted those who had eyes to see and ears to hear.

Joseph sat back in his chair and stared at a point above Alex's shoulder. Anastasia had said that it was an ancient symbol, the origins of which were lost in time. Its use by the Visitor as a greeting carried suggestions of bygone encounters or landings on common inner shores. Or perhaps both. It conveyed intimations as to the Visitor's agenda. It insinuated the mechanism that connected the advent of the Visitor with Joseph's dreams and other experiences. Also, it once more demonstrated how its arrival was weaving together many strands into a synchronous whole. He again recalled Alex's conviction that the Visitor must have known that the two of them would meet, although his friend had never fully explained why he believed this so firmly. Joseph became aware that Alex was watching him expectantly. He pulled Anastasia's drawing directly in front of him, then looked up at Alex and smiled.

"I think I'm beginning to understand," was all he could think of to say. Alex did not reply, but watched him expectantly. Joseph took the hint. "There's more, isn't there? It's not only this."

"Remember, Father Joseph, great beings rarely speak to us in crude literalisms," Anastasios rumbled. "They prefer questions to answers and delight in symbols. They seek to draw from within us that which they would have us know, for in so doing we grow."

Joseph looked at the Hegumen and nodded. He then cast his mind back again to the Visitor's arrival, seeking what he had previously failed to see. The others kept silence, allowing him to think.

The first sighting was on the moon. Was there anything about this that carried symbolic meaning? He tried to remember all he could about the myths and deities that human beings had associated with the moon over the ages, but there were so many that his mind quickly became confused. All kinds of subtle connections could be deduced with the Visitor's lunar arrival, yet it all felt dead in his mind. He had long ago learned that this was a sign that he was on the wrong track, even when the logic was impeccable. He went back to the beginning and tried to find a new angle. He replayed in his mind all that he had heard about the first sightings - and then something finally clicked into place.

He remembered the same astronomer saying that she had watched the point of light perform its strange maneuvers over the Sea of Tranquility. This was a place that needed no introduction to Joseph. It was one of the most famous locations in human history. It was where a human being first stood on the surface of another world. It was the site of the first Apollo landing and of Neil Armstrong's immortal words. The connection was obvious. A visitor from another world using a symbol of humanity's own space exploration to make itself known.

Yet although Joseph felt that he was now on the right track, he knew he had still to properly hear what the Visitor was saying.

He refocused and tried to remember every detail of that extraordinary arrival. In his mind he saw more observers being interviewed and government officials being grilled by the media. Then he latched onto something. At first he was not sure what it was. It was like trying to recall a telephone number that remained just out of reach. Then suddenly it was there, clear as daylight. A disheveled and rather distracted scientist, who looked like he was only speaking to the press under orders, was being asked by a journalist about the moment when he had become aware of the Visitor. That particular piece had stuck in Joseph's mind because it turned out that the scientist ran a laser ranging station aimed at the moon. The man had irritably recounted how having aimed the laser at the reflectors left at the Apollo Tranquility base, the measured distance then began to decrease rapidly. In that instant, he had realized that something strange was happening. Joseph tried to see why this particular incident was so important. The deep levels of his mind seemed to know what he needed to see and were leading him to clues. He thought about the laser. He could see that by placing itself in the beam, the Visitor could show that it was real and on the moon, before demonstrating that it was unequivocally moving closer. Again, though, he knew that there was more than this. Then he remembered something else that the scientist had said. He recounted how the Visitor had subtly changed the reflected beam, almost as though it was sending a message, but careful analysis had revealed nothing. Joseph's mind lit up as he finally understood. The Visitor had used Apollo to send the message. The message was the messenger.

"Apollo," he suddenly said out loud.

There was a tangible sense of relief around the table and the three of them smiled at Joseph.

"I had complete faith that you would get there eventually, Father Joseph," Alex beamed, while trying to give the impression that he had not believed this at all. "I had hoped, though, that it wouldn't take quite so long," he continued mischievously. Then he became serious once more. "But this is only a first step."

Joseph knew this only too well. The surge of satisfaction at having seen the importance of the Apollo link quickly subsided as he realized that he still had no idea what this meant. The room returned to silence as he sank once more into thought. It took only a few moments for an eerie sense of synchronicity to arise. Apollo was, of course, one of the most important gods of ancient Greece, where Joseph now found himself, surrounded by Greek friends, having met Alex seemingly by chance in far away England. He began to glimpse what Alex must have realized in the hermit cell. Difficult though it was to grasp, the Visitor had apparently seen in advance that the two of them would meet. Joseph marveled at this, but at the same time understood how it could be. Just as Anastasia and Anastasios had seen the approach of the Visitor prefigured by movements within the inner tides and currents of reality, its "bow wave" as they put it, an advanced race might well be able to discern more detailed probabilities. They might be able to make out the sub-currents and ripples that would spread outwards from the main event. But these would only be probabilities, not certainties, for humans were creative beings. In other words, they were capable of unforeseen reactions and thoughts. If they could surprise God, then they could most certainly do the same to lesser beings, no matter how advanced.

Then something deepened within Joseph's mind and new insights arose. For a few moments he began to think in shapes and images, rather than words. An intuition arose that this explanation was true as far as it went, but that at another, more profound level, the Visitor had not been discerning the future but remembering the past. That it could experience the arrow of time both forwards and backwards. That in some unfathomable way it was also journeying backwards in time, as if from the far future towards the present moment, watching as the threads that in normal human perception spread out from each moment reassembled themselves. This was how it had been able to see the likelihood that Alex and he would meet. Yet, paradoxically, there was still unpredictability. The creative impulse of humanity could still work its magic even in this direction. And, just as paradoxically, this understanding did not invalidate his first insights. Each was true at its own level. How the images and shapes that he was seeing conveyed this, Joseph could not say. Somehow their composition and movement induced such understanding. He began to feel disorientated and knew that he had to return to normal awareness. He was tasting a quality and depth of consciousness that he was not used to, like a teenager experiencing strong alcohol for the first time. He focused his will and forced himself back to an awareness of the room.

Joseph found his three companions staring at him with interest, but he had no inclination to share what he had experienced. There was something too personal about it. Too much would be lost in the telling. Instead, he focused his eyes once more on the wall behind Alex and tried to reassemble his original train of thought about Apollo. The great god was fresh in his mind. He and Clare had been reading all about the Greek myths in preparation for their visit. As he recalled this, his mind tasted sadness once more. But he also again felt a sense of having been prepared for this moment, of seeds planted in the past now bearing fruit.

He recalled that Apollo was the child of Zeus and Leto, and one of the most important of the Greek Gods. Over the centuries he had been given many attributes. He was the god of light and sun, of truth, prophecy, music, the arts and healing. Apollo was nearly always represented as the beardless youth and associated with objects like the lyre on which he was supposed to play wonderful music. But nothing he could remember seemed to connect with the arrival of the Visitor. He tried to think back further, beyond what he had read in preparation for the holiday.

It was then that Joseph recalled something that sent a shiver of excitement down his spine.

It was an old memory, from his teenage years, of endless hours in a dull classroom studying Homer, the great Greek poet. The Iliad should have been fascinating to a young male with its stories of battle and heroism, but the teacher had managed to drain all life from the epic saga by proceeding from the premise that it was only written in order to be analyzed in as abstract a manner as possible. It was, though, not Joseph's memories of the Iliad that had triggered his epiphany, but a lesser known work by Homer that the teacher had also required them to study. It was called "The Hymn to Apollo".

It told how the great god swam in the sea as a dolphin.

As soon as he recalled the verses, Joseph could see in his mind the vision from the hermit's cell. Once again he was leaping and surging through the waves, overflowing with the joy of being alive. He was also filled with purpose. His oceanic journey was not random, he was heading somewhere. And the verses of the Hymn to Apollo told him the destination. They recounted the legend of how Apollo, in the shape of a dolphin, carried Cretan priests on his back across the sea to the place where one of his greatest temples would be founded.

Apollo took them to Delphi.

Of all the places in Greece that he and Clare had wanted to visit, Delphi was second only to Metéora. Its story had fascinated them and they had felt very drawn to go there. Built on an array of terraces that clung to the southern face of Mount Parnassus, Delphi was the most important oracle of the classical world. It had been sacred to both Greeks and Romans for at least a thousand years, before the advent of Christian power in the Latin empire led to its dissolution in the fourth century. It had been a complex of magnificent buildings, now ruined, that zigzagged up the mountain side, following a switchback processional path. It occurred to Joseph that building on mountains seemed to be in the Greek blood. The heart of the complex had been the Temple of Apollo, which was now little more than an impressive base made of large stone blocks with a few columns left standing. As a picture of the ruins appeared in his mind, another strand of the hermit cell vision erupted into consciousness. It was the most disturbing image. It was the woman, with the disheveled hair, who stared into the distance, lost in other worlds. Involuntarily he took a deep breath and realization dawned as to the meaning of the face. It was the Pythia, the oracle, who sat in a fume-filled room below the temple dispensing obscure advice and guidance to those who came to see her. Perhaps her trances were the product of hallucinogenic gasses that flowed out of the rocks beneath, but whatever the cause, her enigmatic words changed lives, as even Socrates himself had discovered.

Joseph could contain himself no longer.

"Alex, it's Delphi. The Visitor is pointing me towards Delphi. The dolphin is Apollo on his way to Delphi and the strange woman is the oracle. I'm being told to go to Delphi to … hear words of guidance."

Alex jumped slightly at the sudden outburst. Joseph realized that he must have been absorbed in his thoughts for a long time.

"It's more than just the dolphin, Father Joseph," Alex replied having quickly recovered his composure. "You saw shining cliffs with the sun rising above. These are the Phaedriades, 'the shining ones', the two rock faces on the southern side of Mount Parnassos that overlook Delphi. In the legends, the sun is Apollo in his chariot. Everything points to Delphi."

Joseph absorbed what Alex had said and looked thoughtful.

"It all makes sense, Alex, but there are also other layers to the symbolism. There is a great emphasis on light ... and messages being hidden in light."

"This is true my friend, but I have a feeling that these other layers of meaning sow seeds for the future. For now I think we have to concentrate on the more literal understanding - you are being asked by the Visitor ... the Messenger ... to go to Delphi. It is where you will meet."

Joseph knew that Alex was right, although the thought made his stomach churn.

"There is nothing that tells me when to go. Do I just turn up and wait?"

Anastasios interrupted.

"Oh no, Father, I think that we can assume that our strange friend is more precise than that." The Hegumen paused and took a drink to wash down the last of his food. "In ancient times the pilgrims would come to Delphi on only one day per month to seek guidance - the seventh day." He paused again and looked straight at Joseph. "Tomorrow is the seventh day."

This time Joseph's stomach did a somersault. Everything had suddenly become very real. He found himself taking a deep breath.

"Right," was all that came out.

Anastasios pressed on remorselessly.

"We have made arrangements for you to be taken to Delphi before first light. You will leave in a few hours with Alex. It is important that you are there before the sun rises over the Phaedriades, for it is then that we think the Messenger will come. You must be waiting. We have also arranged through our more influential ... friends ... for you to have private access. The site will be closed due to unexpected safety issues. Our friends will also make sure that television cameras are present. Whatever happens must be seen by the world, although until that moment all will be kept secret."

Only now did Joseph realize just how far behind the curve he had been. Alex and his friends had been waiting for him to catch up. He felt slightly embarrassed. He also felt irrationally annoyed that so many plans had been made without consulting him. Anastasia seemed to sense his feelings. Once more she placed her hand on his arm.

"Please forgive us, Father, for taking so much for granted. We just felt that there was so little time."

Anastasios and Alex looked surprised by her words. It had never occurred to them that Joseph might feel disturbed by their planning. But her concern melted his irritation.

"Please don't worry about my ingratitude. Sometimes I feel that despite being at the center of all this, I have the least control over events."

"Perhaps it is better that way, Father Joseph," Anastasios replied. "You can then come to everything as a child, unencumbered by detail."

Joseph looked at the Hegumen seeking any sign of disrespect in his words, but instead glimpsed a trace of envy in the big man's eyes. For the first time, it occurred to him that others might long to be in his shoes. He was humbled. He looked at each of them in turn.

"I am truly grateful for all you have done."

The atmosphere lightened. As if taking this as a sign, Anastasia rose to her feet and began gathering the plates and bowls.

"Before you leave us, Father, we must prepare for what is to come. We have fed our bodies. Now we must feed our souls with the bread and wine that the Christ offers."

Chapter 21

Anastasia led them back into the refectory. It was clear that the other monks and nuns had been awaiting their arrival. The monastics were still in silence and Joseph wondered whether the whole meal had been eaten in that atmosphere. He had a feeling that this was indeed the case, for it was now a mature silence, nurtured by time. Then, without words or any visible sign, the robed figures lined up behind the Hegumen and Hegumeni, women on the left and men on the right. Joseph and Alex went to the rear of the procession, only to be waved to the front by Anastasios. He signaled that they should stand immediately behind him and Anastasia. Joseph sensed that Alex was uncomfortable with such prominence and what must have been for him a disconcerting break with convention. He had also ended up on the women's side.

Then the chant started. Once more the primal rumble of Anastasios' astonishing drone reverberated through Joseph's body, as mysterious words poured forth from the Hegumen. Within moments, the sound was been picked up by the other monks and their combined voices seemed to send subtle vibrations through the stones of the building. Joseph recalled reading somewhere that great religious buildings had been deliberately constructed so as to amplify chant. He wondered if this was another attribute of the refectory, and perhaps the whole monastery.

But the procession did not move.

All stood perfectly still as the cavernous drone gradually filled their consciousness. Joseph was aware of the effect it was having on his mind, yet could not have resisted even if he had wanted to. It would have been like King Canute trying to hold back the sea. Slowly, the sound imbued a profound inner stillness, combined with intense alertness. It also brought a sense of community; of togetherness. He discovered an unspoken sense of companionship with a group of people he barely knew. Such was the power of sacred sound.

Joseph became so absorbed in the chant that it was a shock when, led by Anastasia, the nuns suddenly broke into song, their higher pitched voices combining with those of the men to transform the sound into a multilayered harmony. It was like spring bursting forth from winter. This was the moment that the procession started to move, the robes of the monks and nuns swaying gently as they walked with a slow undulating gait. There was no conscious decision to walk in this fashion; it was a natural response to the rhythm of the chant.

With Alex at his side, Joseph followed the Hegumen and Hegumeni out of the large double doors at the end of the refectory, very aware of the line of robed figures that followed. For a few moments he remembered his dream of the community of monks in the forest, his brothers, and how they had followed their leader to the clearing. It was a ghostly echo from the depths of time. Once through the doors, they turned right down a wide candle-lit corridor that Joseph had not had time to explore during his brief stay. The walls and the stone beneath his feet were rough and worn, unlike the polished precision of the refectory. He sensed that they were moving into an older part of the monastery. In the flickering light, with the chant resonating ever more intensely in his mind, he could just make out faded ancient paintings on the walls. The colors must once have been glorious. There was also a smell of incense, despite the fact that the monks and nuns were not carrying any. Joseph realized that the aroma could only come from the walls themselves, soaked in sacred fragrance for so many centuries that it had become part of their fabric. After about a hundred feet, the procession turned left and descended a broad staircase. Each step had a small hollow worn into the center by the countless feet that had trodden that way. So marked were some of the depressions that Joseph was occasionally thrown slightly off balance. As they progressed downwards, in the illumination provided by wall-mounted candles he could see faint frescoes of Bible scenes painted into the ancient stone. He realized that Alex's work in the entrance corridor was the continuation of an artistic tradition in this place. At the bottom of the stairs a pair of mighty wooden doors stood open, framed in an arched stone surround, through which the procession wound its way.

The sight that greeted Joseph's eyes took his breath away. Strangely, for a brief moment, it reminded him of the hermit's grotto through which he and Alex had escaped. It had the same enchanting, cave-like atmosphere. Passing a stand that held an icon of an unknown saint, painted in the most brilliant golds, blues and reds, they entered a room about twenty feet long and thirty wide. Ahead of them, across the center, stretched a broad red carpet, at the end of which were two more impressive doors, opened wide to reveal an even greater chamber beyond. As they moved along the red carpet, the sound of the chant subtly altered by the new surroundings, Joseph could not help but look around and absorb what he was passing through. From his scanty knowledge of the Orthodox Church, he knew that this anti-chamber was called the narthex. It symbolized the point of connection between the mundane world and the sacred space of the monastery chapel. It was like a spiritual airlock, a place of transition from one expression of reality to another. Traditionally, it was the place beyond which non-Orthodox could not pass, yet no one was telling him to step out of line. Once again, he realized the extraordinary generosity with which he was being treated. Against the wall on either side he could see a row of high-armed chairs, elaborately carved out of a dark wood that exuded gravitas. From the dregs of memory, he recalled that these were called stacidia and were provided for those few parts of the Liturgy when sitting was permitted. The high arm-rests could support standing when necessary. For most of the service, which could last several hours, the Orthodox stood before God.

Within moments, it seemed to Joseph, they reached the double doors on the other side of the room. He knew that these were called the Royal Doors and marked the entrance to the nave, the main part of the chapel. On either side of the doorway, as they passed through, stood two large candles on beautiful stands, their flames burning brightly. These were the menalia, representing the pillars of fire which in the Bible led the Hebrews into the promised land. It reminded him that virtually everything in the Orthodox tradition had symbolic meaning and pointed beyond the literal to the hidden. Joseph had no doubt, however, that this community related to such symbols in a far more nuanced and esoteric way than did their more traditional brethren. Then they went through into the nave to be greeted by the pungent, evocative aroma of incense, this time fresh, not some fossilized relic of long-ago prayer. The new chamber was much larger than the first and was illumined by what seemed like hundreds of candles. Through the faint haze of incense smoke, Joseph could see before them the iconostasis, a large screen that stretched from wall to wall, covered in exquisite icons of Jesus and other holy figures. The vivid colors of the stylized paintings were astonishing and the images were a feast for the imagination. The work looked new and, glancing over at Alex, Joseph had no doubt as to the identity of the artist. It was clear that the aim of such a room was very different to that of the refectory. Here the idea was to inspire the mind, not lead it to stillness. But it was a focused energizing, to enable a creative reaching out into deeper realities. As Joseph looked closer at the rich technicolor screen, he could just make out the three doorways that were always traditionally present. At the center of the screen were double doors, often called the Beautiful Gates, that led through to the sanctuary, the third element of an Orthodox church together with the narthex and nave. It was there, hidden away from general view, that on a square altar the bread and wine would be consecrated.

East or West, despite different language and understanding, it was the universal rite at the heart of Church. The exception was that in the Western Church, the community that had its roots in the Roman lineage, the consecration took place in full view. But for the Eastern tradition, this was such a special, mysterious event that it must be performed hidden from the eyes of all except the privileged few. It was the moment when the bread and wine became the spiritual body and blood of Jesus. It was the great sacrament. Joseph knew that whilst his understanding of what took place might be different to many other followers of Jesus, at a deeper, more soulful level, they all had felt its ineffable power.

The main area of the nave was almost square, with a small, semi-circular apse on either side, each containing a chair and lectern made out of the same dark wood as the stacidia in the narthex. On each side wall were more similarly dark stacidia, but it was what stood at the end of each, prior to the apses, that really caught the eye. Two magnificent canopied thrones faced each other across the central space. Painted gold, with a bright red cushion lining the back and seat, they contrasted sharply with the dark wood of the other furniture, while complimenting the imposing iconostasis. Joseph had seen similar thrones in western cathedrals, where they were reserved for the bishop. But here it was different. Without pausing, Anastasios and Anastasia each made their way to one of the thrones, he to the right, and she to the left. Having been walking directly behind them, Joseph was not sure what to do, so he just stopped. It turned out to be the right thing, as the monks and nuns fanned out around him, roughly keeping to their male/female demarcation. The only exceptions were a monk and nun who positioned themselves at one of the lecterns in each apse, the female to the left and the male to the right. Joseph guessed that these individuals had been chosen to be deacons for the liturgy. As the nun turned, he saw that it was Adriadna. He was not surprised. He had a strong intuition that tonight's liturgy was intended to have a power that required only the most senior to preside.

As movement ceased, the chant stopped of its own accord, leaving a silence that was thick and sensuous. Joseph's eyes wandered across the chamber and he noticed an incense burner to the side of each deacon. His gaze lazily followed the swirling smoke upwards, until he stopped in amazement at what lay directly above his head. The roof above the Nave was domed and looking down at him was the face of Jesus, picked out in the same blue, red and gold as the other icons, only on a far vaster scale. It was as breathtaking as the ceiling fresco in the entrance corridor, but carried a very different, transcendent energy. The offering of bread and wine that dominated the former had a great earthly feel to it. What lay above him now, evoked that which was not of this world. It was the ultimate Jesus. It was Christ in Glory. The eyes peered down into Joseph, transfixing him despite his aching neck. He had no idea who, or what, Jesus was, or what it meant to be "the Christ". But he knew in that moment that the meaning of these words was touching his soul, expanding his consciousness. He was brought back down to earth by the voices of Anastasia and Anastasios, in perfect harmony, chanting a short proclamation in what he guessed must be liturgical Greek. They were immediately followed by the two deacons, who embarked on a long litany, to which the assembled monks and nuns responded from time to time. It was clear to Joseph that everything in this community was performed jointly by men and women, reflecting the polarity that was central to their understanding.

As the rite went on, Joseph had little idea what was happening except that on several occasions he picked out his own name from the torrent of Greek that assailed his ears. He was humbled to realize that they were praying for him. On one occasion he heard Alex's name alongside his own and, glancing over, saw his friend look down, his face filled with emotion. Joseph lost track of time and, for a while, became an empty space through which the words and rich sensory experiences simply passed. His body ached from standing for so long, yet it did not seem to matter. The discomfort was in a distant place in his mind, too far away to disturb the flow.

When the prayer suddenly stopped, it took a few moments for his mind to register the fact. It was like a sudden awakening from a dreamy sleep. As he brought his eyes into focus, he became aware that there was movement in the chamber. It had been so long since this had happened that it was almost shocking. As Joseph watched, the two deacons moved slowly over to stand shoulder to shoulder, facing the iconostasis. Then Anastasia and Anastasios moved towards each other and, to Joseph's surprise, stopped and looked directly at him. Surprise turned to apprehension as, with a discreet movement of the hand, the Hegumeni signaled that he should join them. Joseph hesitated, confused by the unexpected turn of events, until a nudge from Alex got him moving. He walked forward and found himself being subtly shepherded until he stood behind the two deacons, and sensed the Hegumeni and Hegumen form up behind him. This was the cue for the community to begin chanting once more and, in response, the deacons moved off to their left, towards one of the side doors in the iconostasis. Joseph followed, assuming that this was what he was meant to do. With dignity and grace the deacons led the small party through the door and into the sanctuary behind the iconic screen. Joseph's mind was reeling. He knew that in the Orthodox tradition only a few were allowed to enter this inner sanctum. That he, a non-Orthodox, should be allowed to do so was almost unthinkable. Directly in front of them was a table covered in red brocade, on which rested a paten with small particles of bread heaped at its center and a chalice about half-full with wine. It was the raw material of the Mass, which had seized his soul as a young man. It was what he had shared with the forest community in his

dream and had celebrated in his own church on the very morning
that the Visitor had arrived. He saw in that moment that there
could be no better preparation for whatever was to happen the
following morning.

Anastasia and Anastasios moved to the table. He reverently
lifted the paten while she took the chalice. Turning, they made
their way back out of the door by which they had entered, while
Joseph was guided by Adriadna to follow immediately behind.
The two deacons then fell into step behind him. Re-entering the
nave, the small procession wound its way around the edge of the
chamber, chant and incense filling the air, as the bread and wine
were held high. Eventually they stood once more before the
iconostasis, with the Beautiful Gates before them at its center.
Anastasia and Anastasios paused and Joseph could sense the
eyes of the great painting of Jesus looking down from the domed
ceiling above his head. Then they moved forward through the
central doors of the screen, entering the sanctuary once more, but
by a different route. The deacons closed the doors behind them
and the chanting from outside stopped.

What was about to happen would not be seen, only heard.

The deacons moved to each side of the altar while the
Hegumeni and Hegumen placed the bread and wine at its center.
Joseph had a suspicion that he was about to watch something
unheard of. For all of its emphasis on the equality of men and
women before God, in the Orthodox tradition only male priests
could pronounce the "Anaphora", the great prayer of consecration through which the bread and wine were spiritually transformed. The ancient line of reasoning was that the priest took the
place of Jesus, a man, at the re-enactment of the Last Supper and
also chose only male apostles to take his work forward. Joseph
had no doubt as to the views of Bishop Jennifer on such a justifi-
cation, but that was not what was stirring his interest. It was quite
clear from their positioning that Anastasia was going to preside
jointly with Anastasios. Joseph was about to witness something

that should not be. Yet it was logical. Such a fundamental breach with Orthodox tradition followed naturally from their views on polarity. Joseph stood expectant, astonished that he should even be in the sanctuary for the consecration, and even more amazed at what he was about to see.

But the next thing that happened shook him further. Anastasia turned and beckoned him to the altar. He was too stunned to react, so she waved him forward again. Numbly, he felt his legs carry him to the Holy Table and he found himself standing at her side. The three of them stood before the bread and wine, the female priest with a man on either side.

"We would be honored if you would concelebrate with us at the moment of epiclesis," she whispered to him.

"Of course," he found his mouth saying, hiding his surprise at the request. For a non-Orthodox to be asked to participate in the greatest mystery of the Divine Liturgy was an honor beyond words. He had little time to think further as, in perfect harmony, the Hegumen and Hegumeni began to chant the anaphora. Once more, Joseph could not understand the words that poured from their lips, but the basic elements of the great prayer were common to all of the traditional churches. It was reasonably easy, therefore, for him to follow each stage and he began to feel slightly nervous as the epiclesis approached. Then Anastasia and Anastasios paused and he knew that the moment had arrived. In a single movement, the three of them reached out and held their hands over the paten and chalice while, in low pitched voices, the Hegumen and Hegumeni pronounced the words of invocation, asking that the Holy Spirit be sent down onto the bread and wine. This was the epiclesis, the moment of transformation wherein the simple food became spiritual sustenance. It was the priestly moment. It was a moment that, for Joseph, seemed to last an age, yet within seconds he was withdrawing his hands as the great prayer moved on. It was a moment that would live with him for ever.

The rest of the prayer passed by him in a daze and it took a few moments for him to realize that it had ended. The deacons moved to the altar, soaked the small pieces of bread in the consecrated wine and handed them to Anastasia. Taking a small ceremonial spoon, she scooped up one of the pieces and held it to Joseph's mouth.

"Father Joseph, receive the body and blood of Jesus."

"Amen," Joseph replied as he received the sacrament. The taste of the wine was sharp and lingered for a while after he had swallowed. He then stood back to allow everyone else to receive, but once more Anastasia beckoned him to rejoin her. She held out the chalice and spoon for him to take.

"Father, on this of all nights we would be honored to receive the sacrament from your hand."

Joseph had no words for the trust that was being placed in him. He almost felt that he wanted to cry. He controlled himself, took the chalice and spoon and began to share the sacrament with the others in the sanctuary. The deacons then led them back into the nave and, with Anastasia and Anastasios on either side, he distributed the bread and wine to the rest of the community. As he did so, he could feel, almost physically, the presence of his brothers as in their forest, on some inner plane, they too celebrated the mystery of the Mass. He knew that as he placed the spoon on the lips of those in this remote part of Greece, so they also were tasting sharp wine and rough bread. There was a joining across the ages and through the depths of reality. He knew also that they, like him, were preparing for what was to come. And everything was overseen by a presence that words could never approach.

It felt like the most holy moment of his life.

And, unknown to Joseph, a silent observer watched and marveled.

He had not wasted his time.

As he waited for events to unfold, he had connected more intimately with the land below and the waves of awareness with which it had been, and was in relationship. He had admired the building, so obviously the out-picturing of arcane resonances within the consciousness of those who built it. He could sense its atmosphere, which vibrated at the boundary of this plane of reality, accumulated over centuries from minds seeking to touch the Source of All. With the help of the fellowship who reached to him across time, who knew this place long before the building existed, he had absorbed the sacred story for which it was a gateway. It was an extraordinary mythic tale that had moved him deeply. He had encountered many such stories in his travels, each in their own way pointing towards the truths of existence, but rarely one that so emphasized the road of vulnerability and seeming weakness. The awesome being around which the story was woven filled his mind for a while. He knew that he had met a profound manifestation of the living spring from which all poured forth. Occasionally, rarely, he had been touched by such manifestations, wearing different masks. Although the form and dynamic were so different, so alien, he knew beyond doubt that he had been blessed.

At other times he had monitored the continuing reaction to his presence through the electronic media that permeated this world. He had enjoyed Joseph's appearance and been intrigued by his thoughts. This was a being of great depths, only now beginning to suspect that he was far more then he had ever dreamed. Since then he had seen how his lack of activity was changing the collective mood of the world. It had become increasingly suspicious and resentful. This interested him, for on other worlds his silence and stillness would have enabled a growing acceptance as he became part of the general background to life. Mind structures could be so different. He had tried to understand the causes of this world's reaction and concluded that, perhaps, there were elements of pride and power at work. To be ignored could be seen as the greatest insult and to be able to do nothing about it a shocking emasculation for a race so accustomed to dominance. But his presence was meant to disrupt and disturb. This is how it had to be, for he was midwife for a new expression of consciousness that could only grow out of the ruins of the old.

As his time over the church had lengthened, he had watched with some admiration as brave souls approached to stare at what he knew must be a nerve-jangling sight. The light vessel still provoked awe in him, who knew it so well. So he could imagine how it must appear to the beings of such an undeveloped world. There were two such visitors who intrigued him. Two females who came much closer than the others. One he had encountered before on the night he had joined with Joseph in the blue light. She had stood nearby, different to the rest, seeking to meet with him in the depths of the moment. They had touched lightly and he had sensed her connection with the land and openness to other planes of being. In their brief encounter he had sensed how she embodied an older story to that of the sacred building, but no less powerful. Her spirit had enlivened him and, in turn, he knew that she had glimpsed something of his own truth. Now she was back and he felt glad.

The other female was very different and he was at first surprised that they should be together. She did not have the same feeling for the land and the life force that flowed through it. She was a creature of thought. Her mind was powerful and clear, but deeper, natural currents were suppressed. Yet when he considered the two of them, he saw that unconsciously each needed what the other had and that the inner tides had brought them to swim together for a while. Without at first knowing, and undoubtedly resisting, they would influence each other and both would become more than they were. But as he looked closer, he saw another connection also. They both felt strongly about Joseph. He touched something within them, reminded them of a loss, a hole inside, and through him each sought to heal their heart.

So he had waited and learned, and time had become a distant river, until the fellowship of the forest had returned with power. They had invited him to share in ritual and to this he was not averse for, although unimaginably different, ritual was fundamental to his own people as a way in which they opened to the mystery of being. And now he was immersed in the movement of power and the connection with the ultimate Source of All, that they invoked. Of course, he could not directly experience the bread and wine, but felt its effect on them.

It was in this moment that he knew the reason for their invitation.

They did not dance alone.

Others on his plane of existence kept perfect step and, in so doing, embraced their fellows across time and space. Caught up together in the stately movement, tendrils of consciousness entwined and from his position of solemn witness he recognized the being that led the dance. His awareness touched Joseph's in a new way and fresh connections came alive in his mind. He saw that his message had been understood and that he must soon move to another place so that great things might occur.

But something else happened that took him by surprise.

As the ritual came to an end and his ancient friends faded away, he found himself going far within and, awakened by the intimacy of his encounter with Joseph, dreamed again of what once had been.

Chapter 22

The stone seat felt cold even through the thick coat he was wearing. It belonged to Anastasios and was much too big for Joseph, but he was grateful for its warmth in the pre-dawn chill. The rain of the previous day had given way to a crystal clear starry night that had brought freezing temperatures and frost to the slopes of Mount Parnassus. The moon, now past its fullness, hung low in the sky, throwing long silvery shadows through the ruins of Delphi. From his high perch on the side of the mountain, the distant lights of the port of Itéa on the Gulf of Corinth sparkled brightly through the translucent ice-cold air. Joseph knew that between where he sat and the town lay a drop of two thousand feet and a journey of ten miles. For the ancient pilgrims arriving by ship, it would have been a demanding climb to Delphi, but the testing of body, mind and spirit was an essential element of pilgrimage shared by all religions.

For a long time he had not been able to take his eyes off the stars. He had an irrational feeling that they shone for him that night and their beauty made him want to cry. His life-long yearning to plunge into their midst, filled him with its delight and frustration. Then it had occurred to him that though he might not be able to travel to the stars, it seemed that they were coming to him. The thought stopped him in his tracks and awakened another deep-rooted feeling that had dominated his life; his sense of unknown purpose; of having something important to accomplish. In a moment of profound stillness he saw that these two great themes of his life were connected. He had not been able to think properly after that. The thought was too enormous and seemed to have short-circuited his mind. After a while, with considerable effort, Joseph had pushed the unthinkable to one side and refocused. He would need his wits about him for what was to come.

He was not alone. Alex sat a little way off, silent and invisible. He seemed to think that Joseph needed space, both psychological and physical, to prepare himself. Somewhere in the darkness, also, further up the slope, was a television crew. They had no idea why they were there, having been told only to be ready at an instant to broadcast whatever occurred. Their presence and the private access to Delphi spoke of the power of the shadowy fellowship to which Alex and the Metéora community belonged. The arrival of the television crew had been a shock to Joseph as they had brought with them a reminder of the normal human world. In the short time he had been at Metéora, he had too easily forgotten how it made him feel. Joseph had hidden from the crew in the darkness so as not to give the slightest clue as to what might be about to transpire. Every now and again a faint conversation drifted down from above and, although he did not speak Greek, Joseph was in no doubt that they were not enjoying their latest assignment.

Actually, Joseph did not need to prepare himself. There was no way that he could. What was about to happen was too unimaginable. So he was just allowing his mind to drift, to go where it would as he waited for the sun to rise above the unseen cliffs that lay behind him.

At first, his mind had been full of the events of the previous evening and night. He had found himself replaying the conversation with Anastasia and Anastasios, savoring each astonishing insight that they had planted in his mind. He realized that it did not matter too much at the moment whether he fully understood the ideas, or even agreed with them. Their most important effect was to blow his mind open, to shake the foundations of his thought structures, so that his consciousness would be more receptive, more sensitive than it already was. The Divine Liturgy had multiplied the effect exponentially.

Perhaps that was the best way to prepare for the unimaginable.

As he remembered the conversation, however, one particular question kept coming to mind, needing to be resolved. For some reason he needed to know what to call the being that still waited, as far as he knew, in the strange vessel of light above his church in far away England. Up until now, along with the rest of the world, he had called him or her "the Visitor". Anastasia and Anastasios, though, had used the term "Messenger", and had good reason to do so. Yet neither description felt quite right to Joseph. They were too impersonal. All words paint pictures in the mind, which in turn influence what we think and do. So to have the right word mattered. He wanted another word, but nothing satisfactory came to him.

It was not so dark any more.

He had not noticed the shift, it had been too gradual, but it was definitely lighter than it had been. Joseph looked over his shoulder at the mountain and there was a faint glow just peeking over its top edge. He looked up at the stars and their pinpoint light was not as sharp. Dawn was approaching and with it the incredible unknown. But it was still quiet and Joseph slipped back into his thoughts.

After the Divine Liturgy the farewells had been short but intense. As soon as the rite was complete, Anastasia and Anastasios had led the way to the main entrance to the monastery. Two silent men waited. The Hegemeni had taken the hand of himself and Alex and looked deeply into their eyes.

"These men will drive you to where you need to be. All other arrangements have been put in place." She had then paused and glanced over at Anastasios, before addressing them again. "Know that we are with you, even though we will be far away. Remember that you are never alone." She had then turned and walked swiftly back into the monastery, with Anastasios following more slowly behind.

The descent down the steep rocky path in the darkness should have been nerve-wracking for Joseph, but he had walked like an automaton. His mind was elsewhere, floating in a stream of consciousness that swept by. The Liturgy had worked its magic in him and its afterglow had still to fade. By the time they had reached the car he had returned to almost normal consciousness and the reverie had been replaced by exhaustion. He could remember nothing of the journey to Delphi, awakened only as they had pulled up at the entrance by an irritable conversation between the driver and a custodian as the gate was reluctantly unlocked.

But he had dreamed.

It was the dream he had experienced before, of the ancient city that stood between two rivers. He had dreamed of the person who always spoke to him, yet this time it had been different. There had been no conversation. They had just looked at one another. It had felt intimate, like an expression of the deepest friendship. Also, strangely, Joseph had the strongest feeling that it was a shared dream. That they dreamt of each other. He still had no recollection of the person's face, but somehow knew that their relationship was now different and transformed.

The ringing of a mobile phone shattered his musings. It came from above and Joseph guessed that it belonged to one of the television crew. He sighed, at first irritated that the stillness should have been broken, but then he sensed the sudden tension in the voice that answered the call. He heard what sounded like urgent instructions shouted in Greek and the crew sprang into life. In that moment he knew that the Visitor was no longer above his church in England. And from the reaction of the crew, he knew that it must be very close. The shock was almost physical. When an idea turns into reality, no amount of forethought can anaesthetize the moment. Involuntarily he turned once more in panic to look at the sheer rock face behind him, almost expecting to see the light vessel appear. But although it was by now even lighter, the sun had still to rise over the edge of the mountain and, deep within, he knew that it was then that his second encounter with the Visitor would take place.

In order to relax, or perhaps to avoid thinking about what was to come, he looked around in the early morning light. No decision had been necessary as to where to wait among the ruins. His vision in the hermit cell had made this clear. He sat in the semi-circular amphitheatre at Delphi, high up on one of the top rows. Directly below him in the gathering light was the paved half oval performance area where the actors would have given their all. For the Greeks, theatre was a natural expression of religion as it brought to life vivid stories of gods and heroes, and explored great moral questions. At its best, theatre opened the imagination and thereby consciousness. Bordering the theatre at the rear was the processional way that meandered up through the complex, terminating above where he sat at the amazing sports stadium, able to hold thousands of people, that had been carved into the mountain side. But it was what lay on the next level down from the theatre that was the heart of Delphi. From his seat, Joseph had a birds-eye view. Little was now left of the Temple of Apollo, the dolphin god of light, except for a long rectangular base of large grey stone blocks. Only the irregular remains of six rebuilt columns at the eastern end broke the horizontal monotony. Long gone was the famous portico which displayed the eternal spiritual teaching "Know Thyself". And it was there, right in front of him, in what would once have been a magnificent building, that the Pythia had given out her ambiguous guidance to supplicants. Joseph wondered if his vision of her in the hermit cell bore any resemblance to what the reality would have been. He stared at the ruined temple for a while, moved by what it told him of the material world and the affairs of human beings. The once magnificent building would have awed those who approached, finding their way upwards along the processional route, past the lesser shrines and buildings. It would have seemed indestructible and eternal, yet had now lain in ruins for millennia. So also the worries, ambitions, hopes and fears of all the human beings that had sought the oracle. All-consuming at the time, now completely forgotten. The ruins were a warning against hubris and taking one's thoughts too seriously. It was a warning that helped Joseph as he sat on his cold seat and brought some sense of relief. It caused him to lift his eyes from the sight of human ruins and look gratefully at the grand natural spectacle that lay beyond; the mountains, the valleys filled with olive trees, the birds that were now circling in the sky and the distant sea. They knew nothing of the human soap opera. Joseph reflected that this fact alone should help human beings not get too full of themselves.

The flash of light behind his eyes brought an end to his musings.

It was blue light.

His stomach clenched and he felt his pulse start to race. Even though it was cold, he suddenly felt hot and broke out in a sweat. The moment had come. By an act of will, he controlled his breathing and looked over at Alex. His Greek friend had his eyes shut and appeared lost in some kind of trance.

"Alex, it's here."

Alex's eyes opened slowly and he turned to look at Joseph.

"I know, my friend, I saw it too."

Without more words they stood and turned to face the mountainside that lay behind where they had sat. In that moment the first sliver of sun broke across the ridge. A few seconds later it was not alone in the sky.

The light vessel slowly rose over the crest of the mountain, a swirling elliptical kaleidoscope of soft colors set against the dark blue of the early morning sky. Vaguely, in some distant part of his mind, Joseph heard distant shouts coming from the television crew and knew that this epoch making moment was being witnessed around the world. He knew that this was how it should be. But such thoughts passed swiftly and vaguely as he became transfixed by the second sun of the morning. He watched as it paused, as though to heighten the drama of the moment, and then glided silently towards where he and Alex stood with their necks craning. It passed overhead and Joseph felt a gentle breeze of displaced air. Then it lowered itself gently into the space where Grecian actors once spoke their lines and fired imaginations. The short journey was completed so quickly that Joseph was left just standing on his stony tier, staring at the pulsing vision that filled the ancient stage, no more than sixty feet away. He had the distinct impression that it was looking back. There was a pause while his mind tried to absorb what lay before him. It was Alex who broke the spell.

"It is time to go, my friend."

The words knifed into Joseph and fear seemed to grip every part of his body. Yet something deeper was also present and he found himself walking over to where Alex stood. He took off Anastasios' tent-like coat and handed it over.

"I don't think I'll be needing this."

"No, I am sure that any civilization that can construct such a vessel will also have invented central heating."

Joseph founded himself laughing at the absurdity of Alex's joke. It was the perfect medicine for the tension that gripped him. Alex started laughing too and grabbed him in a huge bear hug. It occurred to Joseph that the watching world must think them mad. With a final squeeze, Alex released his grip and looked into Joseph's eyes.

"Go with God, Father Joseph, and remember what Mother Anastasios said. You are never alone."

With that, Alex stepped back and returned his gaze to the light vessel. Joseph knew that he was deliberately giving him no opportunity for further prevarication. Joseph turned and began to descend the steps, moving ever closer to his destiny. It was a short journey, but it felt for him almost timeless. A profound feeling arose that the whole of his existence had been leading to this moment. Memories of all who had helped him - who loved him - came to mind. He saw Leola, Bishop Jennifer, Alex, Anastasia and Anastasios, and knew that he stood on their shoulders. Yet he also knew that the moment went far beyond this life and this cold sunny morning. He felt the deep currents and tides that had surged to the peak on which he now surfed. He sensed the flow of time that now reached culmination. And there was one face that stayed with him. Her love filled him as he reached the vessel.

The pulsing light now filled his vision and he knew that the next step would take him into another world. He cautiously pushed his hand into the light and pulled it quickly back as an electric tingle shot down his arm. But it was not unpleasant and, pausing to remember to breathe, he pushed out his arm again with greater confidence. The tingling returned and also a feeling of slight resistance. He withdrew his arm once more and knew what was required of him. He turned and looked at Alex, their eyes meeting for an instant.

Then he stepped into the light.

Chapter 23

He stepped into soft, undulating pastel light, which hinted at colors without quite becoming them. The effect was, in a subtle and delicate fashion, almost kaleidoscopic. As he moved forward there was a sense of resistance, as though he were pushing through something. Joseph was momentarily puzzled as to how light could have substance. Then the resistance gave way and he was through.

He was met by extraordinary silence and stillness.

And suddenly he had never felt so alone.

His most primal instinct, honed over untold generations on the land of Earth, told him to return immediately to what he knew; that this place was too strange; that his mind would disintegrate if exposed to something so profoundly alien. In the moment he emerged from the wall of light, he had a sense of having died. That everything he had ever known had ended. Worse than that, he had an overwhelming feeling of having been imprisoned. He was filled with panic and his hands started to scrabble at the cascade of light to find his way back to the known.

And then, just as suddenly, he knew that all was well. He was not alone. Friends stood with him. He was once more back in the forest clearing, on the edge of the cliff, lying in his grave. But he was also out of the grave, standing at the center of the circle of monks, his brothers, whom he knew were with him now. A knowledge infinitely beyond his deepest animal instinct told him that the past and the present were both fully alive, now, in this moment, and that in this fertile ground an unimaginable future waited. Anamnesis, once more.

He was utterly aware of his brothers' eyes fixed upon him, connecting with his soul, filling him with their presence.

The panic departed, to be replaced by a dilute natural tension. He sensed his brothers' presence moving into the background as this happened. They were there, he knew, utterly supportive, but would not interfere with the journey to come. He must walk the path before him of his own free will, responding from his unique place in existence to whatever occurred. They could not do this for him.

He turned from the wall and tried to take in where he was. He stood at the end of a tube-like passage that ran away to his left, turning into the heart of the vessel. It felt as if he was inside a sea-shell that spiraled inwardly towards its unknown center. He knew that he must walk this path and discover that which lay hidden. With a deep breath, he took a step forward - and then stopped again. The act of movement had revealed something that he had already dimly sensed, but pushed to one side as panic had taken over. There was something wrong with reality in this place. It was not how it was meant to be. Or rather, it was not normal. But who was to say what was normal, Joseph thought. Reality in the corridor of light was somehow thicker, almost dreamlike, although these words did not do justice to the experience. He looked around and sensed an intense aliveness to everything. As he looked more closely, he felt he could detect a faint shimmering of existence itself. It reminded him of a Van Gogh painting. Perhaps he was experiencing that which was always present in the everyday world, but which only extraordinary people like the great Vincent could see. Joseph watched his hand as he moved it in front of his face. It almost seemed to leave a faint trail. It was as though the material world in this place was less solid, more fluid than what lay outside. Boundaries here were not hard, not definitive - it was as though one thing gradually morphed into another. And as he stood there, Joseph had a deep intuition as to how fundamental this fluidity of boundary was. He knew in his bones that even the boundary between the inner and the outer, between mind and matter, was in this place suggestive rather than prescribed. It was a shallow stream, easily forded, rather than an unbridgeable chasm. He pushed gently at the wall with his hand and felt it gradually begin to give way.

Joseph focused on the passage ahead and began to walk slowly on the solid, yet not solid floor. He noticed a growing calmness now, a stillness and inner silence that were in harmony with where he was. As he became aware of this, he knew once more that he was not alone, that he was accompanied from levels of reality enfolded within this one. That he was a doorway, a two-way icon through which realities were encountering each other. He continued walking slowly, gradually turning to his right as he progressed, moving ever closer to the center of the vessel and whatever awaited him. It suddenly struck him as strange that he had not been met at the entrance, until he saw how he had been given time to adjust, to connect, with where he was. The human side of Joseph was grateful that no one had been there to witness his moment of panic. Even intergalactic explorers, he thought wryly, need to retain some pride.

After a few more steps he stopped and his heart leapt in his chest. The passage continued away in front of him, but now he glimpsed its end. Still partially hidden by the remaining curve of the path, he could see a room. He could just make out part of what seemed to be a circular floor, with a dome shaped ceiling and walls. And the light seemed even more intense in the room, with waves of color and faint images sweeping across the surfaces. There was something else. Not strong enough to be called a smell, there was nevertheless an aroma that at first Joseph struggled to identify. Then it dawned on him. It was the primal smell of the sea. That damp fishy mixture of salt and seaweed that always told us we were near the ocean, even when it could not be seen. The aroma brought a new quality to the moment, as only the sense of smell can. In that strange reality, everything was now very real.

He knew the time had come. He had no doubt that the whole point of his life was about to be revealed; that the subterranean inner pressure that had always been with him was about to erupt into the open. He went to move forward, but then stopped. Something was missing. He brought to mind an image of Clare and remembered the taste of her presence. A moment such as this had to be shared with his greatest love and closest friend. He took a deep breath and walked slowly until he stood at the entrance to the room.

At first he had difficulty seeing the room clearly. His mind could not initially grasp the swirling, eddying waves of light and color that swept across the ceiling, walls and floor. Gradually he began to adjust. The smell of the sea, which was now much stronger, seemed to help. It was something tangible and familiar in the midst of great strangeness. He allowed his awareness to follow the smell, trying to sense where it was coming from, and his eyes began to make out shapes in the middle of the room. His perception was adjusting rapidly now and as his vision cleared the shapes took on definite form.

And then their eyes met.

It was the most awesome moment of Joseph's life. Something filled him that was a fusion of stillness, bliss and quiet ecstasy. This is what he was for, this moment of meeting, this moment of relationship. The eyes regarded him steadily and as Joseph looked back he became aware of a deeper connection opening within his mind. There was a new presence floating in his consciousness alongside that of his brothers, not threatening or assertive, simply awaiting an invitation to make itself more fully known. Joseph resisted the invitation for a few moments as he allowed his field of vision to widen. The being that awaited him was bipedal, human-like, but at the same time something else. The face had two dark large eyes, which were hypnotic in their intensity. Membrane-like eyelids would occasionally sweep across them. A short stubby nose ended in flaps that opened and closed as it breathed. The mouth was almost lipless and drew a straight line across the face. But it was the head itself that was most strikingly non-human. From top to bottom it was oval, as though streamlined. The ears seemed to be flexible, capable of being flattened against the head for minimum resistance or maneuvered to enhance listening. There was no hair and the skin was smooth and glistened slightly with a subtle turquoise coloring. Then Joseph noticed something that was also decidedly not human. On both sides of the neck, though closed, he could just make out a series of flaps. He knew that they were gills, although currently not in use. The rest of the body was less challenging and could easily have been mistaken for human, except for the slight webbing between the fingers and toes. Although there were no obvious signs, Joseph sensed a male aura to the creature, but also something else. His intuition told him that gender for beings such as these might be a more complex matter than that with which he was familiar. The being wore clothing of some smooth unrecognizable material that had a sheen dimly reflecting the waves of light in the room. It was sitting in something that resembled an armchair, with a high back and parallel armrests. Although leaning back in the chair, its posture was straight with its arms positioned precisely along each armrest. Opposite, a couple of yards away, was a similar but empty chair. Joseph sensed that the two chairs were exactly positioned around the center point of the vessel.

Without warning the creature raised its right arm, startling Joseph. He calmed a little when he realized that it was indicating that he should sit in the other chair. As he moved forward into the room he became aware of just how tense he was feeling again. His legs were stiff and did not quite seem to want to move properly. There was no panic as earlier - indeed, paradoxically, there was still a deep peace - yet there was also tension. Both were present and, despite the extraordinary nature of the moment, Joseph was fascinated that two such conflicting states could coexist within him at the same time. He found his way to the other chair and sat down. Immediately he realized that it was no ordinary chair. As he made contact, there seemed to be some kind of joining, as though he were connecting with a silently humming vibrancy that was full of potential, awaiting his direction. No, that was not quite right. It felt as though it were waiting for him to suggest something. Joseph leaned fully back and found himself mimicking exactly the shape and posture of the being opposite. The chair seemed to require it of him.

When he was settled, Joseph looked over and once more made eye contact with his host. As he did so, the new presence in his mind gently asked to be allowed to flower. This time Joseph acceded to the request and, in paying attention to the presence, it began to open. With it came a quiet, melodious, slightly hesitant, voice in his mind.

"You are ... welcome. I know that this time you are ... known as Joseph. Perhaps it would be right if you called me ... Sennao."

For one brief moment Joseph again felt panic rising up at this alien intrusion, but it was almost instantly submerged in a wave of stillness from that older, more familiar presence in his mind. He saw, just briefly, his brothers around him, focusing their eyes into his soul. As he calmed, the import of Sennao's words dawned on him. An ancient memory flitted around, but out of reach. Joseph took a breath and searched for a reply, but was not sure how to make himself heard. He decided to speak aloud in the hope that the thoughts behind his words would make themselves known in this deeper way.

"I ... cannot find the words to express what this moment means to me," he managed to say. Sennao leaned his head slightly to one side, suggesting that he was listening. "I know that you will be patient," Joseph continued, "as this is almost overwhelming for me. I am also very ... nervous."

Sennao moved his head slowly back to an upright position and seemed, if it were possible, to open his eyes even wider. Joseph felt a kind of movement within his mind, a different quality of communication to the words he had just heard, and then he saw what he had never expected to see. The awesome mysterious being that looked back, next to whom he felt as a child, was letting him know that it felt just as he did. Joseph knew it when he gazed into those fathomless eyes. He realized also that Sennao very much wanted him to know this.

In that moment something special happened. In their shared vulnerability, they came closer.

The voice, obviously having to choose unfamiliar words, spoke in Joseph's mind. "This is a moment that many ... across time and realms ... have waited for. You and I carry them ... with us into this encounter. You bring your ... fellowship ... and I bring mine. This ... coming together ... is a great occasion and my mind too is not ... still ... in its responsibility and in its anticipation. I hope that you will be ... understanding ... with me."

They began to relax. Each knew it of the other. In their intimate form of communication, words were not necessary to convey this fact. It was a shared experience. Joseph decided to explore this a little further.

"How are we communicating?"

"In a way with which you are not ... unfamiliar. We are ... finding ... each other in that ... level ... of mind where the many begin to become the one. We swim in the depths of the sea rather than ... float ... in our own vessels on the surface. But your words are not mine and I must ... search ... your mind for ... units ... of language that will carry my meaning. This is not always easy as my own ... language ... is more ... poetic ... more flowing ... more watery ... and in this also is meaning. So I must take ... care ... to translate both content and ... feeling."

"Can you read my mind then?" Joseph asked.

Sennao paused before replying. "If I understand your ... intent ... the answer is no. In ... opening ... to my presence you have granted ... permission ... for knowledge of your words to be ... available ... to me. If I were to attempt further ... penetration ... the deeper part of who you are would know and ... resist.

Also," and at this point Joseph caught a whiff of something akin to humor, "the average human mind is not a ... place ... that I would seek to ... spend ... any time. Its ... chaos ... would be ... disconcerting. Nothing can be ... read ... as you put it ... when the words are ... utterly ... mixed up and the ... pages ... are randomly turning at great speed. Of course I should ... add ... that your mind is not average."

Joseph found himself wanting to laugh out loud. He was not sure whether it was because of suppressed hysteria, relief or genuine amusement. Sennao's face was unmoving and gave no indication that his words conveyed humor. Joseph scolded himself for projecting a very human attribute onto something, or rather someone, completely alien. He had to be more disciplined - yet there had been just a fleeting impression of something. There was silence for a while as Joseph reviewed what he had heard. Sennao was obviously willing to go at Joseph's pace. His mind was filling with questions, each clamoring for attention, and he knew he should have some kind of agenda to work through. But he could not do it. He could not impose a manufactured order on something as beautiful as this moment. Without thinking he asked the question that seemed to be pressing the most.

"Who are you? What are you?" he managed to blurt out, although he was not sure if he had actually spoken or was now only projecting the words in his mind. That boundary, too, was blurring.

Sennao paused before answering, gazing intently into Joseph's eyes. Joseph sensed that he was choosing his words with great care. When Sennao replied, it was slowly and with precision.

"I don't know."

Joseph was stunned. It was a reply he had never expected.

Sennao spoke again. "Truly ... Joseph ... I do not know who ... or what I am. It is the ... pursuit ... of this ... question ... that has brought me to ... this moment. It is what has ... brought me to you."

Joseph was silent once more. He had a sense of having run before he could walk. He knew immediately that they had touched the fundamental, profoundly mysterious reason for their encounter - but too soon. Relationships have to be built slowly. The climax must not be rushed. He sought to take the conversation into other, more obvious areas first.

"I ... have a sense of the importance of what you are saying, but perhaps first you could tell me about yourself at a more mundane level. What kind of being are you? Where are you from?"

Sennao's head moved slightly as he considered Joseph's words. Then he spoke. "Ah ... I must ... apologize. In my ... eagerness ... I come to things too soon. We must start in ... the shallows. I must try to ... put myself in your shoes." Joseph had a feeling that Sennao was pleased with having found this phrase. "I am of a ... race ... that evolved on a planet not too different to yours. So as you will have ... noticed ... our physical forms are not that ... dissimilar. And what differences there are ... consist of ... evolutionary ... streams that can be seen on your own world. Nature tends to find the same ... range ... of answers to similar challenges. Our main point of ... departure ... is that for subtle yet crucial reasons my ... forebears ... unlike yours did not completely leave the ... sea. We evolved so as to be ... operational ... both on land and in ... water. The best word that I can see in your mind is ... amphibian ... although the comparison is not ... straightforward."

Joseph was fascinated. In a sense it was obvious from Sennao's appearance. He was particularly interested, when he thought about their conversation so far, how Sennao's choice of language and imagery reflected the environment that had shaped and formed him. His thinking was interrupted as Sennao spoke again.

"There have been other ... encounters with my ... people. Long ago there have been ... meetings. I was once told ... in all innocence ... that your ... kind ... can find our ... scent ... unpleasant. I apologize if this is the case. But I would also ... draw ... to your attention that humans are not ... without their own scent." At this point Sennao's nasal flaps twitched.

Joseph was again aware in his mind of the merest hint of humor, yet still could not be sure if this was just his own projection. But he was far more interested in the meat of what Sennao had said.

"Your people have met human beings before?"

"Mine is an old race ... from an old planet around an old sun. We have ... swum ... in the space between the stars since before humans ... developed. We and others have ... watched ... and sometimes humans have glimpsed ... our presence ... especially in recent times with ... your technological advances. We have watched because ... whilst life is widespread on many worlds ... few manifestations ... of the life impulse have ... the ultimate potential ... to fold back ... upon themselves as we and you can."

Joseph sensed that Sennao had been struggling to find the right phrase to convey what he meant. "What do you mean by 'fold back'?"

Sennao paused, seemingly searching for a way to communicate what he was trying to describe. Then, without preamble, Joseph saw a picture in his mind. It was of a figure, vaguely human, standing by a busy city street, clearly intensely preoccupied with daily life. Then he saw the same figure staring out at the night sky, obviously entranced by the unspeakable majesty of what could be seen. Then, slowly, the figure bent forward until the head reached the midriff - and kept going. It disappeared into the torso and the rest of the body followed until the figure was turned completely inside out. The image blurred for a moment and then there was the same figure, but this time contemplating another vast universe. The image faded and Joseph began to grasp what Sennao was trying to show him.

"To 'fold back' is to become aware of the mystery of my existence," Joseph said hesitantly. "It is to awaken from the intense dream of living, to remember the astonishing miracle that I even am," Joseph continued, the words beginning to flow from a deeper place. "It is to travel within to meet with the source of my being and, in doing so, to encounter new universes. It is to awaken from the enchantment of my outer life and to become amazed that anything actually 'is'."

The words stopped, leaving Joseph trying to grasp their meaning.

"This is the ... potential ... that we share ... your people and mine. We have ... discovered ... that most life forms we have ... encountered ... in our journeying through the universes are ... consumed ... with being what they are. Is this not also ... true of your planet? Do your ... cats ... contemplate the source of their being ... or watch their minds work? It seems to us ... that there are a few ... only a few ... species through which ... existence ... is becoming aware of itself. When we ... encounter such species ... when the time is right ... we make contact so that the great ... search ... may be shared and ... thereby ... magnified."

"So, we are not the first?" Joseph asked.

"No ... there are some ... others ... with whom we are ... travelling companions."

As Sennao spoke a wonderful and monstrous serpent, that had been awaiting its moment, began to uncoil in Joseph's mind. Something that had been said earlier came back to Joseph in sharp relief and memories stirred that had slumbered for eons. A sense of shock began to well up inside. A question erupted into his mind, but he was not sure that he wanted to know the answer, for he suspected that he knew it already and it would be too mind-blowing. Yet if the answer were different, the disappointment would be devastating. His mind started to collapse into turmoil, which he knew could only be healed in one way. With great effort he forced the words out.

"Sennao, right at the beginning when we first met, you implied that we had known each other before, but that I then had another name."

There was silence for a few moments and a quiet panic began to build in Joseph. He needed this question answered as much as he needed to breathe. Relief flooded in as Sennao began to speak.

"Yes ... this is the question that I have ... hoped for. I have waited for the ... inner currents of your mind ... to respond to certain ... stimuli. It could not be forced. All must be ... drawn forth. I am ... grateful for this is the moment when ... veils and ... screens ... may finally fall away and something ... pure ... may take their place. Dreams now come to life."

Sennao paused again and Joseph found his mental turmoil being replaced by a sense of joy, even though he had no idea why. His mind seemed to know something he did not. Sennao's head moved slightly before he continued.

"This is a ... reunion. The individual ... essences ... of what we are ... have been ... friends ... before ... in the ancient times of your race. Those essences now ... enliven ... new forms."

Sennao's words should have been a shock to Joseph, but this was not the case. He had not known this - and yet always had.

"A reunion. How? When?"

Another pause.

"Did you not dream last night?"

Joseph found himself letting out a deep breath. The serpent unwound further and a smile began to form.

"We dreamed together did we not?"

He was struggling to catch up with his words for they seemed to understand more than he did.

"Indeed my friend ... we shared ... old times."

Joseph tried to bring clarity to his thoughts. There seemed to be two levels of knowing at work in him. He knew that Sennao was being patient, allowing something to be born. He decided to let his mouth, if he actually was speaking, lead the way.

"Over the last few years, I have had a dream that returned again and again. It was of a city with two great rivers, where I would meet with someone and be taught."

Another pause.

"We both learned my friend."

A shiver went through Joseph, thrilling and disturbing.

"A dream really has come to life."

"Thousands of years ago ... in another form ... with others of my kind ... I spent time on your world. We saw ... your potential to ... turn within ... and gently watered the garden of your mind. We knew that ... a flowering was long off ... but we did what we could. Now it is time for you ... to remember. I have been helping you ... through dreams and in ... other ways to do this ... or you would not be able to move forward."

The serpent was now almost fully unwound and started to become a living part of Joseph. It brought so many questions that he did not know where to start. Once more, he let his mouth lead the way.

"Why did I not remember this ... previous life?"

Finally the awesome words came out. A Rubicon had been crossed.

Sennao paused again, but this time Joseph had a sense that it was to honor the moment.

"My turning within is older ... more developed ... more sustained than yours and so I may ... reclaim ... memories ... should the inner currents so require. For you such rememberings are a ... darting ... will of the wisp ... that cannot be seen clearly. And this is right for ... to remember such matters ... too soon ... would prevent young minds from ... further learning. Lessons would remain ... surface and not ... sink ... to the depths where they may nurture ... profound change. Nature has ... arranged ... things in this way from its own ... unfathomable wisdom. But there comes a point where it is ... helpful ... to reconnect with ... these hidden parts of the mind. Now is such a moment for you and I have helped. It is a ... holy instant. Also even though your ... recollection ... has not been focused at this ... level of consciousness ... its wisdom ... has still moved in the deeps and produced ripples on the surface. It is this way with many ... experiences ... of your essence. Yet now they are ... coming to focus as needed for this time. The other ... presence ... that joins with us ... your brothers ... is also a sign of this."

Something that had been trapped in Joseph was finding freedom. It rejoiced to be in the open air after so long. He allowed his consciousness to flow unhindered. He was gradually catching up with his mouth, but it was still a little way ahead.

"It isn't just the dreams, though. You've been ... touching ... my mind in other ways."

"I have been very ... presumptuous ... and ask for your ... forgiveness ... but circumstances required certain ... actions."

Time to cross another Rubicon. Caesar only had to deal with one, Joseph thought dimly somewhere in his mental suburbs.

"You are ... were ... the Teacher?"

Sennao's head seemed to nod slightly. Joseph could not be sure, but it was almost as if he was acknowledging the recognition.

"My journey to your world ... at this level of reality ... has taken much time. This has allowed me to ... reforge ... our ancient link and so ... reach out ... on the deeper planes to ... prepare ... you for this ... meeting." Sennao stopped for a few moments. "For otherwise it could be ... too much ... too shattering. So I became your ... guide ... once more so that the ... dismantling ... might be gradual and gentle."

Joseph became whole as the serpent was finally absorbed into his being. To finally have so much explained left an inner spaciousness within which he began to luxuriate.

"Why did you leave?"

"It was ... essential ... so that you would be ... forced ... to draw from your own well ... for what was to come. We must meet

... as equals. Also ... were we still ... coming together in that ... manner ... it would cause confusion for our ... encounter ... on this plane of existence."

Questions still burned within Joseph.

"Why did you bring me to the ... my ... brothers of the forest?"

Sennao seemed to have limitless patience with Joseph's enquiries.

"This is an ... encounter ... at many levels that will ... force growth in the ... deep structures of your mind. For this you need ... buttressing ... that all may not ... collapse. I searched the ... hidden ... parts of your mind ... of which you were not aware ... and found memories of a life ... with close relationship with this ... group ... of profoundly aware souls ... whose hearts are set on fire as is yours ... by the presence of the great teacher of your ... faith story. Your ... interlinking ... was ... and is ... so strong that their ... buttressing ... would be most robust. Through the ... inter-weaving ... doors of time ... I sought their help."

Sennao's words took Joseph back to the forest. Flashes of memory zigzagged across his mind of deep friendship, of love, of shared danger and of a simplicity of life. He knew that there was much more to come.

"But how can that be, for that time is gone? Their ... essences ... must have moved on."

"Time is not so simple ... not so linear ... not so one dimensional ... from a greater perspective ... also it is not ... a one way street."

Joseph knew that he was out of his depth. Yet in the same moment, something inside said that this was only because he was thinking in the wrong way. He recalled his experience the previous evening, with Anastasia and Anastasios, where he found himself thinking in images and symbols about time, and of how strange counter-intuitive insights flooded his mind. But he did not want to be sidetracked.

"Why did you summon me to Delphi when before we met

elsewhere?"

"Because we must move forward ... not backwards. That form of ... relationship has gone ... now we are ... new. Everything is a symbol ... and ... Delphi represents this. Also it is a symbol for ... the world ... which will see the links as you have and ... their minds will expand."

There was silence for a few moments as Joseph pondered what he had heard.

"You are very patient with all my questions."

"It is why ... we meet ... but also you must remember that the questions ... and answers ... are only on the surface and that they ... open up ... vents ... below that move you into ... renewed ... understanding that is not ... of words. This is ... perhaps ... more important."

As Sennao spoke, the truth of his words became apparent to Joseph. He suspected that this was intended. He could feel more serpents uncoiling in his mind; more long-forgotten windows opening. He allowed himself to sink into the process and, as he did so, his mind began to expand more powerfully than it had at any time over the past few days. The deepest sense began to grow of the vastness of existence and of the tides that moved in its midst carrying along everything, from Sennao and he to the greatest galaxy. The sense of mystery and awe were overwhelming. He saw time stretching out from that moment, into the past and into the future and knew that he was also present in both, now. And that as the arrow of time moved through "now", his form, the manifest expression of what he was, refocused and changed, but that "he" remained, evolving towards some unknown state of being. He had a strong impression of life as theatre, of sacred role-play, through the experience of which something fundamental was growing into adulthood. Then he remembered where the light ship lay, in the magnificent theatre at Delphi. He saw that even this was a teaching. Another symbol that Sennao had placed before the world. These insights erupted from the core of Joseph's mind and, for a while, he just had to let the flow have its way. He had learned to do this. Sennao seemed to understand what was happening and waited patiently. Eventually the flow began to fade and Joseph was able to speak once more.

"My world, the world of my mind, has been so small. I have always sensed this and glimpsed that which lies beyond, but now I see so clearly. It is like emerging into the daylight, having lived in a cave for a lifetime. It may take a while for me to adjust."

"And perhaps you should ... consider the possibility that all that has happened is that you have ... emerged into a bigger cave ... that there are more ... births ... to occur."

Sennao's words penetrated into Joseph's mind. True wonder filled him at the magnificence of the journey he was on. He smiled at his companion and said, "And you are to be mid-wife."

"And you in ... your turn."

The smile faded from Joseph's face. Sennao's words lay heavily on his mind. Another serpent began to uncoil, that until that moment had been hidden under a rock. It felt like it carried real venom.

"But of this ... we will speak in ... a while."

The serpent lay still once more, but Joseph knew that this was only a temporary reprieve. Sennao interrupted his darkening thoughts.

"You must understand that we are ... midwife ... to each other. For as you ... evolve ... so will I. This is how it is with ... relationship. And through us ... others will be touched and grow ... for we interconnect at ... many levels. There is ... hierarchy for ... clearly ... my kind are further ... along the path than the people ... of your world. But in another sense all are ... equivalent ... for each individual... occupies a unique ... coordinate ... in existence and sees that which ... no other ... may see. When we ... journey together ... we expand our vision. And the ... total vision ... is more than the sum of the ... individual ... glimpses. As we become more individual ... express more our unique essence ... we also join together more ... into oneness. This is what you call ... paradox."

There was silence again as Joseph absorbed the awesome implications of what had been said. Another question started to burn within. He had a sense that he was shooting around all over the place. It occurred to him that this might be a sign that his mind was operating at its limit - or even beyond.

"Sennao, why me?" Why did you pick me? Why am I here rather than someone else?"

Sennao paused before replying, as though sensing that his words would provoke a response. The malign serpent was about to unwind fully, in the space of a few words.

"You ... offered yourself. We did not ... pick ... you. We work with your ... ancient desire ... as do your ... brothers."

Sennao's words should have shocked Joseph, but they did not. He wondered if he was becoming inwardly numb. As he listened the pressure he had always felt inside, the undefined sense that there was a profound purpose to his life, burst open. It seemed to know that its time had come. He had to speak, but now he was ahead of his words.

"And what is this desire?"

"It is to help awaken your ... world ... from its self-absorbed dream. It is to be a living symbol to your ... people ... of how little they really know ... that they may see ... further ... outwardly and inwardly. It is to show them that ... like me ... they do not know who they are or why anything is ... so that they may take their place in our company that we may ... all see ... better." Sennao paused before continuing. "It is to ... teach and to lead ... in this. We have given you a ... unique and unsurpassed ... prominence ... in your world. This you can use. You will not be alone ... for there are ... others ... ready to help. And we will never ... be far away."

Sennao stopped speaking, clearly knowing the effect his

words would have.

Joseph's eyes were open, but were no longer seeing anything. Deep down he did not doubt having made such a commitment in some long forgotten place. The secret that had been with him all his life was revealed. It had gone from a dream to a nightmare. He could imagine some inexperienced idealistic youth passionately volunteering for such a mission. But now the moment had come and a solitary hermit-like man, who struggled to like his fellow human beings, who was actually frightened of them, was being called upon to fulfill the promise made. As he thought of what would be involved, of the nature of human society in which he would have to operate, he baulked at the prospect. He was not even sure he cared what happened to humanity. He has seen enough of its unpleasant side. Yet more than anything, he felt his own inadequacy.

Sennao sensed what was happening. He did not seem surprised.

"Joseph ... let us take this gently. It is not a ... choice ... you have to make. There are other options. Everything must always be ... free will ... or it is meaningless. Your offer was made ... long ago. It was accepted with ... thanks. But if it is now ... not right for you this will ... be fine. You will still be ... our friend and we will continue to ... grow together. The great ... Will... that lies behind all will find another way ... if it is needed."

But Sennao's earlier words hung around Joseph like a weight, for he knew that they were true. He had made a commitment long ago and this encounter was the culmination of that promise. He could feel how much energy had been given to bringing about this moment and how minds barely sensed awaited its fulfillment. Yet he could find no energy for the task and the prospect daunted him. He suddenly felt a great need for Clare's presence. Sennao interrupted his downward spiral.

"Joseph ... I said there is another ... possibility. Would you like to ... explore it?"

With a great effort, Joseph gathered himself and remembered where he was. He felt his brothers move closer and their presence broke the spell. They whispered in words he could not hear. But something within him heard, for he began to be amazed and shocked at himself. He was in the midst of an extraordinary experience. Only minutes before he had tasted the grandeur of creation, yet could still allow his mind to slip towards the shadows. He took a deep breath and made a point of looking closely at Sennao and a thrill of excitement ran through him. His mind began to expand once more and his long-ago promise did not seem so overpowering. It moved away and became simply one thing set against the vast background of existence. Balance returned and he sensed his brothers retreat a little.

"I'm sorry, Sennao. You must find me ungrateful. But you touched an old ... fear." As he said the words, Joseph wondered quite what he meant by them. The words were beginning to lead the way again.

"I understand Joseph. Remember that I have ... touched ... your mind many times. You are unlikely ... to surprise me often. Let us explore the other ... possibility ... that I promised. It may shed ... new light. I will show you."

Chapter 24

At first, Joseph did not know what to make of Sennao's words, but then he began to sense something happening to the vessel. The swirling light and colors around him started to deepen and the pattern of their movement changed. He also began to feel something in his body. Whatever was happening to the vessel was in some way happening to him. He paid careful attention to the sensation and realized that it was connected with the chair. In some way it joined him inwardly with the light ship. He also became aware of something else. The presence in his mind that was Sennao had changed in its quality, as though it had expanded and, while still one, had two distinct areas. He looked more closely and realized, without knowing how, that the new aspect of Sennao's presence was the cause of the changes that were happening - and that Sennao wanted him to see this. Then the obvious hit Joseph. The ship was moving and Sennao was piloting it. Joseph took a deep breath and tried to adapt to this new challenge. Entering the ship had been daunting, encountering Sennao an awesome moment, but he had still been on the ground with all that he knew not more than a few yards away. But now he was leaving for an unknown destination, bereft of any control.

Yet also his heart leapt, as it sensed that something for which it had always yearned might be about to happen.

"Sennao, where are we going?"

"To see what you have always ... dreamed of seeing ... since longer than you realize. But first you must ... brace yourself for an experience ... that may at first be ... shocking."

Joseph felt a subtle change in the light ship and without warning the entire floor became transparent. He instinctively grabbed the arms of the chair as he seemed to hang over open space. At one level his mind knew that there could not be a problem, but a more primitive layer of consciousness insisted that he must be falling. He closed his eyes for a few moments and, again, sensed something akin to mild humor emanating from Sennao.

"I did ... warn ... you. Open your eyes and ... look down. I am holding the vessel ... steady ... and you should ... adjust quickly."

Joseph slowly opened his eyes, carefully focusing first on Sennao, then on the walls, before finally looking down. He was prepared this time and caught his breath in wonder at what he saw. They seemed to be hovering about two hundred feet above the theatre. In the bottom right he could make out the Temple of Apollo, although he had never seen it from this angle before. Snaking through the picture was the path that wound its way through the ruins that now constituted Delphi. Ruined it might be, yet even from within the vessel Delphi had a power and a presence that was palpable. But what really caught Joseph's eye was the theatre itself and the faces looking up at him - as well as the television camera. Alex was clearly visible, looking worried.

Sennao said, "They cannot ... see us. All they ... behold ... is the vessel of light."

The vessel began to rise and turn to the right. More of the Delphi site came into view and Joseph could make out the Sanctuary of Apollo, then the Sacred Way and finally the Treasury as the craft completed its turn. The theatre was now behind them and, without sight of the faces, Joseph suddenly felt even more cut off. He sensed Sennao making some new adjustment and both of their chairs turned to face the same way, as the section of the wall in front of them slowly became transparent. A magnificent view of the Plistós valley opened up in the crystal clear morning light, an ocean of green olive trees stretching almost as far as the eye could see. In the distance was the turquoise blue of the Gulf of Corinth and slowly they began to move in that direction. Joseph once more had to hold onto the arms of the chair as they progressed. It was like being in a chair lift moving high above deep valleys, except you knew that you were not attached to any cable. But it was still a wondrous experience and his face wanted to break into a large smile. Joseph had no sense that they were moving particularly fast, yet they were soon over Itèa and then the Gulf itself. He realized that they must have been gaining altitude, for he could now see a long way. In the distance to his left he could see the unnatural straight line that was the Corinth Canal, while to his right he could just make out the magnificent suspension bridge at Rio. Then they stopped and all was still. Far below Joseph could see the waters of the Gulf, with several ships moving slowly along. He wondered how the crews would be reacting to the vision of a brilliant light hovering above. Perhaps they were so absorbed in the world of their conversations and duties that they would not be aware of the symbol of a far vaster existence that hung over their heads, waiting to be noticed. In front of him were the mountains of the Peloponnese, home to some of the greatest myths of humanity. Joseph wondered how many of those myths were wrapped around ancient encounters with beings such as Sennao. As this thought occurred to him, he found his head turning to the left and his eyes wanting to see beyond the eastern horizon as dim fragments of memory stirred once more.

Then, suddenly, his mind was wiped clear as the light ship began to ascend straight upwards at enormous speed. Joseph found himself gripping the armrests even more tightly as the Gulf, the mountains and then Greece itself flew away from him, shrinking rapidly. It was like being in a glass elevator hurtling upwards, with no apparent support. He had the distinct feeling that he had left his stomach several miles below. Yet at another level his mind knew that these physical reactions were purely psychological, primal reactions from what his eyes were seeing, for if he paid attention it was clear that there was no real bodily pressure. He realized that he must be protected in some way from the inertial and gravitational forces that he should have been feeling. Then he had an intuition that, in some inexplicable way, the light vessel did not have to guard him against these forces, as it existed in a slightly different level of reality where they did not apply. He was puzzled as to how he could know this.

As they rose, the curve of the horizon became ever more pronounced and he began to make out the shimmering boundary of the thin atmosphere of gases in which all life on Earth existed so precariously. A shallow pond in which he had for so many years been trapped. The light outside the ship was also changing as they moved upwards. The brilliant blue that had filled the sky only a few moments earlier had changed from mauve, through dark purple and was rapidly becoming black. The transition had been so rapid that his mind struggled to take it in. He realized that they must have ascended at fantastic speed.

And while his mind was trying to process all of this, the moment of epiphany came.

The ever-darkening purple became black and suddenly all around the stars were shining, more brilliant than he could ever have imagined. All Joseph could do was contemplate what was before him. Then Sennao brought the vessel to a halt and slowly expanded the transparency of the light ship until the two of them seemed to be just hanging in space, on their chairs, surrounded by the Mystery. There are no words for what Joseph felt. It was a day in which dreams became real. An ancient hunger was satisfied. But nothing he had experienced as a child looking up at the night sky, or in the rectory garden, or in the bishop's arboretum, could have prepared him for the awesome reality of that moment. He found his mind expanding as it was filled by the cosmos. Even though he still had a profound sense of being, it was also as though he had disappeared and the stars had taken his place. Time stopped.

Time started again when Sennao spoke in his mind. "I have

seen this sight ... instances without ... number. But unlike ... so many other things in life ... I never tire of it. Indeed ... it seems more ... nourishing on each occasion."

Joseph could understand completely what Sennao meant. There were many experiences in life that were powerful at first, but diminished when repeated. The taste went out of them. But there were a few, and only a few, where the opposite was the case. Each encounter seemed to reveal greater riches. No matter how tired or jaded one was, it was always fulfilling and meaningful. It was this way when he celebrated the Mass.

"It's a sacrament," he said.

He was aware of Sennao searching his mind for the meaning of the word.

"Ah ... yes. That is a ... beautiful word. In my ... language ... we have a ... term ... for such moments ... that brings to mind ... encountering a gushing spring ... pouring forth from unknown rocky depths. We have another word that ... has the picture ... of breaking through ice and ... falling ... into the watery abyss below. The two ... analogies ... together ... are conflicting yet they ... also ... strangely convey the feel ... of the experience."

The images evoked by Sennao's words appeared in Joseph's mind unbidden and reinforced the sensation of floating amidst the stars. There was silence between them for a while, before Joseph spoke again.

"Sennao, what do your people believe is to be found in those depths?"

Sennao's reply was not what Joseph expected.

"We do not ... believe ... anything. We seek ... to know. We look as ... closely ... as we can that we may see. We ... enhance ... our different ways ... of knowing ... that we may see better."

Joseph was fascinated by Sennao's last sentence. "What do you mean by 'different ways of knowing'?"

"Existence has many ... levels ... and we are ... alive ... in this moment across them all. The manner of our ... awareness ... is different depending on the ... depth ... at which it floats in this ... upwelling. Near the ... ocean floor ... of existence ... all is almost one and so 'to know' is to be that which is known. For example ... in this moment ... as we sit here enveloped in stars ... we are alive. We know this by ... being it. But then ... as one rises on ... the current of being ... the almost oneness gradually changes into the almost separate. Thus awareness becomes ... ever more conscious. At this level ... that of the manifest material universe we can ... also know by seeming to be ... separate to that which is ... known. And between these two ... states of knowing ... are wonderful ... harmonies of both ... which we may call the inner worlds ... which are also ... gateways ... into other outer worlds."

Sennao's words resonated with Joseph. It was what he had been told the previous evening. But, even more, he knew it in his gut. As he sat amongst the stars, he was experiencing a profound sense of oneness, of communion with all that is; a mystical sense that he was a part of them and they of him. At the same time, he could relate to them as being separate to him, the knower and the known, the observer and the observed, and could rejoice in the mighty insights of science and skeptical thought that arose from the strict application of this principle. And between the two, as Sennao had said, there were amazing places where, mysteriously, paradoxically, the two extremes were interwoven. His thoughts were interrupted as Sennao spoke again.

"When we look upon your ... world ... we see all of these ways of knowing ... as present. But you have ... not embraced them all but ... continually swing between them. One is ... favorite ... for a while then another. For some ... it is the way of science and skepticism ... that is the only way. For others it is ... the way of ... the deep up-flowing oneness that is ... the truth. But all are needed." Joseph could sense Sennao searching his mind for an illustration. "I see in your ... thoughts ... a broken picture ... a jigsaw. The individual pieces reveal little ... and can

... even deceive on their own. They must be ... brought together for the ... real picture ... to be seen ... which is always greater than ... the parts."

Joseph remembered something that Sennao had said earlier.

"You said that your people do not 'believe' anything. But surely in the midst of great mystery you must have some kind of map, a collection of assumptions, no matter how inadequate, to help you navigate?"

Sennao's head tilted slightly to one side as he thought about the question and Joseph had the momentary concern that his chair might topple over, before remembering that they were not really floating in empty space.

"I did not use your word ... belief ... for it is a word which causes ... much confusion ... in your world. And from this confusion comes ... great suffering. For you ... too easily ... confuse this state with ... knowing ... and act from this false knowledge. Because your people are still greatly ... driven ... by their primitive ... survival impulse ... which can wear many ... convincing and sophisticated masks ... belief becomes a psychological protector against the hostile universe ... and can therefore be used to justify terrible things. Most sadly belief often reduces ... the hostile universe ... to the shape of your fellow beings ... who may therefore be righteously attacked. Too often ... in your minds ... belief and power are equated ... for both are responses to primal fear."

Sennao paused before continuing.

"But you are correct. We do ... possess a set of ... ever-evolving ideas that guide us as we ... swim ... through the great Mystery. That open new ... channels. We imagine ... all possibilities ... that our minds may be open to ... the strangeness of existence. But we do not confuse our ideas and imaginings with ... the truth ... but as we see deeper we refine our thoughts ... so they may better ... reflect ... the essence of truth or ... if you prefer ... that they may become ... more transparent ... to the shining of truth. Yet we never … forget … that our ideas are not the truth … itself. The truth is … an experience … or better a state of consciousness … such as we share now." Sennao leaned forward slightly, as if to emphasize what he was about to say. "And such experiences are … enhanced by the sharing … as the picture of the … puzzle … only emerges as the pieces are … assembled. Each of us is a … unique coordinate … in existence and brings a … seeing … that no other may. Only as we share our … seeings … can we become … truth. And in this do we … taste … that which we call … love."

Sennao's words moved Joseph deeply and they sat in silence among the stars for a long while. Joseph felt a power moving within, but which had no name. He suddenly saw that it was not *a* power, but *the* power - it was the life force itself, surging and dancing. Although there was no outward sign, Joseph knew that Sennao was sharing the experience. The moment slowly passed and Joseph found his mind returning to his original question.

"Sennao, you did not answer my question. What … thoughts … do your people have about what lies in the abyss?"

Sennao answered only after a long pause.

"Something that … waits for us."

"Something or someone?"

"It is both something … and someone … and far more than either. The source of the spring … is the Source of All that is. It must therefore possess … all potentialities. Nothing can … be … in our worlds that is not a … seed … in the mind of the source."

Joseph hesitated before replying, a little daunted at the prospect of taking the initiative in the conversation, until he felt a subtle wave of encouragement from the ancient presence of his brothers.

"It is the experience of my people that the Source does more than simply wait. Many of us have felt its presence in our minds and lives, guiding and inspiring. Awakening us to wonder and awe. Some of us, of whom I am one, sense that on rare occasions it has stepped into our history in physical form in order to point us in new directions and give us a better ... channel ... through which to relate."

Sennao seemed pleased with what Joseph had said. "Indeed we know ... of this. It is different to our experience ... of the Source. You approach the deeps along different ... currents ... to us. It is why we must ... share ... our stories and visions. For us the source has tended to be more of a ... something ... than a ... someone. The more ... personal ... relationship with the source that some ... but not all ... of your people have experienced is more ... rare ... among my people. Together perhaps we can see more ... wholly. Perhaps we may see ... beyond ... 'someone' or 'something'."

Joseph again caught a faint suggestion of humor as Sennao added, "Joseph ... I do not object if you use the word ... 'God'. After all you are ... a priest." Joseph looked over at Sennao, but the alien face was expressionless, except for a slight twitch of the nostrils.

"I'm afraid, Sennao, that 'God' is a word that is becoming unhelpful on my world. Many who use it confuse belief with knowledge. So often it is a word of control or attack. It is used for comfort rather than the search for truth. It is a word for an ending rather than a beginning. It is confused with an answer rather than a question."

A thought suddenly struck Joseph. It was something obvious, but which for some unknown reason he had never seen before.

"Sennao, why do I experience the source, God, so differently? Sometimes it is as though he ... it ... is a great pressure urging me to go forward, to grow and explore ... to create. But there are other times when I experience God as a great stillness, a deep peace, a timeless, vividly alive emptiness."

"This is a question that ... we ... have also ... encountered. Perhaps we must ... accept ... that the Source shows us ... different faces ... and is all of them fully. Perhaps we must accept that we

... are not in control." Sennao paused. "Yet also it ... seems ... to us that the ... road ... by which we approach ... the source may influence ... our experience. Sometimes we may ... dive directly ... into the ... great presence ... and float in its warm waters ... where there is no time and utter peace. But there is timelessness ... and such peace ... because there is no creation ... no growth. When we approach through the ... inner realms ... of thought and action ... the creative impulse that comes from the ... Source ... is felt as a forcing current ... a great pressure."

Sennao's words brought back to Joseph's mind the conversation of the previous evening at the monastery - the difference between the mystic and magical paths. Perhaps magic was the wrong word. Perhaps it would be better described as the creative path; the way of thought and action. This was the way by which God was experienced as pressure. Yet without it nothing could be.

Joseph leaned back in his chair and gradually became absorbed once more in the starfield in which he floated. Whatever the explanation, in that moment it was the mystical side of him that was wide awake. His mind became very still and his sense of "being Joseph" slowly diminished until he was simply a patch of incredibly aware consciousness floating in the void. Thoughts began to arise in that patch of consciousness, but they were thoughts that were not the product of other thoughts. One moment they were not present, the next they shone with fiery intensity. As he gazed at the points of light that surrounded him, he knew with a childlike certainty that his body was star-stuff temporarily in another form. As he gazed at the black void between the stars, he knew with the same certainty that his body was also space itself, enlivened. He knew that he was the stars and the void being self-aware. And deeper thoughts then arose. Awareness of the physical faded and he became the life force itself that assembled and maintained, for a tiny flash of time, the form called Joseph. And he knew in that moment that the stars and the void erupted from the same force, but in a very different way. As his sense of the life force strengthened, he saw how it stretched out into innumerable realms and universes and how "Joseph's" plane of reality was but a wafer thin slice of something unimaginably vast. He saw that he was an expression of a primal sea of awareness out of which everything emerged in an on-going act of creation. He saw the passingness of Joseph, but he also saw that he was not Joseph but the awareness itself - and everything between.

And so Joseph died in the midst of the stars.

Chapter 25

A little while later Joseph arose from the dead.

The primal creative impulse gently insisted that Joseph be once more, that through him it might uniquely know and love itself. An incandescent patch of consciousness swam back to the surface of Joseph and drew an urgent rasping breath. For a few moments Joseph did not know that he was Joseph. All he knew was a devastating sense of loss. His whole being grieved for something, but its nature eluded memory. With another breath his eyes flew open to be greeted by an aurora borealis of swirling colour and light. He looked around in confusion and found a strange creature with mesmerizing black eyes looking back. Then his mind began to clear as his thoughts became anchored around two buoys that floated in the sea of consciousness. He remembered who and where he was. He struggled back towards normality.

"Sennao, I can't see out anymore. You've hidden the stars." Joseph was now pretty sure that he was not speaking when he addressed Sennao, but was just sending thoughts towards the presence that rested in his mind.

"I must ensure that you do not ... overdose. This is a ... heady wine. You must learn to ... float comfortably ... in this depth of reality. You are like one of your ... undersea divers ... who must take care when moving between ... levels."

Joseph tried to take in Sennao's words, but the sense of loss still threatened to overwhelm him.

"Sennao, what happened ... just now ... I can't remember ... but I'm filled with sadness?"

"Is sadness all there is?"

Joseph thought for a moment. "No, there's also a kind of bliss. It's weird. How can I be both sad and blissful in the same moment?"

"It is because ... you plunged into the ... abyss ... and tasted the Source. Deeper than you have ever been before. You ... visited home and dived into love ... and then came back."

Joseph stared at the ceiling. "I didn't want to come back."

"I ... know."

There was silence for a while, before Joseph spoke again. "The worst thing is that I can't remember anything about it. It's like not being able to recall the face of someone you love who has died. It feels terrible. Why can't I remember anything?"

"It is because your experience was ... beyond thought. Thought cannot contain it ... and memories are thoughts. Memories are ... like wonderful photographs ... frozen moments of reality that may be ... manipulated ... to recreate wondrous illusions of reality. This can be ... most glorious and can reveal much ... but it has its limits. Your touching of the Source will ... however ... leave an afterglow ... an impression that may in time to come ... evoke images and thoughts that ... symbolize the ... merger."

"Why is the experience beyond thought?"

"Because thought is an ... expression ... of separation and time. You can only be conscious of something ... that you perceive as being other ... than you. You tasted 'oneness' in which thought and time ... cannot arise. It is the different ... ways of knowing ... that I spoke about ... earlier."

Joseph lifted his chin and looked straight at Sennao. His question was full of passion. "But why did we ever leave such bliss, for this experience of suffering and death? There have been many times in life when I have struggled to find the energy to continue. So often it has seemed like an overwhelming struggle. Even now, especially now, I don't want to carry on. I want to go back where there is only peace."

Joseph stopped, shocked at what he was saying and the force that lay behind it. He knew that a deep place in his psyche had been exposed. Now it was out and, as he sensed both presences

322

in his mind gather strength, he realized that this had been intended. Delphi's ancient imperative to know thyself suddenly came to mind. He was being given a little help.

Sennao broke into his turmoil. "We know ... and this we must ... help you to see clearly ... for this impulse has worn many ... masks in your life ... which must now be lifted."

"I've often struggled with life, the sheer effort of living. My heart has been broken by the nastiness and suffering all around." Joseph did not need to mention Clare. He knew that Sennao felt his pain. Then an insight came to him. "I suppose that my struggle has been made worse because I've always known there's something better. I've tasted the 'heady wine' as you put it, which has made it even more difficult to live in the prison of the human world." Joseph took a deep breath. "So often I've felt trapped, on a small rocky planet in an even smaller collective human psyche. I want the vastness and freedom that I've tasted. I want to plunge into the Source and travel the cosmos. I want to leave the pain behind." The words poured out and he felt better. He looked at Sennao and managed a weak smile. "I'm afraid I want it even more after this experience."

"And we ... fan this flame ... into a roaring furnace by taking you among the stars and ... pointing you into the glorious abyss ... while at the same time ... we invite you to return to your world ... with all its smallness and complications ... with all its suffering ... so that you may guide your people. Perhaps we don't know ... what we are doing." Once more there was a suspicion of humor, which lightened Joseph's mood a little. Sennao's next comment changed the atmosphere completely.

"Joseph ... we must complete ... our adventure. Would you like to ... fly ... this vessel?"

Joseph noticed how skillfully Sennao took him to the edge of darkness and then brought him back before it became too much. It did not, though, stop his stomach lurching at the invitation.

"What? Me? Fly this? Is that really possible?"

"Not only ... possible ... but easy."

"How can it be easy to fly a machine as awesome as this? Surely it must take years of training and skills I don't have?"

"It is easy because ... it is not a machine. This vessel is ... alive ... you do not operate it ... you enter into relationship."

Joseph's mind struggled to take in what Sennao had said. It was too counter-intuitive. It challenged his most fundamental concept of what life was. Yet as he looked around at the vessel of pulsating light it began to feel obvious and natural. And as his mind opened in this way he began to notice another presence that lay a little distance from Sennao and his brothers. Looking back he realized that it had been there from the moment he entered the light ship and it had gone to another, deeper level when he sat in the chair. But somehow it had not registered properly and had been overlooked. Now, though, it could be seen clearly. From nowhere, he suddenly knew what had happened. He had not "known" this presence before because he had no concept for it. "Living machine" was too alien an idea to have been available in his mind for consciousness to form around. So it had been invisible.

Joseph paid close attention to the new presence and found himself both drawn and repelled by what he encountered. It was so alien that it was almost too alien. It challenged everything in him that thought it knew what life was, yet at the same time its mystery drew him irresistibly. He refocused on Sennao.

"What is ... it? I don't mean to sound disrespectful, but to say 'he' or 'she' doesn't feel right."

Sennao's head tilted slightly as though in acknowledgement. "We do not ... know. In times gone by ... as we explored the ... nature of light ... we became aware of a ... focus of intelligence and intent that ... swam in the waves and particles. We learned to ... communicate and to relate with this ... presence ... and it has been willing to ... shape ... light that it may serve us. We have technology ... far beyond that of ... your people. But this vessel is not primarily technology but ... an expression of relationship." Sennao paused and then continued. "As you have discovered for yourself ... the presence is intensely ... strange. We do not know whether ... it is of the light ... or at some point entered the light. Perhaps this is a ... false question ... for am I not both of and separate to the sea of my world? We do not know how this ... relationship ... serves the needs of the ... presence. We do know that at ... any moment ... it may swim away ... to new places. For now we ... celebrate this beautiful ... encounter."

"How can something live in light? Or how can light be alive?"

"Do you know what 'life' is ... Joseph? Can you tell where ... it starts and ends? All you have is your own ... experience ... and from this you judge. This is a very ... limited perspective that ... cripples you so that you can only see ... what you already know. Your people have to ... learn ... to admit this disability ... to free your imaginations ... that you may see without limit." Sennao paused, but Joseph sensed that he had more to say. "Also Joseph do you know what light ... is? We do not. It seems to answer ... to laws that are ... not of this universe ... yet it is the ... measure ... of this universe. Light is utterly ... mysterious. It seems that in ... touching ... light we reach into that which is ... beyond."

The profundity of Sennao's words brought a stillness to both of them. Then Joseph quietly asked a question.

"How do I enter into ... relationship ... with the light?"

"You have been ... in relationship ... since you entered the vessel as you have ... I believe ... realized. Now it is simply a matter ... of focus ... and the chair in which you sit ... is designed to ... facilitate this process. Surrender to the chair and allow the ... boundary ... between it and you to blur. It is a ... two-way door. Allow it also to ... poise ... the rhythms and energies of your body ... that your mind and the ... light presence ... may swim together."

Joseph consciously relaxed his body into the chair and sensed it react. As he did so, he became aware of the very strange and alien presence in his mind that was the light ship, growing towards him - except he could not say what or where "he" was. Perhaps it would be better to say that it grew within him.

Then it happened.

There was a moment of union, of intermingling, of flowing together that left him reeling. Suddenly it felt as if he was being peered at by a thousand eyes, but Joseph knew that this was just an interpretation of something far too strange for his mind to grasp. Then his thoughts began to play more tricks and he felt as though an endless sinuous worm was weaving its way through his mind and body. He felt panic rising, but at that moment Sennao's voice spoke in his mind.

"These ... imaginings ... will transform in time into something more ... comfortable if you do not ... surrender to fear. Your mind is searching for ... ideas and images from its past ... through which it may ... relate to the light presence."

Joseph tried to do as Sennao suggested and focused on breathing slowly, on watching the breath as it followed its lifelong rhythm. Gradually the images and sensations in his mind began to shift. The joining with the light presence started to feel more like a warm bath, but a bath in which the water seemed to penetrate every part of him. He relaxed again and there was a sense of harmony, of two sounds interweaving to become something greater. He searched in his mind for Sennao.

"Things have calmed down now. What do I do next?"

"You must make a suggestion ... a word or ... even better an image of what you ... want. But you must ... at first ... be simple. This is a ... relationship ... where clear communication is essential ... but not easy. Over time the ... light being ... will learn better how you ... express yourself."

"What if I suggest something that's dangerous?"

"We have ... found ... over our long ... joining ... with the light presence that generally it will not ... allow ... foolishness. It will sometimes ... question us ... about our intention before ...

proceeding. In early times there were ... accidents ... but now this is not so. We ... suspect ... that the presence is learning how to ... relate to us ... just as we are learning how to ... relate to it. It seems that ... through us it penetrates this ... universe ... so that it may travel and learn."

A thought occurred to Joseph. It felt unworthy, but it had to be said.

"Are you sure that the light being can be, well, trusted?"

"Do you mean ... is it ... using us to prepare to ... invade? I have to admit that ... this suspicion occupied ... our thoughts at one point. But ... thousands of years of ... contact has been ... reassuring. As you explore this relationship ... yourself ... you too will find ... contentment on this question."

Joseph focused once more on the sensation of harmony that he shared with the light presence and decided to start simply, as Sennao had recommended. He formed a picture in his mind of the observation window opening again in front of where he and Sennao sat. This was enough. He did not think he could handle complete transparency again with its vertiginous floating in space. Nothing happened for a few moments and Joseph began to wonder if the message had been understood. Then, suddenly, the two chairs turned to face in the same direction and the light directly before them seemed to swirl for a few moments before peeling away to reveal an elongated rectangle of space. The stars still shone with incandescent beauty. Joseph guessed that the vessel had not moved from the place where he and Sennao had sat floating in the vastness. As this thought occurred he realized, also, that he had no idea how long ago that had been. He seemed to have lost his sense of time. How long had he been with Sennao? It could have been days or weeks for all he knew.

Joseph focused on the task in hand and had no doubt what he wanted to do next. It was a particular journey he had longed to undertake since he could first remember. He formed a picture in his mind and held it steady. It was easy, for he had made this journey in his imagination countless times. The response was quicker and the stars visible through the view screen began to scroll to the right as the vessel turned. Slowly, but steadily, the sight he had sought hove into view. From the pinpointed blackness of space the brilliant multicolored sphere of the Earth was revealed. Its beauty took his breath away. About a quarter of the planet was in darkness and beyond the terminator Joseph could just make out the scattered lights of cities. The sunlit part of the planet was a stunning mosaic of blues, greens, browns and whites. He may have regarded the Earth as a prison for most of his life, but what a prison! He looked for Greece, but could not see it. He wondered if Alex was still waiting or had reluctantly left.

For a while Joseph contemplated his home, his ark in space, imbibing its magnificent image and all the memories and meaning it held for him. Then, still with his eyes open, he formed another image in his mind and, effortlessly, the light vessel responded. Serenely, it began to move away from Earth along the orbital plane. With grace and dignity the planet began to slowly shrink. As his vision widened, he saw out to the left a crescent disk that he knew to be his world's only moon. And then he sat, in stillness and silence, as the Earth gradually shrank and he moved away from everything he knew. The escape he had always sought, which previously he had only experienced inwardly, was now his in the physical realm. He felt deep bliss and, also, great sadness. It was unspeakably poignant.

As the Earth and moon shrank, Joseph began to see them against an ever-expanding starfield. He was still close enough for them to be prominent against the myriad points of light, but already there was a sense of their insignificance in the vastness of space. He knew that somewhere to his right, unseen, was the unimportant star around which they orbited. Inconsequential in terms of the mighty cosmos, yet still an awesome outpouring of primal nuclear power, infusing those tiny specks of self-absorbed life that squirmed and died on its third planet. He suddenly felt, strongly and primitively, that he needed to see the sun. The light presence seemed to anticipate this impulse, for no sooner had the thought arisen than the view screen expanded and, there, searingly brilliant, was the source of energy that drove his physical form. Joseph was transfixed by an arresting thought. What was the relationship between the light being with whom he was joined, who shaped and enlivened the vessel in which he traveled, and the source of awesome luminescence at the heart of the solar system? Did it, or some other member of its kind, live and move in that light too? And if so, was he, Joseph, not a creature of that light also? The questions poured into his mind, unanswerable yet consciousness-changing.

A memory from the past intruded powerfully. It was something he had heard years before, that moved him deeply with its mystical intensity. It was star song, vibrations created by the pulsing of stars as their internal processes flowed on their multi-billion year journeys. Captured by radio telescopes and played through audio filters, it was a haunting sound. It was cosmic whale song. Each star had its own unique repeating pattern of clicks. His star, the one he now contemplated, possessed a beautifully deep resonance. It was the song that had spun him into being. Yet it had been another song that had made the greatest impact. It was from a globular cluster of stars and their sound was a celestial harmony, a blending of individual songs into something inexpressively evocative and alien. As he gazed at his own sun, he tasted again the grandeur of creation.

Eventually Joseph's gaze returned to the Earth, hanging brilliantly against its star-spangled backdrop. He was much further away now and the silvery slither that was the moon was no longer a distinct presence. The features of Earth, too, were blurring and it was becoming an homogenous beautiful blue and white disc. He did not know how far out he was and leaned forward to peer left and right on the look-out for points of reference, but nothing could be seen. He realized in a new way just how difficult it was for the human mind to conceptualize the vastness of space, even within a small solar system. In books and his imagination, it had always seemed so crowded. You left Earth, went past the moon, waved at Mars a bit further on, slalomed though the asteroid belt (narrowly missing umpteen collisions) and aimed for the unmistakable bulk of Jupiter. Of course, intellectually, he had known it was not like this. The distances between even the asteroids were huge. Each celestial body, even mighty Jupiter, was just a speck of matter and gas, an occasional island floating in an infinite ocean. It would be quite possible to travel across the entire solar system without seeing more than dots of light in the distance. But the human mind, shaped and formed on a small planet, conscious from its first stirrings of an inescapable horizon, could not grasp the sheer immensity of space. Even moving out along the orbital plane of the planets around the sun, it would be only good fortune were an object to be close to his line of travel at the right time. Nevertheless, there was one object that he was determined to see even if a detour were needed. As the thought formed, he knew that the light presence in the ship had noted the wish and would act upon it.

He estimated now that they must be well beyond the orbit of Mars. He could almost cover his world with his thumb. He leaned back in the chair and allowed the sight of the steadily shrinking Earth, against its magnificent backdrop, to fill him. He had become so absorbed that Sennao's presence, only a couple of yards away, had been completely forgotten. The slow diminution of the extraordinary cyan disk he knew as home began to be hypnotic. His focus on it became increasingly intense and he began to feel as though he were moving along a tunnel away from something very precious, towards something utterly unknown. It was a flow from dying to being born again, in a new way. It was a near-death and a near-birth experience. The mystical depth of the encounter suddenly strengthened and it took Joseph a few moments to realize what had happened. It was now shared. He felt how his brothers and Sennao had moved closer in his mind, inter-weaving strands of themselves with his own filaments. And in the sharing, the power of the experience soared exponentially. Once more Joseph plunged into the timeless.

Joseph re-emerged from the depths a while later. He did not know how long. The nature of the surfacing was unlike anything he had experienced before. He felt like a rope strand untwisting from other strands, which then moved away a small distance to lie alongside. There was no disorientation this time. One moment he was not "here" and the next he was, with complete clarity as to what was happening. He looked out of the view screen. He gasped with delight.

The view was filled with elegant bands of blue light, some wide, some narrow, running diagonally across the screen from left to right. The bands were very close to each other, separated by thin gaps of varying width through which the blackness of space could be glimpsed. The blue was so pure it almost evoked ecstasy. There was such a perfect sense of order, of harmony, of simplicity that, almost bizarrely, it reminded Joseph of the refectory at the monastery. Yet it was not bizarre, for the same principles were at work. He knew that the scale of what filled his field of view must be enormous. But this sense of majesty only became real when a rocky ball, about the size of a small coin from Joseph's perspective, slowly crawled into the picture from the bottom left and moved against the awesome blue-banded background. He knew that it must be one of Saturn's many moons. The giant planet itself was out of view, down to his left. He was too close to the rings to be able to see it. There was time for that in a little while. For now he just watched as the anonymous moon silently and slowly crossed his vision, backlit by a sea of banded many-hued blues. In gentle contemplation he kept company with the solitary lump of rock that had been alone for so long.

After a while, Joseph's silent rocky companion approached the edge of his field of vision. He sensed it was time to move away from the intoxicating blueness of Saturn's rings, in order to see the planet itself. Once more, the light presence seemed to antic-ipate his thoughts and the vessel began to move slowly backwards. As his field of view expanded, the silent moon shrank until it was soon lost against the rings. Then, from the bottom left corner of the view screen, a curved sliver of mauve pink planet began to move into sight, enormous in scale. Very slowly it expanded and the beautiful pastel colored world began to fill the screen. The mauve-pink color was laid down in subtle banding in which delicate shades merged into one another, almost impercep-tibly. As the equatorial area crept into view, the color of the bands changed to a soft-tinted yellow. Joseph was struck by the perfection of the sphere as it slowly manifested. It appeared without flaw, with a smoothness that reminded him of the surface of calm water or an unblemished field of snow.

Saturn now dominated the view screen. The whole of the yellow-banded equatorial region could be seen. The blackness of space, where it could still be glimpsed, helped to give some perspective. As the vessel continued to glide gradually away from the planet, its southern half came into view. The yellow equatorial region came to an end and the mauve pink coloration recommenced. As he continued to feast on the sight, Joseph noticed that the southern pole showed more than a hint of blue. And there was something else that was different, which took a few moments to register. The magnificent rings, now displayed in their full splendor, appeared to have changed color. Gone was the rich blue, to be replaced by beautiful bands of pink, mauve, white and beige. The transformation reminded Joseph that in space color was a trickster, whose appearance depended on a subtle interplay of refraction, medium of observation and unconscious perceptual mechanisms. As he stared at the planet, Joseph was aware that the image was affecting him deeply, but not in a way that he could define. The sight defied comparison with anything in his mundane experience, yet touched him profoundly. It was an unearthly archetypal symbol that pointed towards something that would not register in his mind.

Then the vessel began to move differently. Joseph was momentarily taken aback, as he could not remember planting any suggestion in the mindspace he shared with the light presence. Then he relaxed and trusted that it had a reason for adjusting the position of the ship. Saturn moved away to the right, off the view screen, until all that could be seen was a segment of the rings. The ship then stopped. Joseph sensed that he was being shown something, but was unable for a while to see what it was. The first thing that he saw was an extra ring that he had not previously noticed. It was very faint and lay a long way outside the main colored bands. It resembled a light sprinkling of dust or ice particles, describing a faint but definite arc around the planet. But Joseph quickly realized that this was not what he was supposed to see. Something in his mind was nudging him to look more closely.

Then he saw it - and his heart beat a little faster.

Lying outside the faint outer ring was an insignificant blue dot.

It appeared no bigger than a small seed, dwarfed by even the tiny segment of Saturn's rings that was still visible. It was a sight that aroused the deepest feelings of love in him. Its sheer vulnerability as it hung in the sparkling blackness, like a small child wandering lost and alone, moved him beyond words. He had an irrational sense that in any moment the vast cosmos could crush it like an egg, without even noticing. He thought of all of those miniscule specks of life that were living out their dramas on that small blue dot, even as he sat and watched. He despaired of them, but in that moment loved them also beyond words. He wanted to cup the Earth in his hand and protect it.

"Do you ... struggle with it so much now ... Joseph?"

Joseph had been engrossed for so long that the voice made him jump. He had to think hard to register what Sennao had said.

"Yes, but now I realize that I love it also."

"And what about your people ... of whom you despair?"

Joseph thought carefully before answering.

"They ... we ... are astonishing creatures, capable of the most beautiful insights and acts of creation. Something shines in us that is awesome. We can bring a profound awareness and goodness to everything we touch. In my sacred story, human beings are made in the image of God - we are the Mystery knowing itself." Joseph paused and took a deep breath. "Yet all I encounter most of the time is blindness and self absorption that, inevitably, leads to incalculable suffering. Above all, I get so angry with people for not seeing the incredible puzzle of their own existence and of everything else that is. It is like watching someone waste the most precious gift that can be imagined. And I get the most angry when I see people act from this willful state of ignorance to inflict pain and suffering on others, on animals and upon the planet. I see cruelty and exploitation imbedded into every culture. The problem is that most of my people, despite their protestation to the contrary, seem to want this state of affairs. And I see nothing around me or in history to suggest that more than a few will ever want to awaken to a deeper way."

"Perhaps it is only ... a matter of time?"

"With all my heart, I would like that to be true, but I see no real evidence of a general awakening. I have to conclude that it's just wishful thinking. But also, when I look at that fragile blue dot hanging in the void, I realize that there may not be unlimited time. It's a tiny spark of light that can be snuffed out in an instant." Joseph looked at Sennao. "Or do you know different?"

"I am afraid that ... you are not mistaken," Sennao replied with a hint of what Joseph thought might be sadness. "It is the same for all races whom ... we have encountered. This universe ... and others ... are sown with ... seeds of awareness. Some never ... germinate ... while others grow for a while but then ... wither. Only a few ... flower and in their turn ... throw new seeds into the wind and so ... continue in new ways. Ways that know ... the oneness ... of all things and are ... humble because of this. Your people grow ... here and there ... but as yet do not together ... open their petals fully to the sun." Sennao paused before continuing. "Our searching across the stars ... suggests ... that each race has only so much time. Our inner journeyings ... show us that the creative currents will ... move on if not allowed ... to flow ... possibly never to return. Yet each race cannot ... imagine ... the universe without its presence ... perhaps imagines that awareness ... can only flower fully through it. Only self-absorption can ... nurture such arrogance. Many races have ... come and gone ... but awareness ... or life if you prefer ... is eternal and will always find ... new forms ... in which to break through if ... frustrated."

As Joseph contemplated the tiny dot of blue light against its immeasurably vast backdrop, he remembered what Anastasios had said the previous evening and knew the truth of Sennao's words. He also felt the sadness that lay behind them. He shared the sadness. It then occurred to him that Sennao had probably watched this process many times and that his companion's pain could be far deeper than he was capable of imagining. He was pulled back by Sennao's voice speaking gently in his mind.

"Of course ... Joseph ... there is another way to ... see. And in seeing ... in a new way ... to feel differently."

"What do you mean Sennao?"

"We must remember that our ... seeing ... is shaped by our thoughts. So to change our ... thoughts ... is to see anew."

Joseph was not sure what Sennao was trying to say.

"I don't understand."

"I sense that your mind is ... full of sadness ... because of our words ... and the thoughts and memories ... behind them. But let us ... change the thoughts. Can we not think ... instead of how wondrous it is ... that there is ... anything at all? Can we not remember that life itself ... is an awesome mystery? Can we not be astonished by the ... inexplicable ... fact of consciousness?" Sennao's presence in Joseph's mind suddenly became more intense. "Can we not ... see ... and celebrate the countless acts of kindness ... and love that occur among your people every day and ... entertain the possibility that they are ... firm foundations ... on which to build something wonderful? Can you not ... bring to mind ... those whom you have loved from ... the depths of your heart ... and who have loved you and ... see the world through such enlightened eyes?"

Joseph was taken aback by the intensity with which Sennao was communicating. He realized that he was being asked to know himself more deeply yet again. But there was great resistance in him. Yet Sennao's words triggered pictures of Leola, Alex, Bishop Jennifer and many others to appear in his mind; and especially Clare. To see the worst of humanity and ignore the best had become a habit. He began to feel embarrassed as the hidden workings of his mind were exposed for all to see.

Sennao was unrelenting.

"I ask you to ... deny nothing Joseph ... but to see through a greater ... more complete vision. To see that which ... saddens the heart ... against a greater backdrop ... in truer perspective. I ask you to embrace ... more ways of knowing." Sennao's presence in Joseph's mind became even more intense. " Or perhaps you do not want ... to see differently. Perhaps you ... like ... to see only what is wrong and its ... seeming victory. Is this an ... excuse ... so that you do not have to act?"

Joseph was not enjoying the conversation. A part of him felt attacked. But he knew that Sennao was right. In some ways his despair of humanity had become a friend, who only ever told him what he wanted to hear. It was a friend who always pointed out the ugliness, while turning him away from the beauty, and so gave him every reason to curl up into a hedgehog-like ball and turn off from the world. His friend was a habit of mind that needed to be exorcised. He felt humiliated that others had seen this in him, when he had not. He did not know what to say, but was saved by Sennao's voice reappearing, much more gently, in his mind.

"I am sorry ... Joseph ... it was necessary to show you something ... which we now sense you ... have seen. Your resistance was ... and still will be for a while ... strong and ... power was required. We hope that you will ... forgive us."

"There is nothing to forgive, Sennao. You have pointed me to the truth, but truth can be painful."

"Indeed," Sennao agreed quietly, "and we have all ... felt that pain." He paused before continuing. "But did not ... the great one of your ... sacred story ... say that it is the truth that sets us free?"

Joseph took a deep breath. "Yes, he did. And he sometimes found it necessary to speak with power also."

They both sank into silence and looked out at the vision before them. A tiny blue Earth floated in the starry blackness, with the mighty rings of Saturn shaping one corner of the picture. Joseph needed the silence. He almost felt violated. Some part of himself had been tugged out by the roots, like a bad tooth that had been hurting for years unnoticed. He also felt embarrassed in front of this mighty creature who had seen through him so easily. But after a while a new feeling began to penetrate his mind. Quietly, in its own time, it slowly rose like a gentle tide coming up the shore. Joseph could not find a word to describe the experience. He then realized that this was because it was not the presence of something, but its absence. The bad tooth was gone and the pain, so imbedded in life that it had become normal, was diminishing. What was emerging was something natural and ever-present, but which could only enter awareness through thoughts that were open to its vibration. It was a profound optimism and hope, which was so deep that it was unattached to any event or experience. It shone on whatever it touched, no matter how dark, and illumined it. As he stared at the Earth from such a vast distance, all he could think of now was the wonder of existence and of human life. Knowledge of the blackness of the human soul was still present, but seen in a glorious context in which it could no longer be all-consuming.

As Joseph began to see the transformation that Sennao had wrought in his mind, he wondered how it was possible that it had been brought about in such a simple manner. Then he remembered, almost with laughter, that he was floating in outer space, out beyond Saturn, sharing his mind with at least three other centers of consciousness. In retrospect, it should not be surprising that the hidden layers of his consciousness should be so malleable.

A sense of well-being began to fill Joseph and he knew that, unlike in the past, this would not be a passing experience. He saw that even though he had tasted the beauty of oneness, of God, in other times, it had never been able to shine properly in his life. The deep thought structures through which it must express itself had been darkened and distorted. What was so shocking was that he had chosen this. He had wanted the light and, at the same time, had hidden from it because of what might be demanded of him. "Know Thyself" the oracle at Delphi had proclaimed. Joseph saw even more now the devastating honesty that this teaching required.

He looked over at Sennao and found the hypnotic black eyes of his friend looking back.

"Sennao, why did it take me so long to see what was obvious?"

"It is something you have seen ... before ... in this and other lives ... and then forgotten due to ... terrible experiences. You have tasted the ... worst of humanity. Your reaction is completely understandable and ... there is no blame. This time we could not ... allow you to hide ... because of the pressure of ... this time ... and ... our presence so clearly in your mind meant ... that we could ensure this ... end."

Sennao's reply left Joseph thinking. He had often suspected that his despair of humanity had deeper roots than he knew. That those roots went back centuries, if not millennia, did not raise even a ripple of protest in his mind. Further thoughts were interrupted by Sennao.

"We are now ... able to bring this encounter to its ... conclusion. You must make ... a decision and now you are ... free to do so with a ... clear mind. I will enter into relationship ... with the vessel ... with your permission for there is something I must ... show you before you decide."

Joseph felt his joining with the light presence gently drain away. The vessel began to move and the Earth started to diminish even further. He felt his stomach tighten at the sight.

And at what he sensed was to come.

Chapter 26

They were moving very fast now, away from Saturn and the distant Earth. As Joseph watched on the view screen, both planets shrank rapidly. Within what seemed just a few short moments the Earth had become a tiny pinprick of light, barely visible against the star-filled background. Indeed, had he not watched intently as it receded, he would have lost it completely.

And then, as they continued to travel at enormous speed, the Earth disappeared. He had blinked and when his sight readjusted he could no longer say which point of light was home. Involuntarily, he found himself taking a deep breath, genuinely in shock. Like an ancient mariner, he had crossed the horizon and all connection with his land, with all that he knew, was gone. A picture of Clare came unbidden into his mind and an incredible loneliness filled his soul. His hands gripped the arms of the chair tightly and he looked over at Sennao. But that did not help, for now it was only his alienness that he saw. Every point of reference he had ever based his life on had vanished and his mind was struggling to maintain its coherence. He found himself staring wide-eyed at Sennao, unable to break the link, while his chest started to heave. He could sense his brothers trying to connect with him, but they also seemed to be struggling. Perhaps this onward rush into high strangeness was too much even for them. He wanted to reach inwards to grasp their hands, but primal fear had concreted him into the outer material world, unable to look away.

Then he heard Sennao's voice in his mind, distant and projected with great power.

"Joseph ... look into my eyes ... focus on their depths."

Joseph wanted to do what Sennao asked, but he was becoming frozen like a rabbit in car headlights. The voice came with even more urgency. Joseph had a sense that Sennao was shouting, but was still barely audible.

"Joseph you must ... plunge ... into my eyes."

As he projected these words into Joseph's mind, Sennao leaned forward in his chair and turned his head slightly to one side. It was the movement that helped. It weakened the intense fear that gripped Joseph and, with enormous effort, he focused his vision on the dark pools that were Sennao's eyes. The effect was immediate and it felt as though he was sinking into a healing darkness. His mind began to calm and the fear to subside. His thoughts were caressed into stillness. He sensed that his brothers were there too, somewhere alongside, sharing the healing. The passage of time became hazy and all he knew was that at some point Sennao's voice sounded in his mind again, but with less intensity.

"Joseph ... you must not lose ... contact ... with me in your mind. The thought structures that ... are your model of reality ... have been stretched beyond their ... limit. Some of them ... in the lower currents ... are still primitive in their nature ... formed long ago in the ... collective mind of your forebears ... on the savannahs and in the trees. An experience such as this ... raises them through ... the levels to ... swim on the surface. This is good ... for there they may be caught ... but it should be a ... controlled and gradual process." Sennao paused. "The minds of your people are new and ... were formed to their present point ... by the need for survival ... on the land of Earth. For what is to come ... new structures must evolve. In particular your minds until now have ... been dominated by the outer. This is ... how it should be. But now you must ... allow the ... deep inner to shape how your thoughts swim. You experienced ... terrible aloneness and strangeness ... just now because you were too focused on ... the outer. Had your mind also embraced ... the inner ... you would have been anchored in ... eternal relationship. This your people ... must learn if they are to ... evolve further." Sennao paused once more before finishing. "But I should have ... anticipated and express ... regret ... for your discomfort ... and that of your brothers."

Sennao's apology aroused a sense of injustice in Joseph.

"There is nothing for you to regret, Sennao. I am the most privileged of human beings. I would change nothing that has happened." He sensed Sennao's pleasure at these words.

"You are ... very kind ... Joseph. I ...we ... are humbled by your appreciation."

Sennao's stumble aroused Joseph's interest.

"Why did you say 'we'?"

"This is something to ... explore further at ... another time. But when we first ... greeted each other ... did I not say that both you and I carry ... others ... with us into this ... encounter? My immersion in ... the depths ... is greater than yours and ... often ... my sense of identity ... is fluid."

Joseph pondered Sennao's words and tried to relate them to his brothers' presence in his mind. In that moment, he and they felt completely distinct, but as he remembered his dream vision on the wooded hill, where he was both in and out of his grave, the boundary was far more porous and difficult to define. His thoughts were interrupted by Sennao.

"Joseph ... you must now ... experience ... something and must ... also ... express your ... direction for the future. Please open your eyes."

Joseph was surprised to discover that his eyes were not open. So immersed had he become in the inner world of the mind, since sinking into Sennao's consciousness, that its way of "seeing" had become normal. He mentally reconnected with his body and opened his eyelids. Now there was only a field of tiny points of light set against the blackest possible background. Some of the stars were slightly larger than others, but the differences were barely perceptible in such minute dots. He realized that they must be billions of miles away from Earth. He did not even know which of the stars was his sun. But this time, to his great relief, he was not overwhelmed. He was too firmly anchored within. The awesome panorama was no longer his only reality, but merely a part of something infinitely greater, which stretched away inwardly as well as outwardly.

"Where are we?" he asked Sennao.

"We float at the edge of your ... solar system ... where the influence of your sun ends. Here new ... currents and tides ... of the great seas between the stars ... begin to hold sway. In terms of your ... measure ... we are approximately nine billion miles from ... your home world."

"Is one of those stars my own sun?"

"Yes ... but it is only a ... minor ... point of light. I could ... indicate ... its position to you ... but this would be ... counterproductive. For I have ... brought you here to ... stretch your consciousness. It is very possible ... on your world ... to travel to a foreign country ... but leave your thoughts at home ... and so not encounter the newness. Can you ... forget ... about your sun ... for a while ... and open your mind to the ... all-ness ... of what you see? Can you imagine ... that you have never ... known your world and its small sun ... and see what this does to ... your mind?"

Joseph was taken-aback at Sennao's request, not because it shocked him but because he did not think it would be possible. He doubted that such a fundamental, hard-wired memory could be buried in this way. Yet when he began to focus on the starfield before him, he found that it was surprisingly easy. It was not that knowledge of the Earth left his mind, but that he switched to another frequency - as if he were changing channel on a television. He knew it was there and could be accessed at any moment, but it was not currently playing on his mind-screen. He suspected that had he still been on Earth, or even still floating next to Saturn, it would not have been so easy. But out here, it seemed to be the most natural thing in the universe to know oneself as a child of space, rather than of a particular lump of rock. As he entered into the act of imagination that Sennao had initiated, he felt a rising surge of newborn consciousness enter his mind. He found himself involuntarily holding his breath as though he were being submerged under rising floodwater. It was a consciousness that had no identity, yet was fiercely alive and individual. It was a consciousness that was naturally at home swimming among the stars in the energetic void of space. It rejoiced in the vastness, rather than squeezing into a transient ill-fitting body, in order to walk around on a speck of dust for a flicker of time. It was consciousness of a gaseous or fluidic nature, rather than a solid-state circuit. It could be whatever it chose to be.

After an indeterminate time, Joseph/not Joseph became aware of the stars beginning to move and realized that Sennao was adjusting the position of the light vessel. New points of light came into view and Joseph/not Joseph sensed that something significant had changed. Sennao's voice drifted into his awareness.

"Now we float … on the edge of the … continental shelf … of your solar system and look out into the … bottomless depths … of the cosmic ocean. Though it looks … little different to that which we … previously observed … your mind senses the difference. What do you … intuit … in this moment?"

Words began to lead the way again for Joseph, just appearing in his awareness, without being the product of sequential thought. Some part of him watched this phenomenon with detached interest, keen to learn what he had to say.

"I see the blackness between the stars and am drawn to it far more than I am to them. The stars almost feel like minor irritations in the velvety perfection of the living void. It is the limitless horizon of the eternal that I crave, not the restriction of the finite. I look to the open sea, not the land. I look at the blackness and I see forever."

As these words emerged, Joseph/not Joseph found himself

wanting to dissolve into that eternal sea. There was a powerful sense that it, and what it symbolized, and was a gateway for, was truly home. And he wanted to go home. He had been away too long. Yet as this desire surged within, Joseph/not Joseph watched in fascination as another realization swam to the surface from that deeper place that he knew was home. It was apocalyptic and beautiful. Mind-blowingly obvious when seen, yet seemingly impossible to see when not seen.

He had never left Home.

The deepest truth of who he was still danced in love with its source, as it had from the beginning of time. Nothing else was possible. The created could not leave its author. Existence was One and could contain no gaps. Yet within that Oneness another part of him swirled, enraptured in its own dance. He was called also to create for he was an expression of the eternal creative impulse. So he was the dance and the dancer. He was the Oneness and a unique individual artist - as was every other life form that walked and talked, squirmed or crawled in all the universes. He remained forever in the bliss of Home, yet also wandered as a restless explorer in a place of imagination called non-home. This is how it was meant to be. But the explorer, utterly absorbed in its creative world-forming adventures, had dreamt it was alone and separate in a hostile story of its own making. And in its own way this was right and proper too, for only thus, by complete absorption, could new creation flower. So those transient ill-fitting bodies mattered, for each saw and experienced uniquely and was an unrepeatable, finely-honed evolutionary tool. Each had the potential to craft something new. Together, their individual uniqueness woven into tapestry, they could create wonders. And the experience of that living tapestry was the song of love to which all could dance.

Joseph/not Joseph saw the truth of all this.

He did not see it as an idea, but was reborn into this truth as a state of being.

And as the seeing of the truth filled his mind, he sensed the decision that Sennao was laying before him. "Not Joseph" began to move into the background and Joseph re-entered the spotlight of identity. He took a deep breath as he became aware of his body once more. The feeling of solidity that physical sensations brought seemed oddly new and interesting. Sennao spoke in his mind.

"I now seek ... a decision. We have shown you ... or perhaps it would be ... better ... to say ... evoked from your depths ... glimpses of your truth. We promise now that ... if you so choose ... you may be of our company ... and swim with us as we explore ... the great sea of space and its ... star islands. Has this not always been your ... burning desire? Your time trapped on the tiny ... outcropping ... you call Earth ... will end. You will roam ... the vastness. You will leave behind ... the blind who do not see ... who in their ... blundering and confusion ... attack and condemn ... and you will be with those of ... greater vision ... who will delight your ... soul. We will take you ... also ... into the other universes and worlds that ... are wrapped within and around this one. And we will ... nurture the flame of your ... joining with the great Source of All ... from whence you came ... still remain and will return. This is offered ... for it is your ... joyful inheritance and all ... will celebrate ... with you."

Sennao paused.

"But Joseph we ask that you ... consider ... another possibility. In times long gone you offered ... to help the spiritually blind on your world ... who longed to see. It was to ... volunteer ... for a soul-draining task ... that could easily bear poor fruit. This is not a ... better ... path than to swim among ... the stars ... and to plunge into the depths ... for both are needed for ... equilibrium ... and each individual's ... pattern ... is differently inscribed by ... the source. It was also the exuberant ... enthusiasm of a ... young soul ... not from the wisdom that ... is now yours. A young soul cannot know ... its calling ... with such clarity. Yet the voice of … the Source … may be echoing distantly … in that immature consciousness."

Sennao paused briefly before finishing and Joseph sensed he was thinking about something.

"I intended to ask you to make … a decision … but I see now that this is … not the correct word. I ask you to … discern what was written on your … heart … when your essence emerged. Only you … can do this. But be … assured … that whatever is your path … we will swim beside you."

Joseph did not speak for a while. He simply looked out at the endless Mystery. It was all that he had ever dreamed of from a child. It seduced him powerfully and eloquently. Its freedom and majesty drew him forward. The moment was profoundly still and silent. Then he spoke.

"Sennao, if it had only been the shrill voice of youth you would not be here now. The inner currents could not have been shaped to arrive at this moment were the offer not of God. Only he … it … could have done such a thing. The callow youth had no idea whose words he spoke. Otherwise he might have kept silent."

He had freewill, but saw with absolutely clarity that there was only one choice. He turned to look at Sennao.

"Sennao, will you return me to Earth please?"

They did not speak on the return journey. Joseph simply watched in a dreamlike state as, very slowly, one of the stars began to increase in size relative to the others. For the first time in his life he knew contentment. The restless unidentifiable pressure that he had always carried was gone. He now understood that the pressure had been a question, lost in the ancient recesses of his mind, that had pressed unrelentingly on his thoughts, unrecognized for what it was. It was a question that reached to him from a time long ago when a youthful promise had been given in haste. Over eons, deeply enfolded within his soul, the question had rumbled like a distant earthquake - could he keep his promise or would he, in despair, break the most solemn of vows? He saw that the pressure originated in him, for the promise was an essential strand of his existence. In the course of many lives, deep within, unconsciously, doubts had grown and become fear; a fear reinforced by life experiences. And the deeper and more hidden a thought is, the greater its power. Over the ages, the fear had broken to the surface wearing many masks and been projected onto the outer world. It lay behind his willingness to see the worst of people and not also the best. It enlivened his dark friend, who supplied endless excuses to support his judgments.

It was not that the fear had gone. His promise still filled him with trepidation. It was that Sennao, in revealing the source of the fear, and offering him instead the opportunity to live out his greatest dream, had shown him that this was not what he really wanted. Gazing out into the cosmos, he had known that something at which Sennao hinted was true. His promise had not just been the impulsive enthusiasm of youth; it had also been the faint echo of what was written on the template of his soul. This was his calling, that for which he was made. Now he knew this, he could embrace the task he had taken on. Not because it would be easy, but because he knew it was the only path that would lead to true life.

The sun grew remorselessly in size and, after a while, began to move from the center of the screen, eventually disappearing from view. As it did so, a point of bluish light took its place and expanded steadily. It reminded Joseph of watching a balloon being filled with helium. Slowly, subtle colors became discernible. From the angle they were approaching, Earth was fully illumined by the sun and Joseph could soon pick out the contours of Africa, partially obscured by brilliantly white wisps of cloud, its northern coast reaching to the top of the marble-like disk. Between and through the clouds the mighty continent appeared sandy brown in its northern and southern parts. The huge central mass suggested dark green, but Joseph was not sure if this was shadow created by cloud cover. Having located Africa, Joseph was then able to identify the tan-colored Saudi Arabian peninsular, lying at the apex of the visible planet. Further south, lay the island of Madagascar, a strong shade of olive. At the southern edge of the disk was a mass of white. This was not cloud, but the hidden, mysterious ice-covered continent of Antarctica. Pristine and pure, it seemed to anchor all that lay above. And all of this now hung in the speckled blackness, gradually moving towards him.

A warm feeling stirred at the prospect of walking again on the surface of the beautiful world that lay before his eyes. Now that he did not feel trapped by it, the sight triggered feelings of deep love. He was not naïve. He knew that beautiful though it was from this distance, the world he looked upon was full of human madness and the suffering it caused to all forms of life. He knew that he would soon walk amidst that insanity once more. But this time he wanted to. He wanted to find and celebrate those quiet, unnoticed moments of love that were happening and build upon them. He wanted to evoke within people the grandeur of their own existence, so that those who were not too asleep might awaken to their own glorious mystery and dive into its depths. He wanted to help his people evolve to a new and higher expression of consciousness in which they knew the oneness of everything, as well as its multifaceted uniqueness. He knew that if this flowering could be sufficiently widespread, the insanity and all that it brought would wither away naturally.

And he wanted to do this because, as he now knew, he loved humanity. He knew this to be true because he cared. Only love cares.

But he also sensed that if this did not happen, time would not wait forever and would move on to new experiments. This prospect saddened him, but also felt strangely right. There was something so vast, so awesome unfolding that humanity could not expect anything else. They would be missed as a single violinist in a great orchestra might be missed, but the music would continue and find new forms of expression. For humanity to grasp just this one great truth, that it was not the center of the universe, would cure it of its self-absorbed arrogance. This in itself would be an awakening.

The Earth was now very close and almost filled the view screen. The reality of his return and all that it would bring now filled Joseph's mind. He turned to Sennao.

"Did you know that I would choose to return?"

Sennao seemed to think before replying. The light vessel stopped its progress towards Earth.

"I was not ... sure ... but I thought it most ... likely. There was no ... certainty ... but I had deep ... feelings ... that you would not be able ... to deny that which was written ... within you. I could never believe that ... your coming forward was merely ... youthful foolishness." Sennao turned his head to look Joseph fully in the eyes. "I am truly happy for you ... my friend ... for I have no doubt that ... only this way can you know peace. We can only know peace when we are ... authentic ... but it can take much time and error ... to discover our ... authenticity."

The love behind Sennao's words shone from the blackness of his eyes and Joseph found himself having to turn away to hide the tears in his own. He managed to find some words to cover his confusion.

"Sennao, what am I do to when I return? Where do I start?"

"You must be guided by ... one principle ... of which you must never ... lose sight. Your role is to awaken people ... to a higher state of consciousness ... in which they see ... the oneness and the mystery of all things. From this state ... love will flow and heal ... all things. You must not get sidetracked ... so easily done ... by seeking to make the world a better place through ... social and political action. This is for others ... not for you. Unless awakening happens on ... a significant scale ... there will be good people trying to make the world a better place ... until the end of time. You must focus on the ... cause ... not the ... symptoms ... of the condition."

"How am I to do this?"

"By not having ... a plan ... but by being very still ... and watching the world unfold around you ... and by being silent within ... and listening for the voices ... of your friends ... and the soundless words of ... the Source of All. When you see and hear ... clearly ... you will know when and how ... to act. You must remember that it is ... not your role to ... please people but to ... awaken them. Sometimes you will ... appear unloving in what you say ... or do ... when viewed from the ... unawakened mind."

"Why should people listen to me?"

"Because ... Joseph ... we have made you into the most ... famous ... person on your world ... and the most mysterious. This is an ... irresistible combination."

Sennao paused, clearly wanting to emphasize his next point.

"But what will have the ... most impact ... will be the very fact of ... your presence ... among your people. Even before you ... speak or act ... you are a living ... icon ... a symbol ... that points towards a greater ... human consciousness ... and vast mysteries. The minds of all who encounter you ... will be challenged to their core ... for all will be aware that ... with us ... you have experienced that which is beyond their ... comprehension ... and you still walk among them. In the words of ... the great one of your holy story ... we have made you into ... the yeast in the dough."

Sennao's words hit Joseph powerfully as he saw the depth and subtlety of the plan that was unfolding. He had been made into a living myth, a mystery into which the human mind could plunge and be changed. No one would see him without being reminded of his unfathomable story and the greatness that it suggested. He knew that from now on his life would be governed by the power of this myth. That he would forever be viewed through it. He realized that it might be impossible to ever have a normal human relationship again for, in a way, he had become alien and it would be difficult for even the best-intentioned person to see him differently. A vision of extraordinary loneliness gripped him, until he remembered something that Sennao had said earlier.

"You said that I will not be alone, that there are others who will help me."

"Indeed ... there are other minds that are ... awakened ... on your world. They will recognize what you are ... as you will recognize them. Was there not the questioner ... of India ... at the press conference? They will give you ... companionship and support. And you must remember ... Joseph ... that such people are ... your equal ... for your prominence arises from ... your role ... not from any specialness. But I know you ... sufficiently ... to have faith that this does not ... really need to be said."

"And what about you and I, Sennao, how often will we meet?"

"At this plane of ... reality ... as is necessary. On the ... inner planes ... we are always joined and all that is needed is to ... pay attention to the joining ... for it to ... come into focus." Sennao paused for a moment before continuing. "And there are others ... who wait to help ... at the boundaries between this ... aspect of reality ... and those which are beyond. Already there are ... your brothers. Many others wait ... to help ... for in helping they grow themselves ... in seeing and understanding ... but also they seek to walk with you ... for to do so is the natural expression of ... the compassion that flows through ... an awakened mind."

Sennao's words reassured Joseph, but there was one more question that he needed to ask. It was a question that was charged with desire and emotion, and so was difficult to express. He contemplated the magnificent sight before him for a few moments, seeking the right words.

"Those that wait at the boundary, do they include those who

... are no longer ... in physical form?" Joseph found himself struggling to speak. "Souls who we ... I ... never said goodbye to?"

Sennao did not answer immediately, but Joseph sensed a shift in the quality of his strange friend's presence in his mind. It became softer and, somehow, more vulnerable.

"I have been ... waiting ... for this question ... Joseph. I understand the pain of your ... great loss ... for it comes from a great love ... a beautiful love. I am blessed with ... such a love myself ... in the way of my species ... and so can feel with you. The answer to your ... question ... is that this is possible. Sometimes there can be an unconscious ... summoning ... of one to the other and an ... unconscious response. Sometimes both come to the ... margins ... in awareness. But just because something is ... possible ... does not mean it is wise. This judgment must ... be made. It must be remembered that without ... moving on ... there can be no creation. Without ... endings and new beginnings ... the universes could not be. This process is the ... engine ... of creation ... of evolution. It is through this ... mechanism ... that our essences evolve ... and to work against it is ... a mighty decision. But at our ... individual ... personal ... level this is very hard ... even though we know it to be true. So I cannot ... advise ... you must decide whether to ... pursue ... this possibility."

Joseph paused before replying.

"What scares me is that when I gazed out at the stars with you, I found that I was at peace with Clare's death. Against that majesty, I could not feel that anything was wrong. Her going felt completely natural. But now I feel as though I'm losing her."

"Joseph ... you are not losing her ... for close to the Source your souls are entwined ... love cannot die. But in your ... wisdom ... the deeper part of you is ... letting go of her form ... to discover a joining that is ... beyond." Sennao paused. "And Joseph ... consider this ... could it be that she and you ... have known each other also … in ages past? That you have redis-covered … each other … again … more than once … but each time in a new and deeper way? Perhaps you should … think on this in your … moments of stillness."

Joseph stared at Sennao for a few moments, unable to speak. His words had aroused a memory that could not be pinned down. A distant song too far away to be clearly heard. He looked back at the screen and saw that the Earth had continued to turn while they had been speaking and new lands were coming into view.

"Sennao, it's time to go home."

Chapter 27

The light vessel glided silently into the upper atmosphere, crossing to the night-side of the planet. Within a few moments, Joseph could see large tracts of twinkling lights far below and guessed that already they must be over Europe. It took him a few more seconds to realize that, judging from the direction of travel, they were not heading for Greece.

"Where are you taking me Sennao?"

"To where ... no one will expect you ... to be. To a place where you may slowly ... reconnect ... with the currents of your mind that ... reflect this world. For though you have ... journeyed far in distance ... you have journeyed further in consciousness ... and must resurface slowly ... without being rushed by the swarming of others. It is also a place where ... the veil is thin ... between your outer and inner realities ... which will help."

Joseph smiled. "Sennao, is that a grand way to say that you're taking me home?" He once more caught a whiff of something akin to humor in Sennao's reply.

"Indeed ... Joseph ... perhaps this is so. But ... nevertheless ... each of us has special ... places in time and space ... where the boundaries are ... less than firm. Sometimes we are so ... familiar with them that we ... overlook ... their importance as places of ... refreshment and healing. Your ... dwelling ... and place of ... prayer ... are such for yourself ... as I think you suspect. In your ... dreams ... and in your waking life you ... inhabit ... the place you call home. So it is ... there ... that I will take you ... that you may have a firm ... anchor ... for what is to come."

"Will people not see the light vessel and know I'm there?"

"The vessel is only ... visible ... to the eyes of your people ... and to their ... instruments of detection ... should I wish it to be so. No one will see your arrival ... and as all believe you are ... elsewhere ... you may take time to bring ... stillness ... to your mind ... before making your presence known."

Joseph appreciated the wisdom of what Sennao was saying. Up to that moment, leaving the vessel and re-entering normal daily life had been just a thought in his mind. Now the reality hit him and, with it, a growing awareness of how difficult the adjustment might be. In his time with Sennao, he had come to accept the extraordinary as normal and, without him consciously realizing, the light vessel had become another home for him - perhaps even a place of safety. Yet he was also conscious of the great strain he had been under. Joseph felt gratitude for the care with which Sennao was handling him.

The pattern of lights beneath began to take on definite shape, as the British Isles were brokenly sketched out in the darkness. The outline began to expand as the vessel descended and a question that had flitted around Joseph's mind came to the fore.

"Sennao, how long have I been away?"

"That will ... depend ... on who you ask." Once more a hint of dry humor.

Joseph paused for a few moments, then realized what Sennao was saying.

"Ah, yes, time isn't that simple is it."

"No ... Joseph ... the experience of time is very ... individual. All sentient beings ... taste ... time in some form. It must be so ... for without time there can be no ... creation ... no change. Indeed ... change ... is another word for time. Your relationship with the ... fabric of existence ... has been very different during ... our trip ... to that of your people on this ... world. It will suffice to say that ... for them ... more time has passed than for you."

Joseph thought about this for a few seconds, before asking the obvious next question.

"So from their point of view, how long have I been gone?"

"Three ... days ... but for you ... a few hours. It is one of the ... reasons ... that our time together has been ... limited ... or your return could have posed ... significant problems."

Joseph said no more, but simply allowed his mind to absorb yet one more aftershock as he watched the approach of the illumined landscape below. It was very close now and he could sense the vessel subtly altering itself as it prepared to land. He was making no conscious effort to link with the light being, but a bond of some kind remained. For a moment he wondered if the connection would always now be present, no matter how great the distance between them. For reasons he did not understand, he had a strong intuition that this was so.

Then, without warning, his church was there, looming out of the darkness, its sturdy tower a pillar of strength in the gloom. Joseph's heart leapt with the joy of homecoming. The vessel moved slowly over the ancient building and from above Joseph appreciated its Gothic glory in a new way. Within a few moments they were gliding silently over the graveyard and Joseph's eyes sought in the darkness the particular place of such precious memory. A great sadness almost overwhelmed him for a few seconds as he yearned to share with Clare all that had happened. But then, to his great surprise, it was gone as quickly as it had arrived. In that moment of transformation he knew beyond doubt that something fundamental had changed within him. It was impossible to express, but it carried a sense of the vastness and majesty of existence - and of the immortality of love. In a few moments more they were passing over the rectory, before coming to a halt over the expansive ill-kept lawn at the rear of the house. Joseph smiled to himself as he felt gratitude for the darkness that hid his array of gardening sins. The vessel lowered itself gently and came to rest. Then all was still and silent.

Neither of them moved or said anything. It was too big a moment. It was the end of something extraordinary. Only silence could do justice to what had been. Joseph became very aware of the waves of light and color that moved around him, more sedately now that the vessel was still. Their ethereal unworldliness struck him once more, as the juxtaposition with what lay beyond the view screen entered his awareness. He had adjusted quickly to what was alien, to the point where it had become normality. Now he was remembering the normality that had deeper roots in him. It was time to leave. Joseph looked over at Sennao and found his unfathomable eyes looking back.

"Sennao ... I don't know what to say. There are no words for what I feel. You have given me the greatest of gifts. I will never forget our time together."

Sennao nodded almost imperceptibly.

"Nor I ... my friend."

A lump rose in Joseph's throat. For Sennao to call him "friend' seemed in that moment to be the greatest thing in the universe.

"Sennao, before you arrived at Delphi I was trying to think of how to describe you. For many you are the 'Visitor', for others the 'Messenger'. But I needed something else. I know now to call you 'Friend'."

Sennao looked at him for a few long moments.

"It has been so since ... from ages past ... and now it is ... new again. I am ... honored."

Another pause.

"But ... Joseph ... remember that this is not an ending ... but a continuation and a ... beginning. Our ... friendship is ancient and ... also ... stretches before us. We are now ... joined in deeper ... currents ... than has ever been the case ... before. And through our more ... profound joining ... many others connect through us in ways as yet ... too hidden to see." Sennao's eyes seemed to widen and become even darker pools of blackness. "Joseph ... I bid you ... farewell ... for this time and ask that you ... remember ... two things in the days to come. Remember that you are ... my friend ... and I love you with ... my whole being. Remember also that ... no matter how difficult life ... may seem ... you are never alone. A host of ... other friends ... only await your calling of them ... to rush to your side. And behind them lies ... the great Source of All ... and the great one of your holy stories."

Sennao leaned back in his chair and the intensity of his eyes diminished. Joseph had a sense that there was no more to be said and that it was time to leave. Yet something was missing. Joseph felt a primal human need, but was unsure how to express it. But Sennao seemed to understand. Without a sound he leaned forward and held out his hand. Joseph took it gladly, the cool, smooth and slightly oily touch of the alien hand against his, expressing more than words ever could. They did not move for a while and just allowed the moment to silently speak. Then Joseph gently released his grip and stood up. He looked one final time into Sennao's wonderful eyes, then turned and walked resolutely across the floor to the entrance of the room. He reached the beginning of the spiraled passageway and wanted to look back, but resisted the temptation and kept walking. As he continued along the corridor, the presence of Sennao and the light being in his mind began to fade, as though a dimmer switch had been turned down. His brothers were still there, but even they had moved into the background. He mourned the loss of such intimacy and a strong sense of aloneness filled him, but he knew that this was an act of kindness to allow him to readjust to the human world. He continued to walk slowly, continually turning to the left as he followed the passage. He became aware of the contrast with how he had felt only a few hours before, when he had traveled in the opposite direction with such trepidation. Now he left as someone else, a new person, utterly changed by what had occurred, his mind expanded beyond measure. He was reborn.

Joseph reached the end of the corridor. It was the point where he had originally entered the vessel through the wall of swirling light. He paused, looked down the spiral passageway and remembered for a moment what lay at its end. Then he faced the outer wall and forced his way into it. There was brief resistance and he clenched his eyes shut as they were suddenly filled with intense colored light. Then he was through, and cold, frosty air hit his face. He started to shiver almost immediately and somewhere in its dim recesses his mind regretted that he had left Anastasios' warm coat at Delphi. He stumbled slightly and felt the long strands of his uncut lawn wrap themselves around his ankles, soaking them with freezing moisture. He recovered and opened his eyes which started to water as they encountered the cold air. His discovered a handkerchief in his pocket and wiped them clear. As he did so, the night came into focus and he found himself looking at the rear of the rectory from a distance of about twenty yards. He raised his eyes and looked up into a beautifully clear night, into the starlit blackness in which he had been so recently immersed. He noticed that his journey was already beginning to feel like a dream, as his mind, now immersed again in its normal surroundings, tried to process the utter strangeness of what had happened. He turned around, hoping to see the light vessel to confirm the reality of his experience, but there was nothing to be seen. Then Joseph remembered Sennao saying that it would not be visible, so that his return would be unheralded. He reached out in his mind to ask Sennao that the vessel be made visible for a just a few moments, so that the reality of all he had experienced might be confirmed. But it was not necessary. As soon as he looked towards where the light vessel should be, there was a moment of touching in his mind and he relaxed into its certainty. He knew in that instant that it would now be necessary to accept different qualities of reality, rather than measure all against the crude physicality that had been the norm. Indeed, as he stood there, he noticed at a deep level that, just as the very fabric of reality had felt subtly different as he entered the vessel, it had now reverted to the more worldly texture to which he was accustomed.

Then the light vessel began to rise. Joseph could not see it, but knew this was the case. He sensed it pause a few hundred yards above him as if to say a final farewell, then accelerate away at enormous speed. In his new expanded consciousness Joseph followed its departure across the sky, whilst all his eyes could see were the shining stars that formed its stunning backdrop. Within a few seconds it was gone. He stood for a while staring at the stars in the sharp cold, alone and not alone. Gradually, he became more aware of his surroundings and everything started to assume solidity. He turned his head slightly and could just make out the mighty trees that bordered the garden, dark hulks against the starlight. Then he walked forward slowly through the long grass until he reached the end of the garden, where the ground fell away sharply into the valley. There lay the town he served, with its invisible river meandering its way around the hill on which he stood. He looked out over the town, the street lamps marking out its skeleton, while an occasional vehicle flowed along one of its arteries. Here and there a few lighted windows, the illumination muffled by drawn curtains, broke through the intervening darkness. As he looked out, his mind very still, Joseph sensed the intense, self-absorbed, story-filled lives that slumbered below, walled up in mental prisons of their own making. He looked up for a few moments at the majesty of the night sky and then gazed over the town once more.

He knew that he was now alien.

As Joseph looked out over the town, he also became present somewhere else. He was now on both sides of the veil. In that same moment he was also in a clearing long ago, with the trees behind and a steep cliff before him. Below, a river wound through a forested valley. He did not look around, but knew that he was not alone. His brothers stood with him in that place of death and life.

Joseph closed his eyes and took a deep breath. He opened them and gazed again over the slumbering town. A streaky red dawn was breaking in the east and he was gradually becoming aware of how cold he was. It was time to go inside and begin the future. He turned and, with frozen feet, walked slowly back through the unkempt grass that, unfortunately, was now becoming visible. As he reached the center of the lawn, he stopped. He became very conscious of the particular patch of ground beneath his feet. He felt strangely connected with the rock and the soil. He remained perfectly still, lost in thought; then straightened his back and walked towards the rectory. He fumbled in his pocket and found the key to the French windows. His hand also touched something else. He pulled out the white plastic strip of his clerical collar and looked at it for a few moments.

Then, with it still in his hand, he unlocked the door and walked in.

BOOKS

O is a symbol of the world, of oneness and unity. In different cultures it also means the "eye," symbolizing knowledge and insight. We aim to publish books that are accessible, constructive and that challenge accepted opinion, both that of academia and the "moral majority."

Our books are available in all good English language bookstores worldwide. If you don't see the book on the shelves ask the bookstore to order it for you, quoting the ISBN number and title. Alternatively you can order online (all major online retail sites carry our titles) or contact the distributor in the relevant country, listed on the copyright page.

See our website www.o-books.net for a full list of over 500 titles, growing by 100 a year.

And tune in to myspiritradio.com for our book review radio show, hosted by June-Elleni Laine, where you can listen to the authors discussing their books.

MySpiritRadio